Journeys
to the Edge

Journeys
to the Edge

In the Footsteps
of an Anthropologist

Peter M. Gardner

University of Missouri Press   Columbia and London

62118231

Library of Congress Cataloging-in-Publication Data

Gardner, Peter M.
  Journeys to the edge : in the footsteps of an anthropologist / Peter
M. Gardner.
      p. cm.
  Summary: "Gardner offers a vicarious anthropological experience
as he describes his research trips to study the Paliyans of the tropical
forests of India, the Dene in the Northwest Territories of Canada,
and the sophisticated arts of India and Japan. Reveals both the scientific and the family dimensions of the ethnographer's experience"—Provided by publisher.
  Includes bibliographical references and index.
  ISBN-13: 978-0-8262-1634-2 (alk. paper)
  ISBN-10: 0-8262-1634-X (alk. paper)
  1. Gardner, Peter M. 2. Ethnologists—United States—Biography.
3. Paliyan (Indic people)—Social life and customs. 4. Chipawayan
Indians—Canada, Northern—Social life and customs. 5. Ethnology—
India—Field work. 6. Ethnology—Canada—Field work.
7. Canada—Social life and customs. 8. India—Social life and
customs. I. Title.
  GN21.G37A3 2006
    305.80092—dc22

                                                        2005029154

Designer: Jennifer Cropp
Typesetter: Crane Composition, Inc.
Printer and binder: Thomson-Shore, Inc.
Typefaces: Minion and Caslon Antique

*Front matter illustrations: p. ii, minuscule garden at Daitoku-ji and
the author with his daughter in India; p. v, Mount Kanchenjunga,
viewed from Darjeeling on a clear day, and peering into the Mount
Aso crater; p. vi, the author in Canada's Northwest Territories and
an Arab dhow three hundred miles off the Indian coast.*

In memory of my parents
who showed me the grass
on the other side of the fence

Contents

Come with Me

To the Very Edges of Our World

Have you ever wondered what it feels like to be an anthropologist plunging into an exotic culture? The delights and terrors may be hard to imagine. Let me share some stories about the eighteen months I spent doing fieldwork with hunting bands in the tropical forest of India. These include accounts of dancing under a full moon in a circle of smiling faces, hunting wild boars with spears, coping with elephant herds and army ants, and waking at dawn to find a venomous snake zipped into my seven-by-seven-foot tent. How different my stories are about fourteen and a half months spent with native Canadian hunters in Canada's northern forest. In that research I faced a bitter arctic winter in the wilds, 105 miles from a road. Yet, again, there are delights as well as terrors to describe. Not every project has involved extreme challenges. I have tales to tell of less worrying exploration in the cities of two of Asia's great civilizations, Hindu India and Japan—with their refined sculpture, music, and perspectives on the world. And even that is not the full extent of the travels I am ready to recount.

Imagine what it would be like to take your family to such places. Much of the time, my own family, including children, lived with me in the field, or nearby. These family experiences are part of what I wish to share.

Along the way, I met one of the world's most peaceful and egalitarian peoples, hunters who live quietly near the equator in a thorn forest. I also witnessed spirit possession at night, two magical fights with the strangest apparent consequences, temperatures cold enough to turn heating oil into jelly on a stormy winter night, and travel nightmares galore, including a family trip alone on arctic sea ice during a December vacation. The anthropologist must be game for any and all of it.

Yet anthropologists are not a breed apart. Like you, many of us feel an interest in exotic ways of life when we are starting our careers, and we are likely to have a bit of an adventurous streak. But we go into the field more innocently than most suppose. While well prepared for our scientific routines, we are seldom ready for a fraction of the personal pitfalls and challenges that await us. The time we spend in the field entails almost constant improvising. Unlike TV's Angus MacGyver and Hollywood's Indiana Jones or Lara Croft, we find ourselves muddling through crises as most ordinary people tend to; the last thing you can expect from us is an aptitude for crafting instant solutions to problems on the run, as the screen adventurers do. It tends to be lucky breaks as much as wits that see us through.

One thing anthropologists can be sure of is that, when strangers learn our occupation at parties or in airport lounges, they start pressing for details of our travels. They ask how we find the opportunities and the funding. "Don't tell me people *pay* you to do that!" they say, with awe. They wonder what motivates us to study folk who dwell in jungles, tropical villages, ancient cities, deserts, and arctic wilderness. Inevitably, their main question will be, "What is such work *really* like?" Rare is the anthropologist who is not eventually turned by these inquirers into a storyteller. Given the situations that most of us have faced in our travels, and being scientists, few of us find the need or inclination to do more than describe memorable events as we, ourselves, experienced them. What I offer you here are just such plain, factual tales. I think you will find they need no artificial embellishment.

Beginnings

Although I was born in England and attended high school in a New Zealand Maori (Polynesian) community, in western Canada, and in Kansas, the tale of my anthropological ventures really begins in Philadelphia, where I attended graduate school at the University of Pennsylvania.

Throughout my undergraduate years, I enjoyed reading about hunters and gatherers—people such as Polar Eskimos, Pygmies, Australian Aborigines, the inhabitants of Tierra del Fuego, Japan's Ainu, or the denizens of the Kalahari Desert. When offered the chance, I wrote papers on them. Yet I thought of this as a romantic, personal interest, something I imagined I would put aside once I got to graduate school. After all, given our changing world, those cultures were fast becoming the subjects of yesterday's research. I could hardly miss the fact that many of the well-documented studies of such peoples were crusty tomes from the 1890s to the 1940s.

Putting my fascination aside was not so easy when the time came. At Penn, A. I. Hallowell and J. Alden Mason had each done extended studies of peoples in the Canadian subarctic; Froelich Rainey, at Penn's Museum of Archaeology and Anthropology, was experienced with the Inuit (Eskimo); and Jane Goodale, also at the museum, focused on the Tiwi in northern Australia. I found myself hoping that hunters and gatherers were still available for study in southernmost India, where I planned to do my doctoral research. For some time this remained an unspoken hope.

By 1961 I learned that such ways of life *did* still exist there. The anthropologist Kathleen Gough and a fellow student who had lived and worked in south India reported to me that they had actually seen shy Paliyan hunters in the forested hills during the previous ten or twelve years. And Christoph von Fürer-Haimendorf, at the University of London, wrote to me about his survey of similarly aloof hunting and gathering bands just to their west, the Malapandarams.

The Paliyans were my first choice. They dwelt on the lower slopes of the Palni Hills in the very heart of the area in which Indians speak Tamil, the tongue I had been learning for use in my research.

Their continuing elusiveness was especially intriguing. I wondered what explained their ability to refrain from contact with the bustling outside world. After all, for a good two or three centuries, several relentless processes have been disastrous for the original inhabitants of jungles, deserts, north woods, and other such regions on the edge of the so-called civilized or developed world. Any survivors of this contact were then sucked into the cultures of new and expanding nation-states. European epidemic diseases and the seizure of land by wave after wave of intrusive settlers may have done the most damage on some continents, but we should not underestimate the effects of people being drawn into the world market economy, being exposed to mission schools, and, frequently, being treated as merely one step above the beasts of the wild.

It surprised me that Paliyans had managed to survive into the mid-twentieth century as a somewhat separate people. Their success invited me to ask how they escaped the usual fate. One of my initial hunches was that they might have been holding back from excessive contact with neighbors due to their values. Yet even that needed explanation.

I wrote proposals to four separate agencies seeking funds to study how the Paliyans had managed to survive as long as they had. By the spring of 1962, I learned that two of the fellowship proposals were successful. I accepted support from the Ford Foundation because it offered me funding for eighteen months, instead of the usual twelve, and provided a generous budget for family travel, for travel within India, and for buying books.

Enough introduction! Let's get started on our journey to the tropical forest, then on to other adventures.

With Hunter-Gatherers in the South Indian Jungle

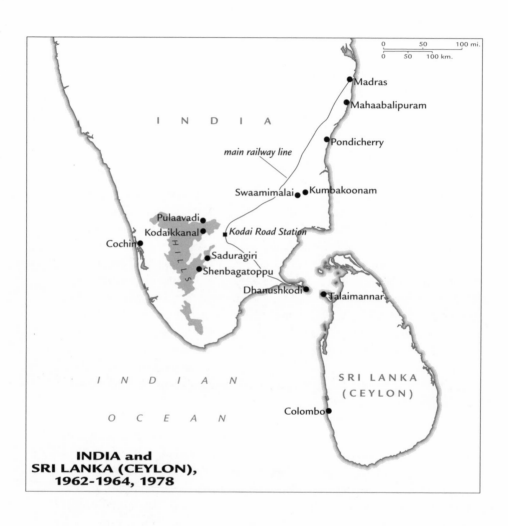

Madras

Mahaabalipuram

main railway line

Pondicherry

I N D I A

Swaamimalai • Kumbakoonam

Pulaavadi
Kodaikkanal ■ *Kodai Road Station*
Cochin

HILLS

Saduragiri
Shenbagatoppu
Dhanushkodi • Talaimannar

I N D I A N

O C E A N

SRI LANKA
(CEYLON)

Colombo

**INDIA and
SRI LANKA (CEYLON),
1962-1964, 1978**

0   50   100 mi.
0   50   100 km.

Stumbling into the Tropics

The Suspiciously Light Suitcase

"Getting there is half the fun," people say. I certainly have had fun along the way, but far more memorable are the awful moments when I was beset by disasters.

Heather was born in early June 1962, just as Trudy, my wife, was graduating with her B.A. and I was completing the preparations for our venture to south India to live among the Paliyans. To be sure, this timing was difficult for us, but we would at least be somewhat free to enjoy our child's first two and a half months before our departure. Part of that time we spent with my parents in Kansas, resting. What a contrast this was with the pace of the past year in school. There was much to do, nonetheless.

One essential task was readying our tiny daughter for international travel. Her tender age did not exempt her from the immunizations that were required by law in those days. The always painful yellow fever shot and the smallpox vaccination were the worst. No handbook told us what to do when not one but two vaccinations refused to take. Doctors and nurses strained to see on Heather's tiny arm an approximation of the reaction they had to certify. It was worryingly close to our departure when they finally declared her legally and medically ready for what lay ahead.

Another basic bit of business was shopping. We needed lightweight camping gear suited to jungle living, camera equipment, tropical clothing, a mosquito-proof foldaway cot for Heather, books, gifts, and much more.

We also needed training. Because we would carry a snake antivenin into the forest with us—one that would be effective against the bites of cobras, kraits, and south Indian vipers—Trudy and I had to learn how to give intravenous injections. My father was a doctor, and one of his experienced nurses solved that problem for us. She rolled up her crisp white sleeves, stuck out both her arms, said "practice on me," and talked us through it. Only then did we know that it was harder to give such a needle than to receive one.

At last our travel date drew near and we were ready. We had an embarrassing amount of luggage to ship, but the crucial items were stashed in a strong little Samsonite suitcase: our joint passport (which now contained our new baby's photograph and my long-awaited research visa), our three World Health Organization immunization records, a thick packet of traveler's checks, Heather's diapers for the first part of the trip, and a good supply of baby bottles and formula. Off we went by train to spend our last ten days in Washington, D.C., bidding farewell to Trudy's family. We would take the Santa Fe up to Chicago, then the Baltimore and Ohio on to the capital.

Two hours after our express left Chicago, I pulled out the Samsonite bag to prepare Heather's bottle. Whoops! The bag was far too light, given all that we knew to be in it. I flipped open the latches in pure panic. All it contained were four cotton dresses and the underwear of a middle-aged woman. Only then did we realize that the suitcase had unfamiliar initials on it.

The staff of the B&O was unbelievable. With an understanding porter's assistance and the train's telegraph, we dealt with Heather's immediate needs at the next two stops. That part turned out to be easy. What really concerned us was the loss of our passport, research visa, and immunization records. It seemed impossible that we could get replacement documents with all the required signatures and stamps in the brief time that remained. Where would we even begin? When we stepped down from the train in Washington, exhausted from worry, it was to unexpected news from Dad. Trudy and I had apparently shared a porter in Chicago with a woman whose bag was the same model and color as ours. Opening what was a puzzlingly heavy suitcase, the poor woman found our passport on top, on the inside cover of which was written my parents' telephone number, to be called "in case of emergency." She did just that. To our relief, the railroad not only took full responsibility for the switch, it also made and kept a promise to have everyone's bags back in their own hands within two days. That innocuous looking Samsonite was clutched especially tightly in my hand the following week as we boarded our Cunard liner, the RMS *Mauretania,* for Southampton, England.

A Stop to Visit the Past

My parents had not been in England since leaving there in 1946. Stimulated by my plan to stop over in England for ten days, they could not restrain themselves from turning the occasion into a full family visit. All went along except my older sister, who by then was married with two young children.

Neither of my grandmothers had yet had a chance to hold one of their great-grandchildren, so Heather's arrival added to the already special event. It was sufficiently special that no one chose to mention our sixteen-year absence.

Trudy and I spent part of our time in Britain doing an American-style "everything tour" by rented car, completing as much in two days as my relatives claimed they would aspire to do in two years. The very idea of it left them breathless. First there was Blackwell's bookshop in Oxford, where fellowship funds allowed me to acquire a number of hard-to-find Indian anthropology books, such as Louis Dumont's valuable monograph on the Kallar, the dominant landholders in the region where I would work. That afternoon we lunched on hearty meat pies in a Stratford-upon-Avon pub, saw one of the Bard's comedies at the Royal Shakespeare Theatre, then pushed on to southern Wales for dinner and a night's sleep.

Dawn found us poking about in the ruins of the thirteenth-century Caerphilly Castle, which a gatekeeper must have left open by accident the evening before. The castle's great leaning tower was wreathed in the morning mist—"dragon's breath," as Merlin is said to have dubbed it. Surely there were knights asleep within, and drowsy guards on the battlements. By midday we had spent time browsing in both the austere Roman legionary post at Caerleon and the ethereal remains of Tintern Abbey in its green, green Welsh valley. The abbey arched up elegantly into a now clear sky, its lofting form still hinting at the ideals of its builders. It was a weekday and there were few other visitors. We lunched there, sitting on the grass to prolong a peaceful moment. Leaving Wales, we made our way due southeast on a little-traveled masterpiece of straight Roman road building, across the Cotswald Hills toward Wiltshire and Stonehenge.

There was an abrupt change in the weather as we neared our destination; a storm swept in with low black clouds, gusty winds, and biting air. This was a stroke of fortune for us. By the time we reached Stonehenge, the only other person there was a keeper who huddled away from the autumn blast and ignored our arrival. We roamed about as we wished, touching the remains of Britain's deep past with our hands in ways that we imagined were not normally possible. Just as happened at Caerphilly Castle, we had a strange sense of being alone with Britain's ages. What an end to our tour! Eventually, though, we had to face up to the demands of the modern world and dash back to the London suburbs, where we were expected for dinner.

We hoped to accomplish one last bit of preparation for the tropics in London before traveling on. Trudy and I both read the warning labels on medicines. The possible side effects of long-term use of the main antimalarial drug were sufficiently frightening (they included irreversible anemia) to suggest that a child might actually be safer forgoing its use. So we dropped in on the London School of Tropical Medicine to see if specialists there had ideas on how best to ensure Heather's protection. Their leading malaria expert put aside his work to meet with us; to our relief, he had something new and relatively safe to recommend.

The Real Casting Off

When we drove to Southampton to board the P.&O. Line's proud new vessel, the *Canberra*, my parents and my younger brother, Don, came to see us off. The moment was surprisingly heavy. It was one thing to say we would sail to India in a lovely ship and undertake well-funded Ph.D. research there; it was an altogether different matter to actually embark on such a venture. I was twenty-three years old with a precious young wife and baby; the Tamil language essential to my study was still not coming easily to me; and I knew little of what really lay ahead. On top of this, as I leaned over the ship's rail and waved to my parents, one of Dad's recent worries came back to bedevil me. He had told me of his fear that Heather would be unable to cope medically with the conditions she faced in India. Were *any* of us up to it? Could we deal with the responsibilities? When the crew cast off the hawsers and the gap between ship and pier grew to ten, twenty, then thirty feet, the full weight suddenly hit me of what I had so long and so thoughtlessly desired. All I really knew and trusted was slipping away, and tears welled up to obscure my vision. Waving blindly for what seemed long enough, I retreated to a more private part of the deck.

Soon other feelings took over, ones of excitement and delight. This was Trudy's fourth ocean voyage and my fifth. Seasoned travelers though we were, the three weeks to come would bring us sights, smells, and sounds that were entirely new: Gibraltar, the Mediterranean, the narrow streets of old Naples, Pompeii, active volcanoes, the fabled passage between Odysseus' Scylla and Charybdis, Messina, a glimpse of Crete at sunset, Port Said, the Suez Canal, the Red Sea, Aden, Socotra, the Indian Ocean, Minicoy, Colombo (where we would leave the ship), and finally India itself.

What were the high points of this voyage? For me they came in Italy and Egypt, where we actually disembarked. Nevertheless, as we left the Gulf of Aden, I did enjoy seeing, in the distance to our south, the island of Socotra. This was the setting for Kipling's fabulous "just so" tale of how the rhinoceros, poor creature, got his skin.

In Italy we took Heather for walks in the streets of Naples, Pompeii, and Messina. Although the Mediterranean summer sun felt fierce, Naples's narrow winding streets offered welcome shade. One sparely built, middle-aged merchant invited us into his shop. When I pointed out that we had only foreign currency he laughed that aside, pushed two bottled drinks at us, and perched us on his shop stools. My father knew this very area. He had been at Salerno beachhead on the first day of the Allied landing, just south of Naples, tending to the wounded who still lay scattered on the beaches. Knowing that many Italians had welcomed the Allies, I decided to try telling the shopkeeper about Dad's 1943 experience. While neither of us knew the other's language, I managed to get the gist of the story across with the help of place-names, cognates between our tongues, and some rather laughable pantomime. He responded warmly. When we continued our walk, Trudy and I knew we had made a friend. In years to come—in India, Japan, and the Arctic—repeated encounters of this sort would leave me certain that people of goodwill abound on our planet.

Italy's volcanoes intrigued and worried me at the same time. They were the first living ones I had encountered. As we strolled about Pompeii,

I kept an uneasy eye on the plume of smoke rising from Vesuvius, for I knew the mountain's history all too well. Yet I yearned to see more. It was only a matter of hours until my itch was satisfied. Tipped off by an experienced crew member, we were standing on a quiet deck after dark that night when we sailed right past the conical island volcano of Stromboli. A sullen glow lit the air above it, and fiery rivers of lava streamed down its sides. Then, just a day later, as we steamed out of Messina, I was to see that same awful glow over Mount Etna. Enough, I thought! Little did I realize that some twenty-one years later I would spend half a day on the lip of an active volcanic crater in Japan, peering down into its sulfurous fumes. That is a story I will return to in a later chapter.

Egypt, for us, was to be Port Said and the Suez Canal. Although this was hardly the Egypt of my dreams, it provided my first taste of exotica since one-day stops in Suva, Fiji, on the way to and from New Zealand in my youth. We were among the first off the ship when it docked in Port Said, eager to experience whatever we could of brass and camel-leather shops, of picturesque residential alleys, and of the passing throng of Egyptians—more than a few of whom were dressed conservatively in red fezzes and veils. I even enjoyed being "gulled" by street magicians, the "gully gully men" who deftly caused coins from the crowd to disappear but scoffed when handed anything less than a substantial British silver coin. These, fortunately for us, were the currency of our ship. Not yet being aware that the prophet of Islam had sported a red beard, I was astonished when one passing man after another looked at my face, stroked his chin with a smile, and addressed me as "Mohammed Ali Whiskers." We spent a few hours soaking up the atmosphere and shopped for practical things, such as toothpaste and a camel-skin overnight bag, with a semblance of effective bargaining.

The canal itself gave us an unspoiled view of Egyptian routines. I must have gazed for hours at the passing river craft with their elegant lateen sails, at pack camels and palm trees, and at people who kept at their toils without a glance at the passing ship. It was a world I had known only from pictures. Now we truly had left the West behind.

Nightmare Heaped upon Nightmare

While we were crossing the Indian Ocean, Heather seemed to have little appetite for her milk and acted colicky. The ship's clinic provided little in the way of effective help, so we had to trust that her distress could be dealt with when we reached Ceylon (now known again by its ancient name, Sri Lanka).

At last, we could see that green jewel of a land, with its graceful palms. How welcoming it looked. We planned to spend three quiet days in Colombo with Joe and Donna, good school friends of mine from 1957–1958. I had been best man at their wedding, and Mum had baked them a three-tier wedding cake. There would be a lot of catching up to do after four years! Joe, native to the plantation country of Ceylon's interior, worked at the time as a probationary officer at Colombo's port.

As the *Canberra* eased around the harbor's breakwater, the ship's loudspeakers notified us that port workers had just gone on strike. There could be delays, and the size of our vessel might render the landing chaotic, but port officers would do their best to stand in for their men on the pier and even on tugs. They finally settled on anchoring the ship far out in the harbor, letting only departing passengers ashore, and transporting people and luggage to the pier on lighters—small open boats. Joe came beaming out of the crowd as we searched for safe footing on the slick seaweedy steps. He was able to spend only a few minutes greeting us and seeing that all our immediate needs were met before he had to rush back to his emergency assignment. Confusion reigned. It took us some time to verify that all pieces of our luggage had shown up in the heaps dumped out of the lighters and to arrange for most of them to be placed in bond until their shipment on to India. By the time we completed that, Joe was able to slip away from work long enough to drive us to his cozy home in a southern suburb of Colombo.

Those we consulted about Heather's tummy told us uniformly that she had a familiar complaint that ought to respond to a patent medicine. Was that correct? We decided to try it as a stopgap measure, and it did leave the child looking a bit more comfortable.

Donna and poor Joe, whose port crisis took up most of his time, were great hosts. They treated us to Sinhalese specialties such as sticky black sea slugs and string hoppers (noodles shaped into the form of loose pancakes). And we reminisced into the night with the help of potent distilled palm arrack that we obtained after nightfall from a bootlegger. While chickens did sleep just through a screen behind our pillow, our compensation when they woke us at dawn was that we could lie listening to new bird sounds outside and the pulse of the tropical community.

As soon as we told Joe about our travel plans we learned we had a problem. First, our Sinhalese visa permitted us a three-day stay in Ceylon, and this could not easily be extended. Second, the ship's travel agent had talked as if we would need only to walk in to the train station, on a day of our choosing, and board a train from Colombo to Talaimannar, then catch the ferry across Palk Strait to connect with Indian trains. We had no reason to question this lovely picture. The truth was that the seemingly simple trip necessitated at least two weeks' prior booking. Joe told us not to be concerned. I have no idea how he accomplished it, perhaps he made a contribution to some Station Masters' Retirement Fund, but on our third evening Joe and Donna whisked us to the station and helped load all our luggage into a spacious train compartment for the night run up to the Indian ferry. Exhausted, we slept.

We woke to the smell of sea air at dawn when the train pulled slowly into its terminus. But how we passengers were treated! Uniformed personnel hustled us from our carriages and herded us in a line, as if we were prisoners, along a footpath to the emigration authorities. Ironically, all this haste was a prelude to their making us stand and wait . . . and wait. We saw that many local Sinhalese travelers ahead of us were being searched. Then, at last we were aboard. The crowded little vessel put out onto a surrealistically glassy sea; momentarily it promised to be a quick, easy twenty-four miles to India. Passport inspection brought an abrupt end to that prospect. It was a sturdy ferry engineer who donned the Indian immigration officer's hat. When he perused our joint passport, he told us with an enigmatic smile that *I* might have a visa to do research in India, but Trudy and Heather were obviously not accompanying me as researchers. Because their names were not mentioned in my visa, he said, they could not enter India without their own visas. He put our passport in his pocket and told us we could retrieve it the following week in the state capital, Madras. If there is one cardinal rule of international travel, it is to *never* let your passport out of your hand.

I felt awkward about having no papers to present when the ferry docked on a sandy spit, a short walk from the huge unventilated Quonset hut in Dhanushkodi that housed Indian customs. But our passport situation was obviously well known to the authorities there. All they sought to do was screen our luggage. Due to the fact that we had so many items to assemble, we were the very last passengers they dealt with. Most others were already on the waiting train or proceeding toward it when the customs officers finally reached me. They put the matter simply: I must write down a list of all that was in our trunks and suitcases. "All?" I asked. "Yes, all." We had packed more than a month before, and my quick recall of particulars has never been reliable. Perhaps I could start with some general categories and go from there. The customs men hung over me as I concentrated on filling in as many specifics as possible. Then a pushy railway engineer joined us and announced bluntly that his steam engine was fired up and ready to go; I was holding up the train. Their repeated chorus of "Aren't you done yet?" only hindered my progress. Eventually, feeling too pressed to think clearly, I ignored the incompleteness of my inventory and handed it in. Everyone looked pleased. The engineer sent Trudy and Heather to our carriage, and the officer in charge seemed ready, I thought, to let me go too. No such luck. He straightened his hat and said, "Let's have a look." We had more than a dozen pieces of luggage, most with color-coded keys and padlocks. He unlocked one big trunk and searched it from top to bottom, then another, then another. After the contents of the first five or six agreed well with my fragmentary list, I was relieved to hear, "All right. You may go." And I should tell you that I realized weeks later that among the things I had forgotten to list were potentially dutiable items, including a movie camera and a tape recorder, both needed for my research. The probable penalty: confiscation and substantial fines.

I was starting to refasten the locks when I heard a change in the sounds outside. The train could not already be moving, but it was, and it was accelerating. Pocketing the locks, I sprinted after our carriage, closely followed by a long line of trotting porters who carried even our heaviest trunks on their heads. I scrambled through the open compartment door, and several porters did likewise, to stack what the others were tossing in on the run. And we made it. But only in one sense. The problem? I had expected to exchange traveler's checks at the border crossing. Because there was no apparent facility for doing this in the customs shed, we had not a single piece of Indian currency with which to pay the men. They were country folk, not worldly gully-gully men, and those who had jumped in to stack the luggage sneered at the English coins I offered them. Acceptable or not, that was all we had. The train was already up to at least ten miles an hour and the porters' angry faces worried us. It had to be English money or nothing, now or never. Thrusting a more than reasonable fistful of large silver pieces into the foreman's hand, we finally induced him and his fellows to leap out the door.

We sat down to enjoy the quiet. After all our harassing experiences, we had much to be thankful for: we were in India, our train compartment was even roomier than the one in Ceylon, a door suggested that we had our own washroom, and Heather's tummy trouble had abated somewhat—she was cooing. It was merely a matter of time until we reached Madras.

After this moment of premature euphoria, we were totally unready for what lurked beyond the washroom door. The doorway had a five-inch-high sill, and when we opened the door it was to confront a five-inch-deep sea of sloshing, stinking wastewater. The toilet and sink were far beyond reach. We did not have a copy of the train schedule, but we expected the 360-mile trip to Madras to take eight or ten hours at the most. It took eighteen. I will not describe how we felt about our surroundings, but believe me that we arrived at Egmore Station in Madras tired, hungry, thirsty, and feeling utterly filthy. We had crept into India through its back door.

An Egmore Station porter assembled a team to deal with our things and told me in Tamil that he could take us to a nice hotel directly across the square from the station. He was right. The hotel stood in a huge, shady, walled compound, away from the street noise, and its manager said he could give us a room for as long as our business took. I asked him if he could pay the porters well and put it on our bill, which he did, graciously. I assured him that in the afternoon we would change some money at a bank. "Today is a bank holiday," he replied. "Tomorrow, then." "No," he smiled, "this is the first day of a three-day bank holiday."

Finding Our Footing

After ten days in Madras our main problems were dealt with. We held a healthy baby in our arms, the visa situation had been rectified and the amended passport was back in our hands, a bank arrangement had been set up for dealing with periodic Ford Foundation checks, I was growing ever more comfortable with Tamil, and I had a sense that the Madras (now Tamil Nadu) State Forestry Department saw no reason either to grant or deny consent for my work in the government forest. It was time to begin the final leg of our journey into the hills, a far happier leg than the one we had just completed. Gorgeous clear weather suited the moment and added to our sense of eager anticipation. We began with a 280-mile rail journey on a rapid and comfortable main-line train. This time we were relaxed enough to enjoy the intense green of the maturing rice and the ingenuity of the diverse irrigation systems: bullock teams hauled huge leather buckets out of wells, human feet moved counterbalanced wooden cranes, and so on. And we were captivated by the tidiness of the tiny mud-walled farm villages that dotted the countryside every mile or so in all directions.

After a few hours on the train, we glimpsed near the southwest horizon what we imagined might be our immediate destination—massive blue hills rising steeply from the plain. It became clear with time that these really were the Palni Hills. All we really knew about them was that Paliyan bands inhabited some of the lower slopes and there was a potential home for us at Kodaikkanal, a so-called hill station, near their summit. Why should we seek a home there? Heather's recent illness had doubled our resolve to make family health a top priority; to that end Kodaikkanal was perfect. In the nineteenth century it had been built as a summer retreat at an altitude of 7,200 feet. Not only was its water supply protected, it lay well above the snakes, malaria, and heat of south India's densely populated lowlands.

A decoratively painted open-windowed bus awaited us at Kodai Road station. Although it was already half full, its khaki-clad driver and conductor wedged in all the new passengers and lashed their luggage onto a rooftop rack bulging with everything from gunnysack bundles to baskets of live chickens. The character of our road toward and then into the hills kept changing. At first we sped along a straight broad highway past lush irrigated fields of rice and sorghum, interspersed with plots of sugarcane and perhaps oilseed. But we also had to pass through two noisy market towns, so thronged with people and animals that, to our delight, the bus was slowed to walking speed. It was the India I had read about, and the people were those Dumont had described so well. I could not take my eyes off it. The men and women were lean and handsome, with weathered skin of various hues. Many walked barefoot; others had simple sandals. Some men were bare-chested, while others sported colored or white cotton shirts of diverse cuts; each man had a simple white cloth wrapped around his lower body, and a few of them wore small towels twisted into elementary turbans. Women wore plain deep red, blue, or green cotton saris. The younger ones, especially, also had blouses. Inexpensive though their clothes were, many women wore enormous geometric gold earrings that, by the time the women were thirty, had stretched their earlobes a good two to two and a half inches. Merchants sat cross-legged in tiny hardware and spice shops. A few old men perched on coffee stall chairs sipping hot drinks. Everyone else was moving. They went this way and that with head loads of firewood, water pots, snacks for sale to bus passengers . . . even wooden plows. And many of the women and children held a fretting naked baby on the left hip.

Altogether too soon we were on the open road again. The steep hillside, when finally we reached it, was dry and scrubby thorn forest for the first few hundred feet of the climb. It felt desolate. Eventually, our laboring bus made its way up into dense, dark tropical growth that echoed with unfamiliar birdcalls. The winding road took us across one stone bridge after another, passing crystal cascades, sometimes near enough to moisten our faces. Our driver had to stop repeatedly in order to negotiate his way past a landslide, an oncoming bus, or a string of straining bullock carts that also claimed the narrow road. Except when we had to deal with Heather's needs, it was difficult to turn away from all this. A little more than 2,500 feet into our climb we entered a brief inhabited strip; the road leveled a bit and we hummed past numerous small thatched huts and modest plantations growing fruit such as red bananas. Then again we climbed, again we were plunged into natural forest. In time, the vegetation grew lighter; by about 5,500 feet we were angling our way across precipitous open slopes of savannah, then just grass, with groves of rhododendrons fingering along the watercourses. In one such roadside grove I glimpsed graceful imported New Zealand tree ferns. As we neared 7,000 feet, we were seeing swarms of people once more, this time wearing sweaters and shawls against the chill. Although our road was as steep as ever, it now wound its way between substantial stone houses and a seminary, a landscape enlivened by pear orchards and flower gardens. Towering overhead were century-old stands of Australian eucalypts. And the air was pungent with wood smoke. We had finally reached the outskirts of our new home, a place we would soon fondly speak of as "Kodai."

It was our good fortune to find a comfortable, conveniently located house within days. "View Cottage" was well named. It had been built on the cliff's edge, overlooking the vast expanse of the plain 6,300 feet below. On the clearest mornings, from just above the house we could see a glistening silver line on the horizon, the Bay of Bengal, 103 miles distant. We were situated but three to five minutes' walk from government branch offices and the main market—with its heavy scents of guava, water buffalo meat, and coffee. Best of all, there was a hospital one block above our house.

Trudy busied herself with making us comfortable. One of the first tasks was finding a person to work in the home, someone who could care for Heather when Trudy went out. She employed Rosalie, a reliable woman who had already brought up her own family. Then she set about cultivating good relations with produce and meat vendors and with itinerant brass merchants. She did it well. In no time at all she proved able to negotiate prices so low they surprised a few of the old-timers. Trudy also befriended diverse and interesting members of the community, those who hiked and those who read and discussed good literature as a group. Her companions soon became aware of her skill with languages and, after a few months, it seemed only natural that she be offered, and accept, a part-time position teaching French at an English-language school in the community.

Seeking the Quiet People

First Steps

With Trudy and baby Heather safely situated atop the hills, I could begin looking for groups I might study. In 1908, F. Dahmen, a Jesuit, published a thirteen-page article on Paliyans, some of whom were employed at a Jesuit-run coffee estate midway up the Palni Hills. Within a few days I learned that the coffee estate remained in operation. Better yet, I heard that a dozen Paliyan families still lived and worked there. Busing part way down the hills again, I walked in through the savannah with an elderly Basque Jesuit who offered to show me the way. He was a good guide, years in the hills having turned him into a fountain of practical lore about the plants and animals we encountered. After half an hour's brisk walk on our grassy footpath, I saw a middle-aged man approaching who could only be a Paliyan. He was diminutive beside the old priest, yet what struck me most was that he stood tall, looked the priest straight in the eye, and spoke in a direct and confident voice. This surprised me, given his people's reputation for being quiet and timid, but I knew nothing at all yet about their manner of interacting with those whom they trust.

It was a great relief to me not to be drawn into their conversation, for many of their words and their pronunciation were strangely unfamiliar. You can imagine my excitement, though, as I watched and listened.

When we reached the coffee estate, some quarter of an hour later, it was more modest than I had expected. I still have a mental image of the compact cluster of simple stone houses, sheds, and a whitewashed church, overhung by ancient shade trees and surrounded by small fields. Because it was Sunday, many of the workers were sitting quietly in the shade. The residents of the estate appeared to be solely Paliyans and European priests. And, the Paliyans . . . oh joy! In their part of the tiny settlement I found men, women, and children of all ages. When I approached them, several adults and youngsters came forward cheerfully to find out who I was, without being bid by my companion to do so. Although the adults dressed in the well-worn clothes of Indian laborers, they were much as I had expected in physical appearance. The tallest men stood barely five-foot-two. Their facial features were diverse, but distinctive; many had short, tightly curled hair, unlike the straight locks of the Tamils; and they were not as dark as most of the people I had been seeing in the neighboring plains.

During the half day I spent there, I learned that one Jesuit was a renowned hunter who knew the hills and forests intimately. He was a person called to help when a tiger in the region became a man-eater. Between them, the Jesuits and the estate Paliyans described the nature and approximate whereabouts of some ten Paliyan bands and then gave me the names of individuals in each locale who could help in contacting the groups I sought. This was a solid beginning. Their leads and the sketch maps we made were detailed enough to launch me on my own effective survey.

Plunging into Another World

Using country buses as far as they went, then continuing on foot or by rented bicycle, I paid brief visits to several of what I judged to be especially promising groups. This survey plunged me into another world economically as well as culturally. I would set out on my survey with a hundred rupees in my pocket (approximately twenty dollars in those days), travel by bus, stay in hotels and hostels, eat in restaurants, and buy such things as cups of coffee and toothpaste along the way. When I returned home, two weeks later, I would usually still have a quarter of my money left! The slow, open-windowed country buses cost only one cent a mile; a three-course dinner of rice with vegetable curry, then with *miLagutaNNi*[1] (literally "pepper water," the basis for the West's mulligatawny soup), and finally with buttermilk, was a mere nineteen cents;

and a brass tumbler of the superb rich south Indian coffee cost but three or four cents. The hotel beds even had mosquito nets. So-called Brahmin eating hotels soon became my favorite restaurants. Their vegetarian fare was always freshly cooked and served piping hot, easily hot enough to be safe for the foreigner's stomach. Yes, I had to get used to sitting cross-legged on a concrete floor for dinner and eating with my fingertips from a banana leaf that I had just rinsed myself. But then taking cold showers discreetly in open public areas in some of the hostels was also a learned art. I loved both the feel of my new routines and the sense of self-sufficiency that grew as I mastered them.

In light of what two old written accounts and the Jesuits said about Paliyan shyness, each visit to a new group was made with someone whom the coffee plantation Paliyans or Jesuits had recommended, or with that person's assistant. Even so, one band was so shy its members would meet us only at the forest's edge long after nightfall. I sensed that they were apprehensive about my guide's rifle, which he told me he carried in case he had an opportunity to hunt a leopard. I learned six months later, however, that the man—a forest produce contractor—had a reputation for serious violence toward tribal people. He was said to have killed three of them when they refused to collect honey for him. It was hard to learn much in advance about those I had been told could aid me in locating Paliyans, but my options were limited; without a knowledgeable guide I stood only a modest chance of finding them at all.

One suggested contact was a prosperous owner of irrigated rice fields and cotton mills whom I knew only by what turned out to be a pejorative nickname, "Mr. Mainar," a name his staff was shocked and mystified to hear from my innocent lips. A Paliyan band was settled on the far edge of his land, obliging me to cross his fields to reach it. I had been cautioned that it was essential for me to meet this man before six in the morning; after that, he would be lost in the mists of his opium dreams. Visiting the man was like tumbling into a Fellini film. His house and the attached family temple were a full block long. Although the building's painted concrete outer walls were unpretentious, one could tell from its dimensions that it might be grand within. I was ushered into a large, cool entrance hall and asked to wait. My first sign of the old man stunned me. His huge body would have dwarfed many a Japanese sumo wrestler; it was so enormous that at the start of each day he had to be carried to his chair on the run by a retinue of burly, well-coordinated servants. He dripped wealth, enough to have a private doctor on his staff, a doctor with a modern car. When I was standing beside the landowner for the very first time, leaning over to explain my needs into his unresponsive ear, I had to cover my mouth to stifle a laugh. His huge chair pointed toward the grand doorway of the entrance hall; directly in front of him, a hammer and sickle had been painted in bold, bold red on the facing building. This, like his nickname (from the British "Minor," equivalent to the American "Junior," but which, I soon learned, carried a local connotation of "immoderate spender"), was surely rooted in resentment. Then, his servile staff sought to honor me by escorting me into the Paliyan settlement like a celebrity. While they meant well, that plan had to be headed off.

When Paliyans and I finally did meet, on the land of "Mr. Mainar" and elsewhere, there were three communication problems. My guides had to be dealt with carefully, or they would bully people and volunteer misleading information about me and about my project to enhance their own reputations. Then, no matter how I phrased my questions, most Paliyans responded to them far too tersely and evasively for me to learn all I sought to know. Finally, Paliyan pronunciation and verb forms differed from the standard Tamil I had learned in class. Two years' study of colloquial Tamil gave me poor preparation for their divergent dialect. Nonetheless, we stumbled along just well enough for me to forgo translation of our general talk. When I told each band that I might come to live with them for some months, people were offhand in their responses. Their manner made it apparent that none of them actually believed I would show up again.

The isolation of one band at a higher altitude attracted me. To reach them I had to start from the top of the 8,000-foot range, descend some newly terraced rice fields on foot, then make my way down into a wilderness that stretched for miles. A man with the unlikely name of Rambo took me in. The last part of our descent entailed climbing down an almost vertical face of granite into a canyon-shaped valley where Paliyans dwelt in loosely scattered huts and rock shelters. Strands of mist across the cliffs gave me the feeling I was descending into a Sung dynasty Chinese painting. Below me stood tall, dense bamboo; above, the air was filled with screaming, wheeling green parakeets.

The inhabitants of the community listened to my clumsy explanation of the project, and no one voiced objections to my plans. They even helped me select a suitable location for my tent near one of their rock shelters.

I hold my daughter outside View Cottage in Kodaikkanal.
I am wearing the problematic faded olive shirt.

By packing in my food I could be self-sufficient for a week at a time. It was manageable. The Paliyans accepted my entry well enough for me to begin by documenting their genealogies. So far, so good. On my third visit, because it seemed silly to enter the forest wearing my tidy white shirts from graduate school, I emerged from my tent one morning in Ivy League denim slacks and a faded olive-colored shirt, much frayed at the collar and cuffs—strictly Saturday wear. People took one long look at me, returned to their huts, packed all their portable possessions, picked up their babies, and left silently in three different directions. Within twenty minutes they had totally disappeared. Following them seemed futile. I was now alone, and unarmed, in what was reputed to be a tiger-infested valley—enough so to keep herders out. Why did they flee? The agricultural people above eventually told me that police had come there six weeks earlier seeking an opium dealer who had run off to the forest following the suspicious death of a rival dealer. They said the police had bullied all they met in their efforts to elicit information, which led, I concluded, to a Paliyan fear of

The valley in which I was abandoned.

anyone who showed up in anything resembling khaki. The valley was to lie empty for some months.

Three anxious days I remained there, huddled in my tent, unable to leave due to torrential rain, a soaring fever, and serious diarrhea. I will not pretend that the proximity of tigers was something I dismissed casually; each snapping twig at night brought ice to my veins.

As soon as the rain let up, I readied every bit of my gear and attempted to stagger out with the sodden tent and two packs slung on my back. A shocking discovery awaited me: my original path down the cliff had been the temporarily dry course of a seasonal waterfall. Searching without success for another way of scaling the cliff, I finally tied my packs securely to my body with tent ropes and edged up slowly through the icy torrent. More than once I thought my fingers, numb with cold, would fail me. The ascent totally exhausted my weak, feverish body. Even after I reached the gentler, friendlier, cultivated slopes, it was a fight to keep my knees from buckling and to stop my feet from slithering off into the rice paddies as I stumbled along the rain-slicked paths atop the terrace walls.

I was beyond exhaustion when, at last, I dragged into the village where

I could catch a midday bus. Then people showed me I would have to climb an additional thousand feet, in gumbo mud, to where my hilltop bus had been stopped by a landslide. Being too dehydrated by fever to face the additional climb to the bus without a long drink first, I went to the nearest house and asked a woman who was cooking there to boil some drinking water for me. She did it graciously. No fieldwork course or textbook had prepared me for all this.

Luckily, when I teetered down out of the bus back in Kodai, a tailor who worked for Trudy recognized me, caught me as I was about to fall, then organized a party to get me and my gear back home. My temperature was nearly 104.

Once over the dysentery attack, I chose another site to restart my research. Three considerations shaped the choice. First came safety. Due to herds of elephants and the huge gaurs (also called the Indian bison), tigers, wild boars, bears, and king cobras, especially, work with an elusive band in deep forest would be foolhardy without the protection of a rifle. It would be particularly so given my remoteness from medical help. Despite my need, friends predicted that it would take months to obtain a permit to carry a weapon and even longer to locate something appropriate. They were right about delays, and the only rifle I could turn up was a monster, a fifty-year-old double-barreled .500 caliber elephant gun. I wondered what it would do to anything less than a tusker. Second, so long as relations with their neighbors were amicable, many Paliyan groups appeared to reside fairly near the forest's edge, in what we might call their frontier with Tamils. If that zone was indeed one of their usual habitats, why not at least begin my work there? Third, due to what I could already see as the slow, quiet character of Paliyan activities, studying one of the smaller groups would yield a relatively sparse set of observations. It would be preferable for me to find a community that was of average size or slightly larger.

A group of Paliyans I had visited at Shenbagatoppu met my criteria. They lived near the margin of the forest, close to a cluster of tiny fruit plantations where some Paliyans found seasonal jobs. Like my first group, they dwelt along the bottom of a canyonlike valley, but theirs was drier and at a much lower altitude—a more representative setting than the one where I began. Although accessible from the plain, the new group inhabited hills more than a hundred miles south of my home; the distance would complicate my travel to and fro. I finally bought a small red Czech motorcycle, which I could use on main roads, cart tracks, and even, with care, on the footpaths between rice fields. It was light enough to be muscled out of mud, too. This allowed me self-sufficient access to all but the most isolated forest groups. It also freed me from erratic bus schedules and from having to make overnight stops en route in communities lacking accommodation for visitors. Once I had had to stretch out in a schoolroom. Another time, a village postmaster invited me to sleep on a bench in his one-room post office, then rendered sleep impossible by bringing in the pride of the village—a grizzled bard who could, and did, regale me for hours with a sung folk version of one of India's great epic tales. With my Jawa motorcycle, I could complete a trip in three hours that had taken me all of twenty-six hours on the two occasions I did it during my survey. The first month that I owned it, I was able to chalk up the bike as my best purchase in India.

Shenbagatoppu bears more complete description. In a recent book on Paliyans I introduced it like this:

> During the early twentieth century a cluster of over 20 tiny plantations grew up . . . where a river emerged from the forest. Prior to construction of the orchards and estates there had been several Paliyan campsites right along the river course. Once plantations surrounded them, Paliyans came to see two of the sites, one a large rock shelter, as uninhabitable [and they pulled back up the valley]. But, plantations provided new kinds of employment and, in the mid-twentieth century, some members of one band then parts of two others coalesced at a spot just 150 m from the new groves.[2]

A two-room government school with a single teacher was to open there a few months after my arrival. This community was where I was to begin my research and learn the basics of the Paliyan way of life. Work with bands in the deep forest came later; so did study of a Paliyan group that had lived just outside the forest for a number of decades.

Utopia in a Thorn Forest

Before getting to the exciting highlights of my time with the Paliyans and in their jungle, I must spend a few pages on something that trumped all the other experiences. It startled me. Paliyans treat fellow humans so considerately that my year and a half with them was unforgettable. They were quieter, more peaceful, more respectful, more egalitarian, and more individualistic than any people I had ever met or read about. Being extreme in all these dimensions, Paliyans were "on the edge" in behavior as well as in geography. Forty-two years later I have yet to see a society approximating theirs in individualism, not even in the proudly individualistic United States. Portraying Paliyans this way makes them sound like those hypothetical, ideal people social philosophers and political theorists love to write about. It also gives the impression that it would be easy to live and work in their utopia. Both matters deserve a closer look, my work situation first.

Initial Obstacles

Far from being easy, getting to know Paliyans was the most difficult task I have undertaken in my professional career. It was slow, too. There was near general acceptance of my setting up a small tent at the end of a row of tribal residences, facing directly onto a small open area in which much of Shenbagatoppu's morning and evening social activity took place. That was helpful, because I could observe a great deal of what went on, and do so discreetly. But the Paliyans initially made it hard for me to use many of the other important means of collecting data I had learned in graduate school. My teachers drummed it into us that we should make a point of interviewing experts. Yet, when I sat cross-legged on the ground in front of their houses talking with them, Paliyans looked straight at me and denied flatly that particular individuals knew more than others about their social structure, foods, medicines, or anything else. They denied it *so* strongly that I soon suspected they were doing it on principle. In addition they acted as if they were offended by the very questions I asked about expertise. This was a crucial lesson for me about values and about the social dimensions of knowledge. In time, I appreciated their view that having specialists and turning to them for advice would create the very kinds of dependency that Paliyans found repugnant. Self-reliance was proper for adults. While some *did* turn out to be more knowledgeable than others, if I made the mistake of commenting to them about their unusual competence, they at once denied it and dropped into confused embarrassment.

Another problem with my techniques was that interviewing anyone at all, on any subject except genealogy, evidently entailed more intense speaking than Paliyans found comfortable. They became restless immediately, and one or two declined further sessions. I could not afford that. Being taciturn by choice, they would have to be won over slowly to my means of data collecting. Modest chatting was fine, but the initial interviews made clear that I should not attempt deep or lengthy discussions right away. When I lessened both my own talk and my requests that others speak, the Paliyans grew more at ease with me.

Two things I certainly could do were to limit my talking to brief conversations or pleasantries and increase the time I spent casually sitting around observing. My eyes became an invaluable tool during the first two months. By simply watching, I learned a considerable amount about ways they cooked, tended their hair, and fashioned hardwood sticks for digging yams, for example, and still more about their quiet, low-key style of interaction. Already knowing each individual's name, I made systematic notes all day on who did what with whom, to find out how friendship and family relationships functioned. It was also possible to keep track of everything that could be interpreted as evidence of social friction. More about that later. In addition, I examined all I could of adults interacting with infants and children. Although mothers talked quietly to their babies and toddlers when showing them things, it eventually became clear that much of a child's learning was done by observation, a technique specialists call "social learning." I mainly saw youngsters just watching others, rather than listening to verbal instructions, as they acquired knowledge about foods and the techniques for obtaining and preparing them. It was my luck that my improvised method of learning—by watching—turned out to be a Paliyan method! For people who are perceptive, speech is less essential than we inveterate talkers realize. Paliyans even had ways of reassuring another person without using words. Merely sitting near someone, either in a patch of early morning sunlight or around a flickering fire after dinner, was enough to convey one's positive sentiments.

As people noted that I never barked out orders the way most outsiders did, that I normally talked in a soft voice, and that I preferred to be self-reliant—these all being proper behavior to them—some did begin to act more confidently and openly toward me, and two or three agreed to be interviewed. It soon became known that I paid people their familiar daily wage (the same they would receive if working on plantations or for forest produce contractors) in compensation when they stayed home for the day in order to give me two or three hours of quiet chatting. Word about this spread. I believe that they, as did I, saw such pay as fair and unproblematic. Several began as well to invite or allow me to accompany them when collecting food—digging yams, hunting, and harvesting wild honey—or gathering plants for trade. They responded to my questions about things we saw while out, treating it as reasonable talk. Although I was to hear more than one disbelieving chuckle over my actions, they also put up amiably with my participating beside them in their work, toward my stated goal of learning everything possible about their forest life so I could teach about it. It helped maintain a good, light spirit when I established a practice of adding my day's take to theirs, as their young children might do. Our increasingly relaxed interaction told me the research was at last beginning to yield results.

Respect and Peaceful Anarchy

It helps explain Paliyan society if we begin with their idea that all people deserve respect just by being people. In their usual way of expressing it, they used a double negative: one should *not* be *dis*respectful toward others; one should avoid what Paliyans, in their dialect, call *tarakkoravaa,* putting another person in a lower position. This respect was not something Paliyans owed solely to males, or solely to adults, or solely to other Paliyans. By "respecting others" they meant, literally, behaving in a respectful manner to *all* others. Readers who have browsed in the social philosophy of earlier centuries may, at this point, remember Lao Tzu's "primal virtue," William Godwin's prescription for "political justice," or Herbert Spencer's "first principle."[1] Each of these thinkers advanced, as one of his central ideals, the notion that people should live virtuously and avoid disrespect, coercion, or domination in social relations.

Can one *really* live that way? Actually, Paliyans showed me that one can. I did not find out about their ideal from their talk; I only heard them speak about it many months after I had discovered their apparent rules by watching their behavior. It was like learning to play checkers effectively by observing silent play, then, long afterward, hearing people speak about moving diagonally, capturing the opponent's game pieces, and making one's own pieces more versatile by getting them to the far edge of the board.

When I mentioned that Paliyans achieved a quiet society by speaking little and using their voices softly, I could well have gone on to say that it would be interpreted as disrespectful merely to speak to others loudly regarding what needs to be done. Demonstrating respectfulness for Paliyans went far beyond restraining oneself from inflicting violence, threats, or embarrassment on others. One should also avoid any self-satisfied verbal assault.

Putting respect first created a system in which equality truly was accorded to everyone, automatically. After studying Paliyans, it astonishes me to read in descriptions of other hunters and gatherers that the such-and-such people "are egalitarian, except, of course, in regard to age and sex." What enormous exceptions! It is hard to imagine how the term *egalitarian* came to be used for people in systems having such asymmetrical statuses and such unequal privileges. But then, even for most American idealists, the wording of their revered Declaration of Independence long expressed the same incomplete standard. Even though the eighteenth-century document spoke of "all men" having the right to "life, liberty and the pursuit of happiness," it was not until the mid-twentieth century that many Americans thought of this as being applicable to everyone.

It is one thing to have ideals and quite another matter to have rights that are protected. How far will Paliyans go to safeguard peoples' right to be free of disrespect? They will go all the way. A case I described a few years ago helps make that clear. "One morning a mother struck her . . . [ten]-year-old son firmly three times for taking food which belonged to his aunt. Another woman who was not in any way a relative and who had several dependents of her own came directly over and led the boy by the hand back to her house. She let him stay the rest of the day and fed him with her own children."[2] What this account does not tell you is that the firm slaps were not hard enough to leave marks on the boy's backside; that the child's refuge lasted about twenty-four hours; that we all watched, but no one spoke to the attacking mother or anyone else about what she had done; and that, minutes after the incident, the mother broke into tears and acknowledged the violence she had inflicted on another human being. This example also illustrates the Paliyan belief that one should immediately move away from an aggressor. Young children have obvious difficulty backing away from parents who misbehave. So available people, especially grandmothers, step in as needed to ensure that they do find refuge. All members of the band, children included, have rights as people that must not only be recognized but must also be protected. The fact that children actually *were* protected sets Paliyan society apart from most others. It is one reason I hold that Paliyans approach an extreme when it comes to equality.

As for equality between husbands and wives, not only did neither partner have greater worth, but mutual respect was obligatory; neither had authority over the other in any regard; and neither had greater property or inheritance rights, greater rights to divorce or remarriage, or greater freedom in sexual matters. How often in this world might we hear anyone other than a Paliyan man say "It's not my business" in talking about his wife's ongoing sexual affair? In the south Indian forest I heard this from more than one person. Then one of the men, a fifty-six-year-old, smiled and went on to say of his marriage, "If I've caught hold of a branch, I shouldn't leave it." These were individuals whom I lived beside for months, and their assertions were not contradicted by their actions. Just as Paliyan parents had no concept of "owning" their children (and would never tell a granny who was trying to protect a child, "Leave *my* child alone!"), neither spouse owned the other. Ernestine Friedl refers to "evidence that a degree of male dominance exists in all known societies," and perhaps because she is a specialist on gender most in my field of study seem to accept her word. Similarly, people seldom question Morton Fried's insistence that prestige is "a real and important factor in all known human societies" and that "most of the simplest . . . societies regard women as inferior."[3] I believe both scholars express the views of the majority of my colleagues. This is sad. My observations on Paliyan marriage reinforced the idea that these hunters and gatherers approached a human extreme in their pursuit of equal rights. For all who espouse gender equality, Paliyan society stands as a rare good example.

Friends and faculty realized, early in the project, that I enjoyed dwelling among people who actually lived a life of tolerance and social equality. My openness about this in letters was fortunate. It provoked Paul Friedrich, a teacher who was well aware of my ideals, to ask if personal "filters" blocked my seeing signs of Paliyan resentment or jealousy. He suggested that I test this by looking at their dreams. Two weeks later, having recovered from the initial shock of his unwelcome challenge, I did as Friedrich proposed with several men I knew well. Their dreams revealed precisely what he had predicted. In a surprising percentage of the cases, a man dreamed of having a revenge affair with the wife of a man who had enjoyed a sexual tryst with the dreamer's spouse, or of flying low over the settlement and taunting those very men whom I saw as living especially effective lives. These details plus their embarrassed laughs as they recounted their dreams to me suggested that they *did* harbor resentment! It was a fieldwork lesson well learned. For the next two weeks I pored over my preliminary field generalizations, viewing them not as summaries of facts, as I had in the past, but as theories in need of testing. While the research benefited from this more cautious stance, I have to confess that it did little to alter my respect for the Paliyan way of dealing with human relations.

Friedrich's challenge reminded me that Paliyans, being people, experienced the usual human feelings of annoyance, frustration, jealousy, and outright anger. I began to see that, like people elsewhere, they sometimes gritted their teeth. What distinguished them from others was that, when trying to deal with negative emotions, they ordinarily restrained themselves from so much as talking back. Verbal retorts would only add to the problems, after all, for they merely increased the number of persons exhibiting disrespect. Moving away and calming oneself down were the proper and usual responses. Paliyans were occasionally killed by outsiders, but I found no evidence of murder within their own society. This is surely the best testimonial for the Paliyan strategy of avoiding all behavior, even words, that might contribute to the escalation of a conflict. Others merely dream of peaceful living; the Paliyans had found a workable key to it.

Just as Paliyan society was peaceful, it was also a functioning anarchy, and a smoothly successful one at that. It followed from the Paliyan principle of avoiding disrespect that no one had legitimate reason to intrude into another person's business. No leader or group had the authority to give an order or levy punishment. People were responsible only for themselves. In most bands one or two men and women did stand out, though. They were people who had "good heads," as they put it, people who were able to distract others with wit or soothing words at times of tension. Two of these wits were wonderful. White-haired Old Mutti was a fountain of original Freudian puns, for instance. They bubbled forth at times when anyone was acting pensively, or when the gods were ignoring Paliyan petitions for help and failing to possess anyone. Young Catayan, by contrast, played the part of a clown. At times of tension, he came on the public stage with exaggerated clumsiness or went up to people and, with slurred speech, pretended that he needed to borrow a common item that he surely already owned. These self-appointed smoothers or distractors are called by two special terms, both of which refer to their good heads. But if we translate the terms as "headmen," we make it seem as if they possess authority. The actual situation is precisely the opposite. When forest produce contractors asked such people to be foremen—as sometimes happened due to their skill at putting others in a good humor—and if they accepted such a role, they tended to do so in a light and self-depreciating way that made it crystal clear that they insisted on being ordinary members of the group.

At times, events felt chaotic to me, the autonomy of each person not being anything I was prepared for. Yet, how sweet it was that no one could give orders, not even to a child of six or seven. A youngster of that age who wanted to make and use a cooking fire did just that. A child who wished to move to an aunt's house could not be told "no" by a parent, although the aunt would, of course, have to be asked. To live properly in Paliyan society, it was necessary only to be careful that one's actions were never disrespectful to others.

I must not give the impression that problems were unknown in Paliyan interpersonal relations. They certainly did take place. I found, though, that difficulties among adults or between adults and children were dealt with in most cases by positive means, especially by self-restraint or moving away. Only in squabbles among young children was there much likelihood of retaliation, and even that would be far too mild to draw adult attention in an American, English, or Indian elementary school playground.

There is more that could be said comparatively. Because Colin Turnbull gave much publicity, a few years ago, to the "mountain people," the anarchic Ik foragers of east Africa,[4] I must emphasize that Ik and Paliyans are poles apart in the overall tone of their social lives. Ik live desperately, for they impose self-reliance on one another by abandoning even their aging parents or young children to their own devices. Theirs is a cold society emotionally. Paliyans, by contrast, have warm relationships. They, too, are self-reliant, but they achieve it in a way that is both positive and principled.

Recent Western political history leads us to regard anarchists as violent. This is a peculiarity of our complex societies. Anarchist theory arose after the societies took form. Think about what would be entailed in a large-scale society if one sought to do away with all the positions and institutions that bear upon controlling other people. It would probably take protracted violence in any populous, organized society for some members to rid the system of such institutions as government officialdom, peace enforcement, imposed taxation, and laws about propriety. Need I go on? There are those who ask, "In an anarchy, who takes garbage out on Thursday?" But does that sort of activity require regulation in a community of twenty to thirty-five individuals, most of whom are intimately related to one another? Surely one master rule on the order of the Golden Rule would suffice. This would accord with Spencer's first principle, that we should have freedom, provided we do not infringe the equal freedom of others. There are several other hunting and gathering societies that achieve relatively smoothly functioning anarchies; but Paliyans, while not unique, are certainly among the extreme once more.

Whimsy, Wild Boars, and Wilder Spirits

An Unpredictable Pulse of Life

Each morning as I sat in front of my tent fixing breakfast, I watched my Paliyan neighbors waking, tending to their babies' needs, then ambling off in search of patches of sunlight where they could squat. Their bodies welcomed the warmth of the sun after a cool night on the ground. They sunned in small family groups or near friends in a quiet togetherness. Twenty or thirty minutes might pass with few other than the children so much as stirring or speaking softly. Eventually, some would wander off to commune with other clusters, followed by yet another twenty or thirty minutes, perhaps more, of idyllic calm. For me it was planning time; not so for them. Most of them expected to spend from about ten in the morning to four in the afternoon intermittently digging wild yams for the evening meal. They anticipated, as well, collecting, and perhaps snacking on, fruit, small game, fish, or honeycombs they encountered along the way. The usual workday needed little advance preparation unless a digging stick for yams had to be straightened or replaced before setting out.

But this would not be the course of the day if rain set in, if the fresh and bloody tracks of an injured wild pig or deer were found nearby, if a family member fell ill, if one person became upset with another, if a honey contractor walked in and convinced some individuals to help him collect honey, or if one of the Paliyan gods descended on a member of the band to help the band cope with a problem. Each day would unfold in its own way, and one had to face whatever it brought without firm prior commitments. All *seeming* Paliyan plans entailed the unspoken understanding that a particular activity would be done *if* circumstances allowed. This openness might seem whimsical, but it is quite serious. Commitments and predictions have to be conditional, because one cannot know in advance what will turn out to be the most suitable or even the most moral way to spend one's time. This holds true even when it comes to marriage; recall how maintaining peace is deemed primary and parties in conflict simply separate, if only temporarily. Should conditions mean that people have to forgo food, work, sleep, or married life in order to preserve the peace that they judge most important, think of the benefits they reap from such an approach.

We inhabitants of big, complex societies may have difficulty appreciating those benefits. We perpetually keep ourselves busy organizing people for collective enterprises that require planning. Yet, think about how keeping ourselves flexible instead would be a principled way for dealing with the unpredictability of life. Staying flexible would allow us to weigh all factors from moment to moment so that we, like Paliyans, could arrive at a course of action best suited to current circumstances. An overscheduled, overcommitted, harried member of Western society can only dream that a supervisor at work would consider it a personal decision, *solely one's own,* as to whether to attend work or stay home with a feverish child.

The ever-changing pulse of Paliyan life can best be felt by describing the events of a few days. While this entails seemingly unpredictable swings from one subject to another, you must understand that this is precisely how I myself experienced life with Paliyans.

The Chase

I have said virtually nothing yet about my hunting and gathering with Paliyans, and a few glimpses of that aspect of life in the jungle are long overdue.

I was just starting to prepare breakfast shortly after dawn one day when I heard a loud and urgent male voice calling us all to a spot about a hundred yards away. The shouter got everyone's attention, too, for he'd found that an injured pig had passed near our settlement not long before. Its fresh bloody trail was unambiguous. Excitement was in the air. Disregarding all else, nine men, aged twenty-three to fifty-five, picked up their hunting gear and set off immediately with two small dogs. No one objected when I put aside my cooking and tailed along. Six of the men carried machete-like billhooks, three of the younger men had spears, and I merely toted a camera. The fresh trail told us our quarry was a medium-size pig. We sped along at a brisk walk, reliant on picking up the tracks intermittently rather than following each print. Where ground vegetation was relatively open, we spread out in groups of two or three, advancing even more quickly than before in a crescent up to a hundred feet wide. Due to the speed with which we followed the trail, my having to double over to get my big frame through the thorny growth proved a boon; with eyes to the ground, I was often the one to relocate the tracks after a gap. The two youngest men, Poonnan and Big Kanni, and a forty-year-old were more vocal than the others, but the party had no organizer or coordinator, and talkative people were not central to group decision making. From time to time theories were voiced about what the pig had been doing, perhaps resting or feeding. The group assessed each of these possibilities in light of actual, visible evidence. I had my own theory, that the pig was dragging a leg. If my hunch was right, this could make it much easier to take; it was time to put aside passive observation. In keeping with Paliyan practice, I tried participating in the hunt by sharing my theory. Several men looked up attentively and asked the basis for my thinking. I showed them that there was a puddle of blood each time the pig crossed a low branch. To me, I said, this indicated that branches were snagging an injured leg, pulling open the pig's wound. They heard me out, but admitted to skepticism.

Near midday, one man, aided by his dog, captured a tiny chevrotain that started from under our feet. Others watched and commented on his actions, but, once he had tucked the diminutive deer in his belt, no more was said about his private take.

Our pig pursued an elliptical path, which eventually brought us back to near where we had been at midmorning. By late afternoon, after ten hours on the trail, we began at last to hear the pig's snorts and scuffles ahead of us. It surely also heard us for, soon afterward, it took refuge in a twenty- to thirty-foot-wide thicket, far too dense for us to see through, and hid in silence. Splitting up into four groups of two or three people each, we surrounded the spot. Three of the men tossed stones into the undergrowth in hopes of pinpointing our quarry's precise location.

When one rock drew a squeal, we all dashed in. There was a whirl of bodies, and a few seconds later the pig lay still. Exhilarated, we reviewed how it had been achieved: Catayan had struck the pig with a billhook, then those who were armed with spears—Big Kanni, Poonnan, and Top-peyan—had pierced its chest in five places. Each of the wounds was probed and discussed. My companions also pointed to a dangling hind leg and flashed me warm smiles; the predator's mauling that morning had done what I theorized. An injury like that is precisely what Paliyans pray for; they ask their gods to send a leopard, a tiger, or a pack of wild dogs to waylay a large pig or deer in a place where they will find either the animal's carcass or its tracks. This happens only a few times a year, but, when it does, it is no less than a gift of the gods.

Four men lifted the pig by its legs, carrying it out onto a nearby expanse of flat granite. Before we did anything else, all of our weapons were propped against the body and a brief prayer of thanks was offered to the gods who had made the hunt possible. People chuckled as the two dogs sniffed at the inert beast, for these hunting companions had done little if anything to help us.

A lanky Tamil lad emerged from the trees during our prayers, so we exchanged a few words with him about what he and we had been up to. He had brought a few goats with kids to browse illegally in the government forest. He had just killed a python, which he saw as a threat to the kids, and very next moment heard *our* sounds of celebration. The happy, lilting Paliyan chatter piqued his curiosity.

Using vines as ropes, we slung the pig from two spears for transport back toward the settlement. When we reached the clearing where the python had been killed, however, we halted to butcher our take. Several men built a fire, singed and scraped off the pig's bristles, removed its guts and edible organs, and carved up the carcass—dicing different cuts of meat into pieces that could be distributed equally to all participants in our hunt. Four of us perched on the goatherd's nine-inch-diameter python as we worked, far too engrossed in our happy activity to bear in mind that our seat was not a trusty log. Not ten minutes later, apparently stunned not dead, the python suddenly regained its senses, convulsed its great body, and slithered away from the scattered butchers, now flat on their backs and laughing. Lesson learned.

We set out big leaves by the work site, one more leaf than there were members in our party; then we portioned the cuts of meat equally onto those leaf plates. The extra share was the customary reward for the person

The end of the hunt for the pig with a broken leg.

who took the risk of striking the first blow. Some people suggested minor adjustments in the portions, but no one reached for a share until everyone had agreed that all were equal. Before we left to carry the meat home, we conducted another, more elaborate ritual of thanks in which we presented a few choice, reserved pieces to the gods who had helped us. This small yet tangible offering would be left atop a roof in our settlement that night for the gods to retrieve at their pleasure.

Back in camp, as the sun sank beneath the hills to our west, bringing the evening cool, we sat around our fires and joyously set about cooking the first meal of the day.

Surprises on "Ordinary" Days

Many days were unremarkable, yet the quiet pace and the self-assured actions of Paliyans were satisfying to watch. And there was always the possibility of a surprise.

Being familiar with images of men hunting together, it shocked me to see women joining in when a mixed Paliyan group ran into game. Digging mole rats out of communal burrows collectively was one thing, but finding that two married couples might go after deer together took me aback. Women do hunt actively in certain cultures—in Australia, in the North American subarctic, among the Agta of the Philippines, and among Aka Pygmies of the Congo. Knowing that now does not mean I was aware of it in the 1960s. As for the parties of two Paliyan couples, one technique they employed was for the men to drive deer through a rocky ambush where their hiding wives could make the kill. So much for simple notions of women doing only safe work and tending to babies!

Another false notion of mine was that the women took responsibility for collecting vegetable foods. That was soon dispelled. Early in my research I went out for a day of digging yams with thirty-two-year-old Lacmi, forty-year-old Viirappan, who was the elder of Lacmi's two husbands, and a slightly younger woman who happened also, coincidentally, to be both polyandrous and called Lacmi. Let me refer to these women by their ages: "Lacmi 32" and "Lacmi 28." The outing was memorable to me for it was the day I learned the strength of these little people, plus a great deal more.

The women planned to spend the day foraging for yams, while Viirappan would divide his time between collecting for a forest produce contractor and digging yams for dinner. A two- or three-mile walk, entailing a thirteen-hundred-foot climb, brought us to our work area by 10:15. The women proceeded a short distance further up the slope; Viirappan and I spent the next two hours collecting *puLukke* stems and roots, loosening their fragrant bark with smooth, five- to six-inch-diameter stones, then stripping it off. Once the bark was packed, we searched a boulder-filled streambed for a water hole where we might drink. We found three five-foot-wide pools. Although each was heavily strewn with floating matter, my companion deemed the water in the third potable when filtered through cloth.

At this point, Viirappan, who had been exchanging periodic calls with his wife, received a request from her for help. Guided by coos, we ascended slowly to where the two women were searching for yam vines, startling a wild pig on the way up. Lacmi 28 had exposed and levered up a huge granite boulder, some sixteen cubic feet in size, simply to extract two yam tubers from beneath it. Even with her companion's help, she couldn't quite complete the job. Their light bodies—for neither weighed more than seventy-five pounds, the heft of the boulder, and intrusive

Lacmi and Viirappan extracting yams from between granite slabs.

four-inch-thick tree roots complicated the extraction of the tubers. We men added our weight to her huge lever, freeing Lacmi 28 to reach quickly underneath and snatch the yams out. Then Lacmi 32 asked our help in separating two enormous leaves of granite, between which two more yam vines vanished. Even Lacmi smiled at the small, flattened tubers she eventually removed. We took a meal break together, after which all spent some time digging. For me, this meant first learning to fashion and use a hardwood digging stick, and then remembering never to back into thorn bushes as I worked. Trial and error can be painful.

About 4:00, the women set out ahead of us toward home. Half a mile along the trail we found them laughing and poking at holes around a ten-by-fifteen-foot water hole, trying to chase off a snake they had seen. Then they spotted some sardine-size fish. Lacmi 32 unwrapped the top of her sari, and the two women swept it three times across the pool, netting thirty-five fish. But all three Paliyans peered down in horror at a freshwater crab they had also bagged. Noting their faces, I couldn't stop myself from telling them with delight that I *relish* crabmeat. They voiced utter disbelief and disgust until it dawned on them that it was just a bad joke; then how they chuckled at the ease with which I had taken them in. "Yes, and you gobble down scorpions, too!" could well have been on the tips of their tongues. Viirappan drank from the pool. Then, while his wife stayed there to wash her sari and her hair, he dug a nearby yam, and Lacmi 28 collected and bundled firewood. At 5:45, after a rest, we set out for home. There was one further stop, to pick and eat fruit and discuss a deer we encountered. We arrived home at 6:45.

Then there is honey. At 6:15 one morning, fifty-year-old Young PerumaL, a lithe grandfather, asked me to come with him on a solo honey-collecting trip. He walked and climbed briskly, stopping only to get me a few samples of medicinal plants we had previously discussed and to show me two kinds of bees at work. So tight was his focus that we strode right past four forest hens. Our path took us across the floor of a valley, then up its wall, a total walk of three miles and a climb of more than two thousand feet.

The ten-inch-diameter comb he planned to take was twenty-five to thirty feet above the ground, in an almost leafless tree. Because of the hills, the sun was not yet on it. In a matter of three or four minutes Young PerumaL stripped down to an abbreviated loincloth, cleared away some tangled branches, and cut a handful of bee-repelling *taraku* grass, which he doubled over and rubbed on a stone. Tucking the now oozing grass into the top of his loincloth, he started slowly up the tree, cutting away all sharp protrusions, dead twigs, and vines as he went to ensure an easy descent. When he waved the pungent grass under the comb, the bees fled immediately, flying back and forth in a tight swarm six feet above his head. He fastened the grass to the tree, snapped off the supporting branch on both sides of the comb, took the stub of the branch in his teeth, and descended without a sting. Within minutes we were back on the trail, comb in hand, walking as quickly as before. Indeed, PerumaL did not stop to don his usual, more modest lower cloth until we heard Tamil voices on the path ahead. The whole outing took just three hours, and, to my surprise and pleasure, he then presented me with his take.

Paliyans collected honey from four different types of bees, ranging from huge, vicious "giant honeybees" with their rich, three-foot-wide combs to minuscule "stingless bees," which make thimble-size honeypots. The first time I peered down at a swarm of stingless bees walking about on my hand—the lovely little creatures looked like miniature bumblebees but were scarcely an eighth of an inch long—I delighted in them even before learning how delicate their honey was.

As the months went by, I found that Paliyans were far too versatile in their food quest for me to describe it in simple terms. They were forever facing new situations and always devising novel responses for handling them. While their work each day tended to look routine at the outset, if I was even modestly observant it seldom appeared that way to me by day's end.

Confronted by Spirits

Protecting *caamis* (spirits or gods) usually respond when Paliyans call on them for help. When a *caami* does "descend on" a Paliyan and take over the host's body, everyone pays rapt attention; those present may be able to coax the spirit to provide information or protection. If people have been behaving inappropriately, the spirit may also detail the behavior that is proper. In forest groups, over a quarter of Paliyan adults of both sexes experience these visits. Sometimes a *caami* visits a person spontaneously at a time of special need. More often, people sing invocational prayers to call down the spirits.

You never know what to expect. Those who experience possession may have a familiar *caami* but can be visited by others as well. I have seen one man drop exhausted after an almost two-hour-long series of unbroken visits, with several *caamis* in turn displacing their predecessors. Another time we had seven people possessed simultaneously, two of them visited by one and the same spirit. But I am not giving a sense of the excitement.

After dark one evening, sudden sounds of consternation rang through Shenbagatoppu settlement. A teenage Paliyan youth who was sitting by my tent ran toward the agitation then doubled back to ask for my bowie knife. Reluctant to relinquish it without knowing why, I accompanied him to the scene of the disturbance. A young woman had been struck by a sharp two-by-three-inch piece of granite that had come hurtling out of the darkness. Everyone was upset, and the atmosphere was tense.

When another stone flew in from a different direction, people began to exchange ideas about who the attacker might be: "Weren't two people momentarily visible to the west?" asked Kritnan. Another man agreed that outsiders might be implicated; hadn't two Malayalam speakers (from the west coast) hung around for no obvious reason earlier in the day? Catayan reminded others of a crank woman whom he had found muttering to herself that day in the settlement. CappaaNi rejected that idea. The previous day he and his daughter's former father-in-law, Poonnan, had seen a *kaTuvaa* roaming about and hiding behind a hedgerow immediately to the south. This giant tiger helps the *caamis* provide game for Paliyans, but it has its troubling characteristics, too: it is subject to manipulation by sorcerers; one can change irreversibly into such a tiger by eating a particular shrub; and the spirit of a dead person can possess a *kaTuvaa* as well. Finally, I recalled, but kept it to myself, that two hours previously forestry officers had placed several head loads of precious sandalwood in a Paliyan house for overnight safekeeping. The worth of a single head load would be equivalent to several years' earnings for any laborer who could put the community to flight.

Poonnan urged that we examine the hedgerow to the south. After much hesitation and discussion, a dozen men, including me, set out with long heavy sticks to see what evidence might be found there. We searched without success. On our return we were told of more missiles being found, both river-bottom and cliff-face stones. Every stone in the open part of the settlement was inspected. We had heard few stones actually hit the ground, and one we knew hadn't been there before had come from the hand of a playful settlement child. He tossed it so openly that we all just laughed. When a dog barked to the north of the settlement, men began clearing bushes on that side and examining the ground there for *kaTuvaa* prints. Then someone said he saw two people on the large rock to the east. We set out in that direction and found toe prints of a running man. It was thought to be a *kaTuvaa* paw mark until a similar but more complete print was found nearby, the footprint of a person much larger than a Paliyan. We marched back to the settlement in a more confident spirit. A long, disorganized conference followed during which some drew figures on the ground as a distraction—I saw line drawings of a human face, an elephant, and a deer with one leg shown skillfully as being behind another. One man's wife tried calling him home several times. After 10:00 p.m. a few members of the group did drift off home, one by one. It was suggested that some stay up to keep watch. Three young men and I got a mat, sat by a tree, and told jokes from 11:00 p.m. onward. There was no moonlight to illuminate the scene and, slowly, the remains of the last evening fires faded away, leaving us in near total darkness. Lacmi 32 walked over to her uncle's house at eleven and asked, "What is there to fear?" One of the young men with me asked her, simply, "Where do the stones come from?"

After midnight three men, CappaaNi (age fifty), Poonnan (age thirty-eight), and Old PerumaL (age seventy), reclined before their houses, praying in song or chant for the *caamis* to come to them and provide help. Extremely long phrases were sung, with no pauses for breath, first in a high-pitched and then in a low-pitched voice. Besides asking for assistance in dealing with the evening's projectiles, one petitioner asked for rain: "The forest is catching fire due to excessive heat. Why don't you give us rain?" One of the singers kept up a simple but loud beat on a single-headed tambourine-shaped drum measuring eight inches across by four inches deep. By 12:45 a.m. the young men on watch predicted *caami* would come to CappaaNi, who was singing in a strained way, broken by great gasps and sobs. Moments later there were two loud thumps. CappaaNi got up, walked a pace or two, squatted briefly, then leaped up and ran three hundred feet or more along a path toward the forest. The distance and the dark soon put him beyond our view. His singing resumed and suddenly stopped. There were piercing screams and other strange sounds, as if from a fight, then silence. Meanwhile, Poonnan was getting steadily more excited. His singing was broken by sobs. At 12:50 he jumped up and took a running leap with both hands on top of his head, his elbows out to the sides. He ran a few steps leaning forward. Then, leaning back abruptly, he stopped. Repeating this leaning run several times, he made his way across the settlement, then he dashed out along the path CappaaNi had taken. We heard singing, a pause, screams, and then silence. Both men resumed singing, with further long pauses.

There was discussion in the community as to whether we should go out to the two men. Some said they would return. KaNNiamma, Poonnan's wife, walked about talking loudly.

Shortly after 1:00 a.m., Poonnan and CappaaNi returned on different paths, singing in strained voices. Poonnan, staggering as before, ran to a spot some twenty-five feet from his home and stood there singing. CappaaNi made his way to a spot ten feet from where he had begun. He was trembling more than Poonnan, his voice was more strained, and his gasps were more frequent. Both were in deep trance states, and their quivering bodies were dripping with perspiration. Initially we could make out almost nothing they said; it was but incoherent screeching. And their arms kept flying up. People clustered around to support them and, although it took much strength to do so, managed to bring their arms back down by their sides. Within a few minutes, we finally got understandable replies to the key question that people kept repeating, "Who are you?" The *caami* who had descended on CappaaNi identified herself as Raakkaacci; the one who had come on Poonnan told us she was Peecciamma.

Two cloths were fetched, men's lower cloths of the everyday kind but very clean, white for Raakkaacci and red for Peecciamma. Another such cloth was tied as a sash diagonally across the chest of each of the possessed. Things became less frantic at this point, and three or four people came and sat near each of the divine visitors. The two *caamis*, who sang in the same manner used by their seekers during the initial prayers, informed us, at last, that two *kaTuvaas* had been sent across the mountains from the western side to devour people. These great tigers had thrown the stones, but they had now been driven back across the mountain range by the *caamis*.

During the next hour and a half the personal needs of nine people were dealt with. Although most of their concerns were serious, others engaged in a good bit of joking and light talk. For instance, nineteen-year-old Veelan three times placed a five-foot stick on the ground straight out in front of the crotch of the squatting Ponnucaami. All seeing it laughed, including Ponnucaami's wife. The victim expressed slight annoyance and pushed it away each time.

At 1:10, three of the people who sought help approached Raakkaacci. Lacmi (aged about twenty) sat before the *caami*, holding her year-and-a-half-old son, and old Raaman lay facedown on the ground with his head by the *caami*'s feet. In response to Raaman's salutation, the *caami* took him by the hair, urging him thus to rise. He rose to a kneeling stance, with his head lowered. The *caami* sang briefly, "Wait. Do not fear. I shall first see to a young banana tree [baby] and next time I will come to you." Raaman lay down again as if asleep and remained there until about 2:00, when he went home. Raakkaacci spent the next thirty-five minutes with Lacmi and her infant son. Lacmi saluted with palms together and said she was unwell and in need of protection. "Don't fear. I will remove all the ailments from your body, the fever and other harmful things," the *caami* replied. *Caami* explained that Lacmi had been bathing at the cistern of a forest temple eight or nine days previously. Hearing a white lizard screeching, she had become frightened and feverish. The *caami*'s whole body was trembling rapidly, especially her arms and legs. As she sang, there were great gasps periodically, for five to fifteen seconds each time. She usually leaned forward quite sharply from the waist while singing, with her hands on Lacmi; occasionally, she stood leaning slightly back with her hands folded in her lap. At first, Raakkaacci put her hands only on Lacmi's head. Later she placed them on her shoulders and chest, then ran them down to her ankles. Lacmi asked about her son's dysentery and fever and was promised a cure. Raakkaacci put her hands first on the child and then back on Lacmi's shoulders and head. Finally, Lacmi requested help for her husband, who had fever and limb pain. Reassurances were offered.

Veelan asked his wife to take their child to Raakkaacci. She brought her forward, requesting the *caami*'s protection. The two-year-old cried as a trembling Raakkaacci leaned over and placed hands on her head, saying, "I'll watch over you and protect you. Don't fear." By now it was 1:53.

A twenty-year-old who had been on watch with me earlier mentioned his injured ankle to a companion and took a step forward. Raakkaacci came to the two lads, placed one hand on the head of each, lowered her head, and held it sideways. Addressing each of them as "younger brother," she offered them her protection. Then she stepped back and extended her left arm from the waist, calling for *tinniir,* sacred ashes, in her cupped hand. A youth fetched ash from the nearest fireplace.

Raakkaacci approached me, so I greeted her verbally and with a salutation of the hands. Placing a thumb mark of ash on my forehead, the *caami* sang that my wife would have a child—as, indeed, she would. Raakkaacci also asked me to watch over everyone in the community and see that no one troubled or beat them. All the while, her hands shivered as she held her ashy fingers in my hair.

She staggered back again and then went over to KaNNiamma. Placing her hands on the woman's head, she called her "older sister's daughter" and cautioned her not to wander in the forest. She promised to watch over her. KaNNiamma asked for help with her fever and the itch and pain of a skin ailment. This interchange lasted until 2:17. Just before departing, Raakkaacci gave a single sharp handclap to get rid of an intrusive spirit, then leaned over and sucked hard on the top of KaNNiamma's head to draw out fever and pain.

Raakkaacci staggered off a few yards and sang until 2:25. Good rain was promised, and something unclear was said about a marital dispute between two elderly people. A young man told the *caamis,* "fine, enough," and two other people repeated that message, adding politely, "go." By now most had returned home for sleep. Raakkaacci half walked and half ran back toward the forest; then, lucid once more, her host CappaaNi returned home.

In the meantime, Peecciamma had ministered to Old Poonnan (aged about sixty) and then left. Old Poonnan had come and sat before her. He told the *caami* he was troubled by evil spirits and requested her protection. The *caami* explained that, a spirit had got hold of him while Old Poonnan had been going to collect honey for an outsider. Peecciamma leaned over slightly from the waist to place her hands on his head. Then the petitioner prostrated himself before her and asked for protection. Near the end, Peecciamma twice gave a single loud clap of her hands. By 1:38, Poonnan had regained his senses. He stood silently with his arms crossed in front of him for a few minutes with Old Poonnan lying as if asleep near his feet. Then Poonnan talked with Old Poonnan in his ordinary voice, and both went home.

This was my first full-fledged experience of meeting the *caamis*. The complexity of the event was exciting, as was the spirit's matter-of-fact attention to me. Both were unexpected.

A later confrontation with a *caami* in a distant, slightly more settled Paliyan band began rather badly by comparison. To make a long story short, we tried for hours at several places in the woods to call three *caamis*: VaNTimaakkaali, Mantu Maavili Caami, and Valayaankaaran.

People laid out offerings of incense, betel leaves, partly peeled bananas, sweets, and a freshly opened coconut on leaves. Several men offered silent or spoken individual prayers; a girl prostrated herself; a woman did likewise; and three men each made small circles of coconut milk on the ground and prayed. Finally, a series of people—a sick youth, two women, seven children, an elderly woman, and others—prayed for the health and welfare of all. The atmosphere, though tense, was full of puns and jokes. But recall that people with good sense create such diversions during times of tension.

Some laughed; others speculated that the *caami* would not come on this day (one hinting that it was due to my presence); yet others called out "Come! Come!" quite bluntly to the *caami* and even threatened him. The sun descended behind the hills, and still this chaos persisted. Most, including me, eventually packed up and set out for home. We had not gone many yards when Valayaankaaran chose to arrive. Perhaps he really had been waiting for my exit, I thought; that possibility left me feeling rather awkward. Nonetheless, I raced back with all the others to watch as people soothed his host's quivering body and sought to ascertain which of their seven usual *caamis* was paying a visit.

Our interchange with Valayaankaaran lasted nearly two hours—on into the dark. The two major concerns had to do with my intrusive presence and the disabling, two-month-long illness of a youth, Young KaNNi. Our trembling *caami* had no sooner identified who he was than he pointed a long, quivering forefinger at me and charged me with trying to catch him with my "dark box," meaning my camera. Suddenly *I* was in a cold sweat. It took the intervention of many people and much loud argument to cope with this, but an immediate chorus of support for me erupted from all those who had approached me quietly over the previous twenty-four hours and borrowed a rupee or two in order to finance their grand offerings. They stated firmly that the *caami* needed to be aware that I had paid for more than half of his gifts. It was an unbelievable relief when the *caami* softened his stance, referred to me as his "grandson," and allowed the community to get on with its requests.

We were to learn during the next hour that Young KaNNi's pale, fragile condition was the result not of possession by a malevolent spirit, as people had imagined, but of his having been cursed by an outsider with whom he and his father had long experienced conflict. No wonder he had not responded to several kinds of recent treatment. The *caami* promised a cure, and the lad did, in fact, improve steadily from that day onward. He became more responsive to others and returned to his work routines within a week.

Moonlit Play

Children played ever changing games during the day. They dog-paddled in icy pools along the mountain rivers, built toy houses, ran together holding reed propellers that spun on thorns, or carried with them colorful tethered beetles that buzzed in endless circles.

Nothing brought out their playfulness better, however, than a full moon in a clear sky. Under such bright night skies youths joined the children in tossing hoops back and forth or playing a borrowed game that they explained in a borrowed way, making it sound exactly like a game I grew up with. But how they actually played it was not at all as I thought. Let me explain.

What looked like two teams stood behind two baselines, each facing the other. With the teams taking turns, players ran out, one at a time, toward the opposing team. They spun and danced as they went, each with a personal style, all the while chanting *cadu kudu kudu kudu* nonstop, but being careful to rejoin their own teammates before their breath ran out. Silly me, a rank newcomer to the community, listened to their recitation of borrowed rules instead of watching what they really did. I asked to join in, which of course I could. Who could say "no" to me? And I started to play what *I* had called "prisoner's base" or "pum pum polaway" in western Canada. My version of the game was highly competitive. So, in my turn, I dashed out, took three of my unwary little opponents as captives (a tiny one tucked under my arm and two others grasped by their wrists), and dragged them all to my team's baseline. Silly, puffed up, self-satisfied me! I was not applauded for this magnificent victory. To the contrary, members of both "teams" looked at me with open-mouthed astonishment, confusion, and horror. The next thing I knew, a delegation of the older players came to ask me, "Please sit over here, be comfortable, and watch." There I reflected, of course, on how badly what I took to be the "rules of the game" conflicted with the gentle Paliyan style of interacting. That explained why I hadn't seen players captured! *Cadu kudu* was really an improvised ballet, each participant in turn being given the happy role of soloist.

Paliyan dance, while similarly joyful, involved a wholly different style of interaction. It exemplified togetherness. When the moon illuminated their camps, the youths got out and repaired their drums in preparation for a night of adult fun. Using many personal variations of a polka step, all-male or all-female circles danced until people had to stop from happy exhaustion. This time I could join the men without problems. And I even had to take my turn on the drum.

Long-married husbands and wives danced as couples, once in a while, in their own small circles. Their beaming fellows would gather around to encourage them, stirred and displaying open appreciation. This resembled the delighted group response I witnessed when my elderly honey collector and his wife (he fifty, she fifty-six) came out of their house one day and went to work in the forest each in the other's clothes. They came home that way, too. As one man put it, they do this because they are happy. Married couples are privileged in their possibilities for such play. Life with another person was not a simple function of survival; it could be savored.

One night, I saw a man I did not recognize dancing in a men's circle.

It took me some time to realize that it was Aame, a twenty-four-year-old married woman, in borrowed clothes and a turban for disguise. Then a second woman did it, and yet another. Although bystanders cheered the dancers on with more than the usual enthusiasm, the cross-dressing was not openly acknowledged as such. Aame and the others were coy with me afterward, but they were adamant that they had neither participated in nor even seen the dances in question. It was not long before two men showed up in saris in a women's dance circle. Then four young women, one holding a sari over her arm, cornered me and said, "You, too." I would not hear of it initially, but they dragged me into my hut and finally got their way. How their eight tiny hands fussed over me to make sure everything (except my beard, of course) looked as it should. I have to admit that my three dances with the smiling women were curiously liberating.

There was a thin, spastic ten-year-old boy who had never known the sensation of dance. I often watched him at dances, sitting on the edge of the group and keeping time to the drums with his hands. Why should he have to settle for that? During one evening of dance, I hoisted his light body up onto my shoulder and we two danced our hearts out.

With Princes into Wilderness

The Three Princes

A great misty-blue range along my route kept beckoning. I felt the pull of Saduragiri each time I passed the midpoint of my ride to Shenbagatoppu. My eyes were drawn to its forested slopes and to its savanna uplands, hidden at times in clouds.

Shy relatives of the people I was studying were said to dwell there, but the blue range was a wild land, without roads or villages, and it was still relatively unspoiled by outsiders from the plains. To ascend Saduragiri I needed to have a rifle to protect myself from elephant herds and other big game. But, when the mountain's magical pull was strongest, my fascination almost outweighed the silly matter of my not yet having procured a gun license or a suitable weapon. I had to go up there.

Some months earlier, I had been told that Periya Raja, the eldest son of a former raja, would be the best person for me to speak with about locating Saduragiri's tribal bands. The Paliyans trusted him, due to his lifelong history of care and kindness toward them. His role of patron was a continuing one, even though his family's rule over the wooded range and nearby cultivated lands had ended in 1947, when India became a republic. Paliyans still came down to his back door at night when needing such things as medicine for a seriously ill child. Given the young prince's reputation as a committed benefactor of the forest people, it seemed only natural that I should pay him a visit, if only for suggestions on how to ascend the range and meet with his reclusive friends.

Motorcycling into his family's former domain, with its modest central town of fifty-one hundred residents, its eighteen or so scattered farming communities, and its lands with twice the area of the European nation of Liechtenstein, I had little sense of what lay ahead. Except for its location, snuggled as it was at the very foot of Saduragiri, the agricultural part of the landscape did not strike me as being much different from the dry lands nearby. Looking down the road, I saw a familiar mix of a diesel bus, slow bicycles (many with extra passengers on the crossbars or back carriers), strings of creaking bullock carts, and farm folk on foot. But it was easy to identify Periya Raja's whereabouts when I finally entered the town, for the burg boasted only two dwellings of any size. They stood apart on the far western edge of the community, surrounded by a grove of substantial trees. The aging father owned a grand house with a pillared porch; Periya Raja resided in a more modern but smaller dwelling, nestled in the trees beyond the larger house.

My host and his wife were lounging on a shady veranda when I motored up their driveway. He was a clean-cut, powerful young man, a former college athlete, about eight years my senior; she was an attractive, sophisticated woman in a lovely sari. As I recall, they brought me the customary brass pot of water to rinse road dust off my feet and invited me to join them in a cool drink. A three-year-long drought was having such an effect on the region's hydroelectric power generation that an iced drink was almost as great a treat for them as for me. Although they owned a refrigerator, their local allotment of three hours of electricity a day was scheduled for nighttime; the machine had to be kept padlocked throughout the hours of heat if it was to be of any use.

I had no sooner mentioned my reason for coming than I discovered for myself the depth of Periya Raja's interest in the Saduragiri Paliyans. His eyes lit up, he was eager to talk about them, and he expressed an earnest hope of revisiting them in the near future. Some months had elapsed since he had last trekked up to see them. There were three bands, I learned—one on the side of the range facing us, another in a high-altitude valley with two tiny Hindu temples nearby, and a third in a more isolated spot at the far end of the range. He went on to tell me that members of the tribe had served as priests at the two Hindu temples for centuries. Perhaps the Saduragiri bands were not as isolated as I had been led to believe. As I grew more comfortable with him, I took the liberty of probing into the basis for the prince's intimate link with Paliyans. He smiled and launched into a tale about events in ancient times involving his ancestors and a Paliyan family, but his wife was quick to cut him off before he revealed much. Given his initial willingness to discuss it, I would have to remember to save my question for a more private moment. There was a lot to learn.

Before I knew it, Periya Raja put a firm proposition to me: if I returned in two weeks, he and his two younger brothers would take me across the range, introduce me to its three resident Paliyan bands, and do some hunting along the way. This was more than I had dared anticipate. I gave him an immediate and enthusiastic "yes." In providing me with safe access to the range, his offer was the realization of my dream.

The prince's garden was chaotic when next I motored in. Members of his staff were scurrying about noisily, and everyone was caught up coping with questions for which they lacked answers. Periya Raja's two somewhat younger brothers came over to my motorcycle straight away to welcome me. They greeted me with warm smiles, but then had to be off again, responsible as they were with organizing aspects of a venture that was far larger and more complex than I had expected. A habitual loner in my work, I found the magnitude of the arrangements worrying. The three princes would each bring a gun-bearer; there were cooks as well, plus laborers to carry our gear and others to clear trails when needed. More than a dozen people would be coming. Given this princely style of travel, it might be difficult to do the kind of interviewing I preferred.

Saduragiri's Enigmatic Wilds

After two hours of trying delays, our troop set out on foot, angling up a shoulder of Saduragiri that had a moderate incline and light vegetation. About one thousand feet above the plain there was evidence that herders had burned off parts of the slope illegally, to encourage the kinds of plant cover their cattle needed. We soon left that behind.

A bit further into our climb we stopped for what amounted to a brunch. While cooks were preparing our meal, I strolled over to where I could get a good view of the plain, only to notice that someone was shadowing me, furtively attempting to get my attention. His clothes suggested he was the senior cook; he seemed to need help with something he had hidden rather obviously in the front of his shirt. I glanced at him and raised a questioning eyebrow. When he pulled out a jar of

English marmalade, I understood his plight without words. How embarrassing. He and his assistants must have been unable to loosen the lid; he hoped I would try giving it a twist myself. It yielded at once, his face was saved, and I watched him sneak back to his post to prepare his special "surprise" for the master's English-born guest.

We resumed our climb. By midday we came across three families from the first Paliyan band. Locating them had been easy, so easy that I wondered whether I needed our great safari to meet my goals. But the interaction between the Paliyans and the prince was well worth watching. As I had seen with the old Jesuit in my very first Paliyan encounter, the tribal people stood erect and talked directly and comfortably with their friend. How different their posture toward the prince was from that of his household retainers! While I had been sharing my first drink with Periya Raja, two weeks earlier, a well-dressed member of his staff who was going off duty approached the veranda, saluted, then prostrated himself full-length upon the ground in front of his master. Now I was witnessing a meeting between equals and noted that Periya Raja gave signs of enjoying and encouraging it. Did he understand their values, or did he just find it a refreshing change, as people tend to do at rituals and in festivals such as Mardi Gras in which the usual order gets tossed aside or turned upside down?

After they had caught up with one another's news—about family health, their recent travels, our present outing, and the whereabouts of band members who were absent—Periya Raja turned and asked me if I wished to interview a few members of the group. I was relieved that others in our party gave us privacy when he and I sat down with them. We collected genealogical data and ran through a list of basic survey questions about their food quest, marriage arrangements, social life, and religious rituals. These would tell me how similar or different their practices were from those of the bands I knew to the south.

A young Paliyan man joined our party when we set out once more toward the heart of his people's domain. The character of our surroundings kept changing as we neared Saduragiri's summit. The savanna vegetation felt ever more wild and natural, the water in the streams became clear enough to drink without taking special precautions, and the birds and small mammals we met were not only plentiful but also unafraid of us. All these changes had to be due to the lessened impact of humans. While huge "footballs" of elephant dung were a familiar sight near my usual work site—the fresh dung often sporting a cover of yellow butterflies—I had never encountered them as profusely as here. It was a land that seemed to require us to traverse it quietly and with respect.

We began looking for a suitable campsite long before evening fell. The princes eventually settled on a sheltered spot, ringed most of the way round by trees. Because it did not especially appeal to me, I said something about wishing to look further, to see if I could find a better place nearby, and walked out of the camp on my own. Off into the mosaic of grass and trees I went. There were campsites with attractive vistas wherever I looked; surely one of them would suit us better. As I was mulling over how I might make a case for such a move, Periya Raja's gun-bearer came up behind me without a sound, tumbled me over into deep grass, and simultaneously put his finger to his lips. I guessed why and kept silent. He pointed back into the clearing I had just passed through, and there it stood, with its head and shoulders emerging from the trees, a magnificent lone bull elephant bearing slender six- or seven-foot-long tusks. Luckily we were downwind. The gun-bearer had tailed me without his usual weapon, so he mimed that I should remain where I was while he crept back through the grass to get a rifle. He returned five minutes later with Periya Raja's gun in his hand, and he and I watched the great beast amble away, still oblivious to our presence. It was my first wild elephant, and I was far too fascinated to realize, until long afterward, how unprotected I was as I sat and watched.

But I was now content to accept a campsite selected by those who knew the land. When we returned to camp, a huge fire had already been built and stocked with wood for the night. Because the mountain air was chill, our fire was kept stoked until dawn as much for its warmth as for its protection.

It became apparent to me after dinner that I was coming down with one of my periodic dysentery attacks. Every hour or so, all night, I had to leave the light and safety of the fire and stumble off into pitch-black woods for another round of fierce diarrhea. Believe me that I never made the trip without the frightening sense that I might come face-to-face in the dark with our huge pachyderm. It should still be in our immediate vicinity.

As awful as the night was, it gave way to a splendid dawn. We were soon packed again and making our way across spectacular parklike country. In the bright light of morning the undulating top of the range suddenly brought back memories of those "lost plateaus" that provided settings for the action in the Tarzan films of my childhood. What adventures lay ahead for us?

One treat was the game. Animal life was far richer than I had appreciated the evening before. We began encountering elklike sambar, a sloth bear, a python, and, in treetops, giant squirrels with heads and bodies the size of large rabbits and tails that were fully two feet long. I seldom saw any of these creatures elsewhere. And my impression of the previous day, that the wildlife lacked its usual wariness, was reconfirmed. It was equally true of the big creatures and the small. Others knew I was lagging behind our bustling troop for bathroom stops; I am not sure they were aware I was doing it for private enjoyment of nature as well.

We reached a cleft in the top of the range soon after midday. Not far below us lay the second Paliyan settlement, with its two nearby temples. It was close enough that we could hear children's playful voices and far enough that it would take us well over an hour to chop our way through the dense foliage that blocked our route down. What we faced was not Indian; it was a veritable wall of a South American weed, lantana. This noxious plant, possibly imported because of its attractive pink and yellow flower clusters, is capable of prolific growth in warm lands. Its ability to strangle native flora has turned it into a blight in Australia, various Pacific islands, and now India. Its leaves and berries are also toxic. What unenlightened soul introduced it to this Eden? Apparently, chopping a path through it was the simplest way down to the village. Members of our party took turns hacking a tunnel with their billhooks, each man working until streams of sweat closed his eyes. Others crawled behind on their bellies, awaiting their turns to come up and chop, trying all the while to disregard lantana's suffocating stench. But we did eventually emerge from our stinking confinement.

Our day's goal was now only a short walk ahead. The small Paliyan settlement was still out of sight down the slope, but we could see two tiny temples, a solid-looking priest's house with an atrium, and fifteen or twenty open-walled shelters where pilgrims could stay. Steep thatched roofs topped all the buildings except the temples, which had tin roofs.

The place was called Mahaalingamkovil, Periya Raja told me, being named for the larger of its two tiny temples. There was a story about its founding. A wandering Hindu ascetic had been seated in meditation here, perhaps four centuries ago. He noticed a stone emerging from the ground nearby, a stone in the common, phallic shape of Lord Shiva. The discovery created a dilemma for him. He believed anything so holy should be worshipped. Yet, as a person who had left society and moved on spiritually to a simple, itinerant life in the forest, the sage could not be the one to stay and conduct appropriate services. While *someone* ought to do so, it was obvious that no one else was even aware of the holy image's existence. So he prayed to Shiva, asking, "What should I do, Lord?" He understood the god's reply to be that he should stop the next passerby and train him to conduct the proper rites. The ascetic remained on the spot until, one day, a Paliyan entered the grove. The hunter was willing to assume the responsibilities of priest, so the holy man taught him suitable ritual techniques. The Paliyan's descendants officiated at the site from that day on, and members of the Paliyan band took up residence at least seasonally in the vicinity.

When people from the plains began making pilgrimages to the spot and donors constructed a temple over the image, a battle ensued over who had right to conduct the worship. It was not irrelevant that temples generate income. The dispute was taken to a ruler, Periya Raja's ancestor. On hearing the history of the holy place, he inscribed his ruling on a copper plate: Shiva's choice of servant should prevail. He named the Paliyan as priest and empowered him to choose his successor. The Paliyan and his family resumed making offerings at Mahaalingamkovil and began to do so as well at the eventual companion temple, a few steps away, Sundaralingamkovil.

The present priest welcomed us upon our arrival. He was a sturdy man of ambiguous age, with curly stark-white hair, and he wore nothing but the Tamil man's lower cloth and a singlet. Our first order of business was to present him with a substantial quantity of rice for offerings at the temples. He and his adult son then cooked a pot of rice behind Mahaalingamkovil and conducted services at both the temples, at the image of Shiva's holy vehicle (Nandi, the bull) that sat before Mahaalingamkovil, and at other subsidiary shrines. Once these repetitious routines were completed, we were able to work in some substantial interviews with members of five families.

It was strange to see a Paliyan conducting Hindu rites, but what really caught my attention was Periya Raja accepting and eating some of the leftover food offerings, and doing so in a pious manner. From a Hindu viewpoint, this should not be. He was a lord of the land; he belonged to a class of people second only to learned Brahmins in their ritual purity. Hindus cannot accept food or drink from the hands of a person of lower purity without rendering themselves polluted. Later and elsewhere I was to see temple-bound pilgrims of high rank asking Paliyans to fetch and serve them drinking water. They, too, were judging Paliyans to be their equals in ritual purity. How could this be?

In a recent book, I have described another puzzling temple scene. It bears repeating. One day I was interviewing a Paliyan youth, Poonnan, near the path to a huge Vaishnava forest temple. An aged Brahmin temple priest came by and asked us to walk the three miles to the temple with him. Our interview was near its end, so we agreed. Vaishnava purity restrictions are particularly strict, but we knew we would not be going into the temple itself with the priest.

> When [the old man] unlocked the temple, the tribal youth and I, knowing something of our ritually impure condition from a Hindu standpoint, remained in the outer precincts, playing with great bells, as the priest took out a series of keys and opened the next set of temple doors, then the next, then finally those of the sanctum sanctorum itself. We watched from a great distance as he prepared the offerings. Suddenly he turned and beckoned to us. We went in through one more of the immense doors. He continued to beckon. Puzzled, after conferring with one another, we went in through another door and stood just inside it. Still the priest called out, so we proceeded right to the threshold of the inner sanctum, as he insisted. Only then we realized that there were three images of the Lord and that the offerings had been separated into three equal parts. The priest asked me to stand on his right and the tribal youth on his left; he requested that we pick up the offerings and do as he did. Stunned and trembling, we stepped with him simultaneously into the holy inner sanctum and concelebrated the [offering].[1]

What accounts for these anomalies? Because they all occurred in religious settings, I suspect that the Hindu participants were viewing the Paliyans from a religious viewpoint. Think of their quiet voices, gentleness, simple garb, untended hair, forest habitat, diet of wild yams, and nomadic life. All of these are traits they share with Hindu ascetics— people who are holy but who do not follow the customary rules of pure Hindus. As for the Paliyans being hunters—eating pork and carrion, foods well outside the pale for Hindus—is it not just the anthropologists' oddity that we tend to categorize people in terms of their food quests? Hindus may find the Paliyan's seemingly religious traits more striking than their diet. Nothing else I know of explains their contextual extension of high ritual purity status to Paliyans.

I had wanted to ascend Saduragiri to meet wild, aloof Paliyans who lived in nature. What I was finding instead were members of the tribe who were interacting in intimate, enduring ways with their civilized neighbors!

While I attempted to catch up on sleep in the priest's house that night, my thoughts kept returning to nature. I had no choice. All through the night we could hear sounds of elephants nearby. Then, at dawn, one of the princes pointed out to me that, only a matter of days before, elephants had scarred the lower ten feet of several trees in the settlement with their tusks and completely pierced another. What a reminder that we were still deep in the wilds.

After observing morning services at the two temples, we were on the move again toward the far western end of the range. All trace of human presence was gone within minutes, for we were entering a vast tract of land inhabited by giant honeybees, hornbills, sambar, elephants, gaur bison, and tigers.

My companions were more alert than before, for this tract was prime hunting territory. I saw that the princes and their gun-bearers had loaded all three of the rifles and were keeping them ready. Well, let me rephrase that: Periya Raja readied his camera as well and confessed to me that he preferred hunting in this new way, visually. How he loved his family's old forest! He and I stood on a grassy crest watching, with cameras out, while his brothers and staff went after a small herd of sambar we had spotted below. I think we both cheered inwardly when the lithe beasts leaped out from the underbrush and made their escape.

We swung somewhat to the north, bringing us into a more open, undulating patchwork of exposed granite, grass, and groves of trees. Periya Raja pointed to the cliffs—below us, to our left—where the Paliyans extracted honey from giant honeybee combs at night. Beyond, to their west, lay miles and miles of forested lowland known as the Varushanad Valley, a further extension of this peaceful Paliyan refuge. Peering down I saw no sign of human habitation, just a carpet far beneath us of lush vegetation that stretched into the distance.

On we strode. In early afternoon we came upon two tiny tentlike thatched huts that told us Paliyans had once been in the vicinity. A scan of the area revealed the dung of elephant, gaur bison, and sambar, but no sign of recent human inhabitants. A good spot for a campsite lay not far ahead, so we kept going, but moving slowly and remaining on the alert for fresh evidence of the local band.

We came upon an elephant herd instead. Advancing toward it in hope of taking photographs, we almost stumbled into a splinter group of the herd that was feeding in a hollow in our direct path—a group consisting of five adults and a calf. The calf's mother reacted to our approach when we were about two or three hundred yards away. She paced back and forth in front of her calf, agitated, with her ears out and her trunk raised angrily to trumpet a threat. She was magnificent. If it had not been for a shallow ravine between us, I would have been happy to make a quick re-treat, rifles or no rifles. Instead, we stood our ground and watched the herd eventually move off. Then, as if to ornament this scene, three huge hornbills took to the air near the herd and flew straight over us. There were lots of firsts for me that day.

We had not seen Paliyans yet, but they had already seen us. As we made our way over to the chosen campsite, someone cried, "There they are." Nine simply dressed Paliyans were walking toward us and passing unbelievably close to the already wary elephant herd. I held my breath. For them, perhaps, it was like walking with self-confidence between pushy, oncoming vehicles—as New Yorkers do. My friends at Shenbagatoppu had told me they did this, but I had dismissed their claim as sheer non-sense.

Periya Raja, who seemed to know each of the nine Paliyans person-ally, introduced me to all and drew me into their conversation. Seven other members of the band were spending the dry season a few miles to the west, they told us, and two more had temporary work elsewhere. All were sleeping at present in rock shelters or in the open, never staying more than a few nights in one place.

Why the scattering and the mobility? They were dispersed simply due to the scarcity of resources during the dry heat, and they stayed on the move for safety. Safety? A forest produce contractor had kicked one Paliyan to death and killed two others with a gun about three years ago, just south of Saduragiri, doing so solely because they balked when asked to collect honey for him. When the band we were talking with got word of their neighbors' fate, they decided it would be wise to avoid all con-tact with contractors for a while. This was the most isolated and self-sufficient Paliyan band I would find during my eighteen months in south India.

I was also curious about their forgoing the use of houses. That was new to me. Rock shelters, where available, were fine for now, I learned. Experience taught them, nonetheless, that there could be landslides during the rains. Monsoon was the only season when they slept routinely in thatched huts.

They gave me a gift of two pieces of cooked yam for a snack. After we made camp, they pulled out several hefty uncooked pieces of yam, each six to eight inches in diameter, and set about constructing an earth oven in which to roast them for breakfast. A two-by-two-foot-wide, five-inch-deep hollow was scraped out in sandy soil. Dry grass and twigs were piled in it to a height of fifteen inches, some thirty stones were placed on top, and the pile was set alight. Once the stones had been well heated, chopped-up tubers were placed atop them and covered for the night with fresh teak leaves and two inches of sand.

We slept that night under the stars on an expansive sheet of granite that would have been of little interest to the nearby elephants. How others dealt with our hard bed I don't know, but I appreciated the padding in my sleeping bag. And I managed to sleep quite well with a cool breeze on my face, despite now having a serious fever to accompany the diarrhea.

The next morning we had a feast awaiting us. We dug out the cooked yams, a delicacy tasting somewhat like baked Idaho potatoes whipped together with sour cream, and we moistened this treat with fresh honey. It was food my poor stomach could manage.

Periya Raja and I conducted some informative interviews afterward. But there was a buzz among the rest of our party; something quite different was on the younger princes' minds. Animal droppings were plentiful here, and this was to be the last morning of our trip. How could we pass up one last hunt?

After stashing our packed gear on the open rocks, the Paliyans and we went into the woods and set up an ambush. The two young princes waited in hiding behind large trees while others circled around and, on a signal, attempted to drive whatever game they could toward the princes. How about me? Being very much a fifth wheel, I was asked to stay out of the way in a clearing. Little did I know I was in for the best view of what we were about to stir up. Moments after I heard the signal to start the drive, four full-grown sambar sped past, but they veered off before reaching our ambush. That was not the end of it. A crashing sound to my right made me think that a mass like a runaway bulldozer was bashing its way bodily through the forest. Ducking behind a tree, I peered around it in time to see a young bull gaur careen through the clearing at full gallop and thunder off into the trees beyond. Its huge hooves shook the ground. Two rifle shots sounded in rapid succession, followed by several seconds more of shattering branches and then silence.

Several of us arrived at the scene before the gaur's powerful body had stopped quivering. What a beast! It had a flawless tawny coat and the hard, rippling muscles of a Mr. Universe. A gaur is close in appearance to Africa's cape buffalo, but longer legged and much bigger. It is, by far, the world's largest bovine. Periya Raja's youngest brother had put two bullets through the bull's heart, we found, yet it had kept on running for almost another two hundred feet. And the rifle the young prince had used was not only the lightest we had with us, but its metal working parts were also so loosely fastened to the stock that it rattled. We stood around admiring both the animal and the feat of the hunter.

We would need porters from the plains to carry out meat and trophies, so someone needed to speed on ahead to arrange this. Because I was to be given part of the liver (a seventeen-pound gift), Periya Raja, several others, and I remained at the butchering site only until the liver was available, then began our descent as fast as my declining health permitted.

A Bone-Breaking Exit

I had a soaring temperature as we began the walk back down. For me, it was just one dazed and protracted slide and stumble. My recollection, though, is that I made it down on my own. We descended partway along the north face of the range, so I knew we faced a several-mile trip along the plain to return to our starting point. You can be sure I was glad to find an elegant little cart waiting for us at the bottom.

Only after clambering in did I learn the nature of our conveyance: it was a galloping-bull cart. I had seen one of these impressive vehicles earlier, miles to the north, speeding along a paved highway. Characteristically, pairs of well-matched, muscular, long-legged bulls, specially bred for the purpose, drew these carts. One had to be a big landowner to afford them.

Although I had an initial sense that a treat was in store for me, it was short-lived. Remember that we were waiting for the monsoon just then. During the hot dry season, our cart track, with its irregular ruts, had become as hard as cement. All romantic notions of speeding along like yesterday's princes dissolved mere moments after we set out on the bone-shattering trip back home.

Bulls, Bites, and Other Challenges

Wild Beasties

What is luck in the forest? Is it having encounters with wildlife? Or is it surviving such encounters? Or avoiding them altogether? Surely that depends on one's personal goals and interests. Little more need be said here about my two brushes with elephants on Saduragiri, other than that they were stimulating and, in retrospect, a bit frightening. Back at Shenbagatoppu we had a small resident elephant herd in our valley, usually at a higher elevation, in the vicinity of the Vaishnava temple. They were audible at times, and it was routine to have to step over their fresh droppings on the trail as I accompanied Paliyans to work or went out for walks on my own. Given that all I carried on my lone walks was a notebook, a pen, snacks, and a bowie knife, I suppose I may be deemed fortunate never to have come face-to-face with the creatures themselves.

Once, when I went off to the forest alone to experiment with fashioning and using digging sticks, I saw a small herd of wild pigs only seventy or eighty feet away; I climbed a tree as a precaution, but they soon trotted off. The main result of the experience was some teasing that evening about my inexpert woodwork. Not only did a young neighbor find my discarded working materials, bring them home, and exhibit them to others, making them the community's grand joke of the day, he must also have seen me clamber up the tree. He asked me later, with a grin, about my reason for going to join the squirrels. Did he think it had been unnecessary? Perhaps I will never know.

After I bought my elephant gun and had moved my work site to a place called Pulaavadi, a Tamil hunter who admired the weapon asked if I would join him in a nighttime hunt for pigs. His goal was to intercept pigs that were trampling maturing rice fields along the forest's edge. Farmers of the area loved him. I was as intrigued with his gun—an archaic muzzle-loader—as he was with my double-barreled piece, so I told him I would come along. Let it be a night off, a night of fun. We set out from the Paliyan settlement an hour or two before the waxing quarter moon was to set. Because it would be a dark night, we tied white rags on our sights. Oh, there were pigs! They were coming down in some numbers that night. But they were wary. We found ourselves, time after time, unable to get close enough for an effective shot. After midnight, we finally called a halt to our hunt. It was now so dark that we followed the trail by sensing with our sandaled feet when we had strayed off into taller grass. Halfway back to the settlement we heard a deep, loud pig's snort a mere thirty feet ahead of us, right on our path. It was no longer possible to see the rags on our sights; we would have to rely on our other senses when aiming. My companion was ready first, but a dull click told me that he had misfired (we found later that his flint had fallen out). It was up to me, and fast. I did an instinct shot from the hip. When my ears stopped ringing, I heard pig hooves thundering away, far to our left. Seconds later there was a bright flash in that direction. Another hunter had fired a muzzle-loader, and he was more successful. We heard the next day that it had been a large boar; it rolled the hunter with its tusks before it died, but the fellow had no serious injuries, and he took away more than a couple hundred pounds of meat. This all occurred close enough to Pulaavadi that the deafening roar of my gun woke many Paliyans. Perhaps they considered me overly proud of my rifle, but for days I suffered constant teasing from the women about the enormous quantity of meat I had brought in for everyone.

During peak rains, within a single week, we saw and chased ten snakes in the Shenbagatoppu settlement. Evidently, they were seeking refuge from wet burrows. Several of them were poisonous—cobras, saw-scaled vipers, and kraits—and most managed to escape from our uncoordinated pursuit.

One was *my* snake. I had been ignoring a cool, persistent drizzle all evening and recording songs beneath a sheltering tree beside my open tent. When children began to doze off on parents' laps, I took the cue, put my tape recorder away, closed the tent, snuggled into my warm sleeping bag, and fell asleep. My right arm was stretched straight out sideways from the sleeping bag when first light woke me the next morning; though I could not see whatever it was, I sensed that there was a snake curled up beneath my wrist. Being zipped into the sleeping bag and tiny tent, I could not leap up and flee. And I could ill afford to jostle my right arm. I lay as still as possible and thought. Due to the rain, I had stored dry branches in my tent for my morning cooking fire; reaching ever so slowly and blindly with my left hand, I found I could *just* reach one. Grasping it, once I had estimated its dimensions from its heft, I swung it across my body forcefully while simultaneously lifting my right arm. The uninvited visitor was a krait, the same serpent that is responsible for the vast majority of snakebite deaths in nearby Sri Lanka. It was stunned enough for me to unzip the sleeping bag, unzip the tent (which I had to do slowly with a fingernail because the zipper handle was long lost), and carry it out on a stick. My immediate neighbors saw what I was doing. They ran over to my tent excitedly, and cried, "Don't touch! Don't touch!"

There was a night when I faced a wholly different kind of beast. Long after dark, I was awakened by a distant noise that sounded more like the hum of a motor than anything else. Peering into the dark through the screen windows of my tent I saw nothing out there, not even headlights in the distance. Most puzzling of all, it was hard even to get a fix on the precise direction of the sound. So I lay down again. The noise persisted. Twice more I got up, each time more curious than before, and looked out every window, the final time with a kerosene lantern in hand. Ready to give up, I lowered my gaze to the illuminated earth near the tent, and there it was! A thirty-inch-wide column of black army ants came straight toward me out of the distance, walked directly under the sealed floor of my tent, emerged from beneath it on the other side, and disappeared into the trees beyond. My sleeping bag weighed down the tent floor right across their path; it was the millions of scraping backs beneath me that had generated the sound that roused me from sleep.

Another major challenge in the forest was food. The monitor lizards and other small creatures that the Paliyans ate were more than palatable, so I imagined I would be able to eat almost anything that came my way. Early in the study, I was called over to join several people who were cooking recently obtained pig meat. Surely it would be another treat. Others were already feasting happily when I arrived, and I tucked in without thinking. The first mouthful was so horrible, so disgusting, that

I refrained from swallowing it, excused myself with a mumble, went off into the dark, spat it out, and put my finger down my throat to vomit out any particles that might have found their way down, before returning to the feast to say thanks, I'd had enough. A lesson I had failed to learn was that Paliyans include carrion in the food sent them by the gods. What they were devouring was a pig carcass that had lain rotting on the tropical forest floor for at least three days by their estimate. Although I was born in a land where people "age" pheasant and other meats for days on end, I discovered that, for me, eating fetid carrion pork was totally out of the question.

My reaction was similar when Kaamaacci, a young Paliyan friend, invited me to dine with his family. Dinner was centered round a lightly cooked stew of sardine-size whole fresh fish that I had helped catch. They were so small that they had been sun-dried for two days without first being cleaned. Again, they simply tasted rotten; I ate a few before realizing that I ought to bring them up right away for the sake of my health.

Long-term residence in a seven-by-seven-foot tent, nine degrees from the equator, was difficult. It was an extremely light mountaineering tent. I bought it for its portability, not appreciating the fact that it was neither sturdy enough for protracted use nor waterproof enough for tropical rain. It was also dark green, which meant that it heated up quickly in the sun. Water was the worst problem. When the monsoon season arrived, I had to cope with more leaks than the manufacturers had led me to expect. Even with a top fly over the tent, to double my protection, there were nights during the rains when I had only four or five square feet of dry floor; if I was to sleep dry, I had to fold my sleeping bag to a quarter of its usual size and curl up on top. Then, when the ground was sodden and a strong wind swept down the valley, I had to be certain there were substantial rocks on all my lightweight tent pegs to prevent the tent from breaking loose and rolling balloonlike across the landscape. Field methods courses never mentioned hazards like this!

My second main community, Pulaavadi, was more settled than Shenbagatoppu. I stayed in a recently abandoned, somewhat decrepit mud hut for the first two weeks, then accepted the people's offer to erect me new one, similar to theirs. Well over a dozen adults pitched in, so it took a mere four days. It was done in a wonderful spirit, and those who were too old or too young to participate dug yams or fished to feed the others. I helped them realize the inaugural ceremony they wanted: when construction was complete and they had decorated the house with flowers,

I brought in a large goat, vegetables, rice, condiments, and fruit for a feast—which we all ate sitting in a circle. Then we danced. The eight-by-ten-foot mud house had a well-thatched roof and the only real door in the village. Others merely dragged a dead thorn bush in front of their entrances if they wished to keep animals out. I furnished my abode with two woven-string cots, which I had made for sixty cents each, and a small kerosene cooker. Thus began several relatively comfortable months—except for the mosquitoes that plagued me each night. I learned to sleep inside my sleeping bag with only my nose sticking out. But I was never successful at slapping down the last persistent mosquito that buzzed around my snout hole. In desperation, I purchased a hand-pumped spray gun and a can of repellent in the nearest market. That very evening I sprayed the inside of the roof thoroughly. So many mosquitoes rained down that I decided to mark off a square foot of floor and count them. There were 117 in that one patch. If they had fallen evenly across my eighty-square-foot floor, I had just killed 9,360 of the intruders!

One of the most awkward episodes in my relations with Paliyans began when Old Poonnan accused me of causing an epidemic by eating forbidden food. He made his allegation after the illness had already sickened many children and killed one of them. Old Poonnan told several people that I was eating beef in my tent, right there in their community; it was meat that had long been forbidden Paliyans by their *caamis*. All I could do was deny the charge publicly. When two quite different theories about the epidemic eventually took firmer hold, I heard little more about my alleged behavioral lapse.

Perils in Indian Society

Motorcycling on Indian roads was problematic. I had one "three-bull day," when my red motorcycle kept angering bulls I passed. The first one was in a big herd that some youths were escorting down a highway. I was concentrating so hard on weaving through the herd quietly, without spooking the cattle, that I failed to notice the bull until he tilted his massive head my way. That changed my priorities! Yes, I did scatter the herd when I gunned the engine, but it was no time to be altruistic. The bull was a scant five feet behind my rear fender when, at last, I emerged from the milling mass, but an escape is an escape.

The second and third encounters involved a large, nasty bull at the end of what had been an exhausting day of travel in heat and blowing dust. My destination for the night was a market town I had never visited before, and I missed the spur road into the town because I was preoccupied with evading an aggressive lone bull just when I should have been paying attention to road signs. My mistake became apparent several miles later. It would be necessary to turn around and brave the bull once more. However, he must also have been on the move, for he was no longer at the intersection when I returned. I breathed a sigh of relief and turned down the narrow road I should have taken earlier. Just as the town came into sight, there was the beast again on the roadside; I was sure it was the same bull. This time he was facing away from me, which helped. Zipping past him in high gear so that my engine would be quiet did not work as well as I hoped. I got by him all right, but realized he was pursuing me again just as I had to slow down my machine to enter the pedestrian-thronged main street, alive with people because I was arriving at the peak of the late afternoon market activity. Our entering the crowd made no difference whatsoever to the bull; he showed no interest in slowing down or giving up. For the second time that day, I was weaving through chaos with an angry bull only a matter of feet behind me. As one might expect in such a setting, everyone was ignoring the overused and pretentious bicycle bells and vehicular horns. Few even noted the great creature on my tail until after we had passed. Just as I despaired of winning round three of the day's contest, I was able to spot and swerve into the gate of my intended hostel.

When cycling in and out of Pulaavadi, I forded two seasonally variable rivers, with from eight to twenty-four inches of water in them, when not in flood, and ever shifting sandbars. A couple of good soakings taught me to be cautious, especially when crossing the bigger river. If I had not sized it up for a couple of days, I would park the cycle, examine the river bottom, and plan a zigzag route around the deep spots. Going toward Pulaavadi, I descended to the big river along a winding ramplike cart track some two hundred feet long, fifteen to twenty feet wide, and with six-foot-high banks where it finally reached the river's edge. Along its whole length both sides of the ramp were hedged with prickly pear cactus. There came an afternoon when I motored down this track, turned off my engine, and looked at the river too lost in thought to realize I had company at the water's edge—a large agitated bull. The monster was already pawing at the ground when I noticed it, and it was no more than forty feet away. My motorcycle was a devil to start; wasting time on that could be fatal, and my options were limited. I made a snap decision to walk briskly up the track. But the bull was already on the move. Hearing it behind me, I broke into a run—my specialty in high school had, thank goodness, been the hundred-yard dash—and looked desperately for a gap in the cactus hedge as I went. Yes, partway up the incline on the left side there *was* a hole, a small one, conceivably big enough for me to do a racing dive through. So, I veered right, veered left toward it, dove through, heard thundering hooves pass by, caught my breath, then sat and plucked out cactus spines for the next fifteen minutes. Better thorns than horns.

I used this route several times a month. Not knowing who owned the bull, almost certainly a prime breeding animal, I put out word that I would carry an elephant gun with me in the future; if the owner did not keep the beast off the public path, he ought to expect me to defend myself. My message must have reached the right ears.

Then there was a domestic water buffalo, her mouth lathered with excitement, that charged my laden and laboring motorcycle on a sandy track and very nearly caught up with me. Was it my bike's wonderful chrome-plated handlebars that stimulated her? After all, they emulated her bull's horns. It is easier now than it would have been then to write off all these chases as learning experiences.

I should not leave out the hazards of the inanimate, for there were mechanical behemoths on the road as well. One particular encounter with buses bears mention. I was cruising along a familiar stretch of paved main highway, doing at least fifty-five miles an hour. Each side of the road had been planted, years before, with a row of shade trees, grown massive and stately with time. Eighteen-hundred-year-old poems tell us that benevolent kings of the Tamil country used to provide such shade for travelers, and recent administrators had kept up the practice. Usually we regarded the trees as wonderful, but the close spacing of the nineteenth-century plantings and the maturity of the trees could transform bends in the road into blind corners. We had more than a few of those. Imagine approaching a corner at speed only to realize that an oncoming express bus was trying to overtake another such bus as they careened around the bend. The two flat-fronted monsters were precisely side by side when I first saw them coming toward me, and they took up every inch of the road. Because we were closing in on one another at about 160 or 170 feet per second, we were only moments apart. This was not only my first motorcycle, I had never dreamed of jumping one at any speed, and I happened to be cycling that day with an unwieldy load lashed on the back. There was no time to ponder the situation: my choices were to attempt a leap across the wide ditch alongside the road or say good-bye. I swerved left, flew forever, and landed upright, but came down hard on earth so damp and soft that my overloaded machine soon bogged down and stalled. Both bus drivers screeched to a halt; that was too late to help me, but well timed to give their hundred passengers a great view of the foreigner they had forced off the road. As I said earlier, the motorcycle was difficult to start, and especially so with a hundred gawking onlookers. I finally turned toward the road fuming, shook a fist in the air, and repeated the gesture until the embarrassed drivers pulled away.

One thing I neglected to mention about the timing of my Ph.D. research was that we arrived in India only days before the October 1962 Chinese invasion. Tightened security procedures went into effect almost immediately. India asked that foreign visitors register with the police and report all their movements to local police stations if they intended to stay anywhere more than three days. I had no trouble with that requirement. During my work at Shenbagatoppu, though, I had the misfortune to be under the jurisdiction of a probationary subinspector of police. People told me that he took his probationary status more seriously than most, and I can believe it. He set out to demonstrate his fitness for an officer's responsibilities by doing every task with more than the customary zeal. In order to learn all he could about his one foreigner, me, he went around grilling all those he could find who had had any dealings with me. Word soon reached me that my associates found it distasteful and frightening.

I walked one evening with some Shenbagatoppu Paliyan youths to a fair in a village a few miles away. We arranged to spend the night in a schoolroom and come home the next day. It was my bad luck to encounter the subinspector there. He collared me, demanded that two chairs be brought to him and placed under a streetlight in the center of the village's main intersection, and ordered me to sit down. He could not have chosen a more public spot. Most activity in the area halted for fifteen minutes for the crowd to watch him grill me. Why was I there? he asked. Who was I with? Where was I staying? I answered each question as accurately as I could. Then he went on to ask why had I not come to his police station in Srivilliputtuur first (it was several miles away in another direction and I was on foot!) to inform him of my movements?

When I replied that the law did not require my reporting a one-night trip, he went into a rage. "*I* require it," he bellowed. What a show! I would not have minded it if he had not then called up my companions, one by one, and grilled each of them in the same fashion. The balloon and knickknack sellers worked our crowd of onlookers at first, and then they, too, joined it, gaping at the smartly uniformed officer throwing his weight around.

This occurred a few weeks after I first got word that he was interrogating people I knew. Until experiencing his style myself, I had not appreciated how repugnant and threatening it was. It was a revelation that made me worry about the long-term impact he might have on my work. The Paliyans themselves were used to Tamil bullies. If anything, seeing me pushed around in a way that was familiar to them may have brought me closer to the lads. It was worrying, nonetheless.

On my arrival in the country, the American in New Delhi who headed all of the Ford Foundation's activities in India had written me expressing interest in my dissertation project. He had shown my research proposal to a friend of his who held a top post in the central government bureaucracy and had found him equally interested. The fact that this bureaucrat was peripheral to the Cabinet meant I had a substantial connection with the nation's capital. I decided to see if that could be put to use to rein in the mad dog. I wrote a polite, informative letter to the district superintendent of police telling him that police inquiries into my research were directed at people who had no real knowledge of what I was doing. If he desired accurate information on my research goals and procedures, he should contact —— ——, —— commissioner of India, who was well acquainted with my work. All harassment ended at once.

There were challenges of other kinds as well. In late November, a Kodaikkanal store clerk made us the surprise offer of a Thanksgiving turkey. It would not be expensive by our standards, so we leaped at it. On American Thanksgiving Day we were enjoying a second coffee after breakfast when Rosalie came in from the kitchen to say she had "prepared the turkey." Doubting that she knew how we cooked it, we asked what she meant. She told us she had done it "the usual way." What did *that* mean? We dashed into the kitchen to discover that she had cut the bird up as one would a frying chicken. Our grief and consternation reduced the poor lady to tears. Something had to be done, for her as well as for us; what might it be? An idea came to me. I eased the two women out of the kitchen and located the large bodkin and string we kept on hand for securing parcels in cloth the Indian way. Orthopedic surgeons would blanch at my slack and lopsided creation but, with surprising ease, I stitched the pieces back together into the rough form of a turkey, doing so sufficiently tightly that we could even stuff it. The bird arrived at the dinner table that afternoon a rich, golden brown. My job at the head of the table was easy: carving consisted of little more than a few quick touches of the knife tip.

Health

Family health problems cannot be written off in the same fashion. When Heather was nearly a year old, we took her to Pondicherry, the former French enclave, for a seaside vacation. The trip itself was wonderful. We strolled on immaculate beaches, enjoyed an airy suite of rooms overlooking the sea for about fifteen dollars a day, with all meals included, and dined on French delicacies. When the hotel served us squab, they had the sense to prepare calf brain for our child. Yet the cost of this outing for Heather's health was considerable. She returned to our hills with painful blisters on all parts of her body. They were neither chicken pox nor any other familiar infectious disease, they were not bites, and they resembled no heat rash anybody had ever seen. Although Heather's doctors found them baffling, once she was back home in the hilltop cool they disappeared in a matter of days. Other than that nasty experience, she came home healthy.

Four months before we were to leave India, Eric was born. The family doctor who had taken responsibility for Trudy's prenatal care broke the news to us only a few weeks in advance that he would be out of the country for a couple of months right at the baby's due date. This was an awkward development, but the community's government doctor said he could cover the case. That sounded all right. When labor began and I tracked down the doctor at his home, he claimed to be unavailable. He was about to leave for the district capital to take a driving test. What is more, he revealed for the first time that he had no training or experience in obstetrics. When I told him that was unacceptable because he had given us his word, he relented and came. Our son's birth was a rare and life-threatening "brow presentation." By facing in the direction of the birth canal, he quickly became wedged in the pelvic opening. Yet the doctor did little more than hold my wife's hand.

After hours of this, now late in the evening, the head nurse came to me worried, pleading that I go at once to see if an obstetrically experienced Indian woman doctor, sometimes resident in Kodaikkanal, had returned from her recent travels. If so, I must fetch her at once. I did find her, though fast asleep, and explained the situation. She threw a coat over her nightwear and ran with me to the hospital. Physically ejecting the government doctor from the delivery room, she washed her hands, worked the baby further up into the uterus manually between contractions, reoriented him, and delivered him in minutes. Mother and son were fine, but totally exhausted.

As for me, due to being overly trusting of my food and water, my main problem was intestinal. I suffered dysentery attacks once or twice every month from early in the work right through to the close of my project. It tended to be bacillary dysentery one time, amoebic the next, then back to bacillary. In my attempts to be personally courteous and for the sake of rapport with Paliyans, I considered it awkward to turn down food that was offered me by my forest fellows, even if food such as the carrion pork reeked. I also judged it to be a hundred percent safe to eat piping-hot food in Indian restaurants when I traveled. And I felt there was no need to take precautions with river water that had been aerated by cascading down from high in the almost uninhabited hills. Perhaps it wasn't the food or drink that got me. Another possible source of the infections was the banana leaves from which I ate when traveling. The dysentery was debilitating, and it cost me a lot of time.

Motorcycling on the highway one afternoon I found myself weak, unbearably hot, and having hallucinations. It was my luck, however, to be near Srivilliputtuur, where I knew an aged Brahmin doctor. He told me I was lucky to have come in. My temperature was approaching 106 degrees, and his diagnosis was pneumonia. The old man tucked me into a cot in his home, gave me a massive dose of penicillin, kept me under observation for a few hours, then sent me back to my tent with firm instructions to rest for a couple of days. While that is not at all how I would be treated in the United States, I was soon able to return to work.

My biggest scare concerning my own health came from an insect bite. I began itching all over one night, about midnight, while I was out with some Paliyan men. Those with me shone my light on me and told me that my whole body, from my scalp to the soles of my feet, was a single allergic welt. My throat was swelling, too. Breathing became difficult, and I felt too weak to motorcycle to a hospital. Even if I had had the strength to start the machine, reaching the nearest facility would have required miles on rough cart tracks, plus fording in total darkness the two rivers with their ever-changing channels and sandbars. It was time to lie down on my cot and let go. What a shock to wake up the next morning with nothing wrong but a hot welt on one calf.

It was illness that finally ended my fieldwork. I had been experiencing abdominal pain on and off for months and made the mistake of connecting it with my dysentery. When the pain was at its peak at Shenbagatoppu, I lay in my tent for three days, without eating or attempting any work. Three Paliyan men came and asked me to describe my symptoms. They went off to the forest and returned three hours later with a handful of *malandangi veer*, or "stomach ache root," and asked if I had honey or sugar on hand. I gave them the sugar I used in my coffee. In a few minutes they delivered a drink of ground roots, water, and sugar. Despite the huge amount of sugar they used, I have never, ever tasted anything so bitter. I did finish it, though, and, to my great surprise, within three minutes the abdominal pain was totally gone. The concoction gave me about two weeks of total relief.

Later, in Pulaavadi, I was having similar distress and feeling extremely weak as well. A middle-aged Paliyan woman sought diagnosis and protection for me one night from one of the visiting *caamis*. While the *caami*'s effort to "drive away the intrusive spirit that caused the pain" was no match for the earlier treatment by roots, I was touched by my neighbor's voluntary efforts.

Some weeks prior to the scheduled close of my project, the illness became too much for me; I motorcycled home. Finding no one there, I rode straight on to Kodaikkanal's four-bed Van Allen hospital. I was so weak by then that I dumped my motorcycle on its side, rather than parking it, and staggered through the door in search of help. It turned out that I had a heavily bleeding duodenal ulcer. Although I had already lost a good deal of blood internally, the ulcer kept on bleeding in the hospital for another eleven days. It meant a week and a half of lying still, with elevated feet, abdominal ice packs, and nothing to eat or drink but milk and vitamin K. Luckily, I had reached a good time to stop work. Although deep analysis of my field data had barely begun, I lay in the hospital bed confident that I had the materials to answer those questions with which I had set out. My full understanding of the Paliyan cycle of movement, toward and then away from the edge of the forest, took some years to develop, but I already had a good sense of how aspects of the Paliyan way of life fitted together, plus a preliminary sense of how and why the tribe had managed to persist into the modern era on the very edge of bustling Eurasia.

Rewards of Fieldwork

I can't tell you that *everything* was a disaster. To start with, there were two extraordinary pleasures: spending eighteen months in the company of tolerant people, and discovering I was making sense of a wholly alien way of life on my first try. And my other rewards were many; I will describe just three of them. It slowly became apparent that Paliyans were weaving me into their social fabric; several good friendships developed; and I was able, by project's end, to set out for home with a relatively healthy family.

Never Quite One of the Boys, But . . .

If my living in a Paliyan community was problematic at first—for them as well as for me—by working on it we fostered a relationship that felt quite comfortable. People became less apprehensive as I learned to avoid acts that might worry or offend them. Even when I noticed lingering remnants of guardedness, I had no reason to take it personally. After all, weren't Paliyans only protecting themselves in a time-honored way from the assaults that the world passes out to them? In time, my interview sessions became more relaxed, and our interpersonal relations took a warm and positive turn.

Regardless of what you may have read about the tendency of anthropologists to "go native," most in my field who have done studies in cultures so different from their own are likely to be viewed by their subjects as childlike in their innocence and as thoroughly alien, as much so as green Martians would be. I know I was. That doesn't mean, though, that we are unable to develop warm relations. Wasn't ET of film fame lovable?

One measure of my improving situation was that, during visits of the gods, four of the conservative, wary Paliyan *caamis* addressed me. Two of them spontaneously came over to me and took up matters of my family's and my welfare and responsibilities. The third *caami* needed no prolonged coaxing to respond to a woman's enquiries about my abdominal pain. And the fourth one, after some negotiation, went as far as including me among those whom he addressed as "grandchild." Better yet, the people around me nodded, smiled, and voiced their approval of my being referred to in this way. Although *caamis* both tell Paliyans not to mix with outsiders and tend to refrain from making an appearance when strangers are present, *caamis* proved accepting of me in two different Paliyan communities. I read this as an encouraging sign that my quiet behavior had earned me a degree of social inclusion.

When we are thousands of miles from our homes and family doctors, illness is doubly nasty. It creates a feeling of being not only unwell but also lost and vulnerable. So you can imagine how wonderful it felt to have Paliyans extend me their unsolicited help when I was flat on my back with ulcer pain. The concern on their faces was real and reassuring; it gave me a sense of being among caring friends. Knowing my various needs, they shared even minor health measures with me. Recall that we were moving about for part of each day, usually without footgear, in a tropical thorn forest. It became my routine to examine each of my soles two or three time daily to pluck out thorns and treat as best I could all the accompanying infections. The young people soon introduced me to a small plant our botanists know as gigantic swallowwort. From its cut stem drips a powerful astringent latex that blanches and puckers the skin; within fifteen minutes of applying a drop of it, the thorn will emerge and all signs of infection will vanish.

I chose to be self-sufficient with my food. This turned out well, for it was exactly what Paliyans expected of their fellows. Paliyans did, however, make at least some gifts of food to close kin, say to adult siblings of the opposite sex, to elderly parents, or to grandchildren. It might have been as an extension of that practice, or because people grew used to sharing their observations with me in the forest and sharing information in interviews, that I was occasionally offered food gifts in a similar spirit. Someone would come to me with a warm smile and say, "Eat this!" Thus it was that I was given tasty roots, many types of fruit as they came into season, nearly half of a monitor lizard, forest hens, and delicate honeycombs.

I have already described how, on clear moonlit nights, I put my notebooks aside to participate in the young people's games and in adult songs and circle dances to a drumbeat. When I was passed one of the shared drums, it felt natural to take my turn with it. Noting that everyone had a personal style of performing on it, I was not inhibited by any ignorance of some "correct" manner of doing so.

And my participation was taken for granted when we were on a pig hunt, or under attack by the stone-throwing giant tigers. My social inclusion may well have been partial, but it was not imagined.

Making Friends

Rewarding social relations went much further than being surrounded by accepting individuals. Although Paliyans steered away from bosom friendships, I believe because favoritism might cause others to feel socially excluded, I developed particularly good relationships with a few individuals. Three of these plus a group relationship bear description.

Viirappan and Lacmi, husband and wife, were a bright, interesting, nearly middle-aged couple. When the three of us were alone during workdays in the forest, we had lively two-sided interchanges.

I must tell you, first, that Lacmi was an enigmatic figure. Already a grandmother who functioned smoothly and intelligently as a conciliator, she was also vivacious and quietly playful. Indeed, Paliyan men treated her as if she was the most attractive woman in the community; they seemed unable to take their eyes off her face. This was surely due to her having remained both physically lovely and as coy and lighthearted as any maiden. It didn't surprise me that Lacmi had two current husbands and continued to enjoy the greatest array of lovers of any Paliyan woman I knew—young or old.

Her play knew no bounds. Once, when Lacmi was talking with another woman in a large, strung-out party walking out for a day's work in the forest, she made a remark that puzzled me. She referred to someone (content told me it could only have been me) in a veiled way, but within my earshot, by an epithet meaning "lover." This puzzled me, because her relationship with me was businesslike, and I must have been the only man in our party who had *not* had a liaison with her. Not knowing whether her comment was meant for my ears, I decided it was in the interest of my research to act as if I had not heard it. But, as I joined the other men in watching her during a work break that day, I was man enough to appreciate why she was the blossom that attracted the most bees.

When Viirappan, Lacmi, and I were working in the forest as a three-some, Lacmi explained the practical uses of plants to me in her uniquely light, witty manner. There were times when she worded her thoughts as if she intended to tease. I treasured these interviews as much for their double entendres as for their factual substance.

Viirappan—Lacmi's first and senior husband—was a lightly built man of about forty, even quieter than she, and every bit as intelligent. It soon became evident that he had a grasp of my goals and my methods. I imagine it was because of this that he was patient with me and exhibited unusual responsiveness to my routines. He was an anthropologist's treasure. More than once, he and I found ourselves resting and chatting by a shaded forest pool toward the end of a day we had spent working together in the forest. As evening fell, I watched him flip around the daylong interrogation to learn what *he* could of *my* world. By generalizing from my behavior, he went as far as trying to conjure up an image of a whole society of Peter Gardners. He was astute even about what our institutions might be.

I should not have to tell you that the time I spent with this couple, whether singly or together, was guaranteed to be a social delight and an intellectual stimulus. It helped keep me going. If it were not for their cultural differences from us, they would be completely at home in a free-ranging conversation over good coffee or wine at some Western university.

Little Carosa toddled over to my tent from time to time to talk. She was an adorable little girl, two and a half or three years old, shy, with a devastating smile and a perpetually runny nose. Carosa used her pudgy hands, one morning, to make shadow images on the tent wall—as American toddlers might do—then she explained each of them to me. The two of us found our quiet talk comfortable. I wondered if the ease we experienced was due in part to our sense that we were at the same level in our mastery of the Paliyan tongue. Even though I knew Carosa's parents well, her trusting, smiling visits surprised me. After all, I was a faded color and a good head taller than anyone else in the community. Having grown up with scant exposure to death, I was shaken and pained by her sudden loss a few months after we developed our friendship. Carosa died while I was at home, ill. Because Paliyans consider it improper to speak about the recently deceased, I visited her tiny grave without ever hearing what had happened.

When I was working in my second main community, Pulaavadi, several young men and women, all in their late teens and early twenties, began frequenting my little mud hut. We were age mates, I being in my midtwenties at the time. Their visits exposed me to evenings of light, unguarded talk about work and marriage. There was also considerable youthful dallying with words, often on sexual themes, inoffensive teasing or horseplay, and budding courtship activity among them. It gave me unexpected access to their private thoughts and aspirations, and it provided insights into subtleties in the words of the elders.

Up to that time, I had stuck to a routine of remaining alone in the communities I studied for periods of five to ten or twelve days at a time, then spending a few days at home, up in the hills, with my family. Such a schedule allowed me to make steady progress with my work, but it often left me feeling lonely during the time I was away from my home. Once I became integral to the Pulaavadi youth group, any hint of feeling isolated was rare. This change, although it was good for me personally, had its costs. Now there were occasions when I yearned for more control over my time; and I missed having long, uninterrupted evenings when I could catch up with documenting my day's observations in detail.

In the course of coming and going, I occasionally gave a man or a boy a lift on my motorcycle. Light drizzle one morning in Pulaavadi convinced everyone that they should take a day's rest. One of my youthful friends who had never had a chance to ride with me chose that day to ask if he could take a spin with me on the back of the machine. Why not generalize the experience that a few others had found fun? I laid down a safe but fast figure-eight track in a nearby fallow field, so all comers could enjoy feeling the wind in their faces. After the young men had ridden, a few older men claimed their turns on the back of the bike. Although they gripped my belly more tightly than the youths did, they voiced the same pleasure. Finally, egged on by their male relatives, the women lined up too. I admit to having felt awkward, initially, over the intimacy of the women snuggling behind me in the presence of all their relatives, but that was my hang-up, not theirs. People watched in sheer delight as everyone got the fastest ride I dared give. Fourteen and a half years later, while engaged in a summer project on south Indian sculptors,

I looked in on what was left of the community. During our opening greetings someone said to me, "Mutti [one of the youths who frequented my place in the evenings] will ask about your motorbike." True to this prediction, she walked up ten minutes later, grinned, hugged me, and did just that. The motorcycle rides had turned an unpleasant, drizzly day into a time that was memorable for all of us.

Friendships were certainly absent from my original list of expectations for the Paliyan project, but they played a big role in transforming what might otherwise have been an academic experience into a personal adventure. Could I have tolerated the isolation and other stresses without them? I do not believe it would have been easy. From a purely academic viewpoint, the social experiences served to round out my knowledge and understanding of the Paliyans as people.

Surviving

Our health was not something that we took for granted. Not at all; not at any point along the way. Remember our initial inexperience and our worried visit to the London School of Tropical Medicine. And recall the twenty-three-year-old who leaned on the ship's railing while leaving Southampton harbor and recalled his father's fear that baby Heather would be unable to cope medically with the conditions she would face in India. That was a frightening moment. And we *were* all confronted by medical problems during 1962–1964, serious and difficult ones. Nonetheless, by the time we finally set out for Bombay, Suez, Italy, France, and home, my ulcer diet was the only remaining tangible evidence of those problems. The ulcer was annoying, coming as it did just as we were on the verge of returning to the delicacies of the Western table, but annoying is altogether different from frightening.

Travel, Paris, and the Devil's Advocate

Travel Pitfalls Once More

Paul Friedrich, by then at the University of Chicago, suggested I seek an extension of my fellowship in order to spend time in Paris on the way home, at L'École Pratique des Hautes Études, discussing my Paliyan materials with Louis Dumont. Motorcycling regularly through the area of Dumont's Kallar research made it apparent to me that his *Une Sous-Caste de l'Inde du Sud* (A south Indian subcaste) was the most incisive and perceptive piece of scholarship on the region. It had given me by far my best preparation for doing research there—best in its general perspective and best in its fine detail. I held Dumont's judgment in the highest regard. Because there was no longer an India specialist in Penn's anthropology department, Friedrich's suggestion was a helpful one. I sent a letter to Dumont proposing a two-month stopover. He welcomed my coming. The Ford Foundation also saw the point and granted me the fellowship extension I sought. We were amused, though, that the staff member who penned Ford's letter of award made snippy reference to our "springtime in Paris," as if we had pulled off a vacation in disguise.

While not yet fully recovered from my ulcer, I had regained sufficient strength for our packing and travel to proceed on schedule. We were to make our way home by a new route: by rail up to Madras then across the Indian peninsula to Bombay, by a small Italian passenger ship from there to Genoa, by railway to Paris, and, finally, by the magnificent SS

France from Le Havre to New York. Once more, the trip sounded far simpler than it turned out to be.

Going north to Madras was straightforward. Our express train clipped along, getting all of our luggage and us to the state capital intact and right on schedule. But a surprise awaited us at our travel agent's downtown office. I walked in, identified myself, and was on the verge of asking the coach number of our compartment on that evening's train to Bombay, when the clerk burst out with, "What are *you* doing here? Your train left three hours ago and we couldn't find you." I told him he had the facts wrong and handed him the itinerary his manager had sent us; it listed our Madras-Bombay train as departing about nine hours hence. Frowning and muttering "impossible!" to himself, he vanished with the itinerary into the recesses of the office.

Well, our train *had* already left. Not only that, but there were only two trains a day and it normally took a good week or two of advance notice to book a compartment on a main-line express. Since our ship was to sail from Bombay in four days, we wondered what the travel agency would do. At last, an all too casual senior clerk ambled over and told us everything would be all right. We should meet their company's agent on the platform half an hour before the departure time for this evening's train. He would tell us then what they had been able to arrange. I stood there with a fussing child in my arms not believing a word he said. How had something rather similar happened to us twice? It was little consolation that it had been their mistake this time, not ours.

As in Ceylon, a year and a half earlier, we never found out how our problem was solved. Needless to say, however, the travel agents managed to bail themselves out. A roomy compartment bore a "Gardner" name tag by the time we reached it with all our luggage.

Once we had settled the children down, there was time to think about what lay ahead. For one thing, we looked forward to traversing a great stretch of south-central India we knew only from books. Our eighteen-hour trip was to take us across a dry, yet once wealthy, expanse of land in which Hindu kingdoms such as Vijayanagar had managed for years and years to hold off the expanding Muslim empires of north India. But, due to the stresses of the day, we fell asleep from exhaustion almost immediately and awoke in time only to catch the last half of the journey.

What a dry land it was! Being used to the green irrigated rice fields of the Tamil coastal plain, what we woke to looked brown and dreary by comparison. Yet the stations were lively: coffee, snack, and fruit vendors did a brisk business; smiling travelers stopped by our windows to greet the foreigners in English, Kannada, or Marathi; and wary monkey troops on station rooftops sat watching for opportunities to snatch bits of food. On one desiccated landscape, I spotted what looked like Golgumbaz, not far from the rail line. If it was Golgumbaz, this huge, boxlike seventeenth-century Muslim tomb, familiar from architecture books, was capped by one of the world's largest domes. Surely it warranted at the very least a sign saying, "Here it is! Wonder of wonders!" No, it merely sat there, anonymously, in the middle of dusty nowhere.

Victoria Station, in busy Bombay, was enormous, chaotic, and deafening. Now we were in a land where railway porters all appeared to be speaking Marathi . . . a problem. But there were *so* many of them, with their khaki uniforms and red turbans, it struck me that it might be worth calling out in Tamil, "Does anyone here know Tamil?" One skinny fellow off behind the others looked up in surprise, grinned at me, and bellowed "*Aama saar, TamiR teriyom.*" His fellows made way for him to come forward, and it was clear immediately that I had a dedicated, cheerful overseer to help me forward our trunks to the dock and then get the overnight bags to a taxi.

As we checked into our hostel, Heather finally came to the realization that she had been snatched away forever from her adoring ayah, Rosalie. She was stunned. After all, hadn't Rosalie fussed over her for the whole waking day, six days a week, during the past year and a half? For Heather, that was all she remembered of her life. Oh, did we see tears—and not just tears. All night, then all the next night, our daughter screamed and wailed until her poor little body was exhausted. Her cries must have echoed through the building, because people in the dining room looked daggers at us, meal after horrible meal.

We loved Bombay otherwise. Despite being a port and one of India's great industrial centers, it had an attractive downtown, tall palm trees, gorgeous beaches, and fresh sea breezes. If I had been transported there in my sleep one night and awoke not knowing where in the world I had landed, I might have thought I was in a gorgeous Mediterranean city. We hoped to come back someday.

All too soon we found ourselves at the pier where the *Sydney* was moored. This modest little ship did a regular run between Australia and Italy, by way of Bombay, Suez, and Malta; it was half full with prosperous Italian-Australians who were on their way to pay visits to siblings, parents, and grandparents in the home country.

Because of my convalescence from my ulcer, I had put off one bit of official business until the last minute—ascertaining whether India would tax my Ford Foundation income. We would not be able to leave India, it seemed, without a tax clearance certificate. Just before we left Kodaikkanal, I finally went in to see the district's income tax officer. He turned out to be a cheerful, educated young man who had been sitting in his office for I don't know how long, yearning for conversation with anyone who shared his concerns about our troubled world. We chatted over snacks about everything *except* taxes for an hour or more. When it was finally time for me to leave, he told me that the fellowship, being educational, was in his estimation tax exempt. Because our departure from Kodaikkanal was imminent and his bureaucracy was guaranteed to be slow, he promised he would have our certificate sent by express mail to our travel agency's Bombay office the moment it was issued. A telephone call to the office once we reached Bombay assured me he had kept his word; the morning we sailed one of the staff would deliver our certificate to the dock. Sure enough, someone was waiting for us there, holding an official looking envelope that bore my name. All we needed to do was turn it in to the emigration officials and we could get on with boarding. Imagine my horror when I opened the envelope on the wharf, now packed shoulder to shoulder with frantic passengers and shouting porters with carts of luggage, and found that the tax clearance certificate belonged to *someone else*. And it was embarkation time! I battled my way to the front of the emigration line in a sweat and told one of the gray-haired senior officers, "This isn't mine. How can I find who has *my* certificate?" All I got from him was a laugh. But it turned out to be a friendly laugh, for he went on to say, "I am sure that somebody else here has your form. We'll straighten it up. Just give us what you have and be on your way."

Once our luggage was stowed in the cabin and we were a bit calmer, Heather finally settled down enough to stand with us at the railing, waving good-bye to the India we had each grown fond of. We now faced fifteen days of total rest, our first such break in a year and a half.

The next morning, some three hundred miles out into the Arabian Sea, we spied three small Arab dhows plying their way eastward toward India under full sail. The sight took my thoughts back to earlier times, when Europeans were learning at last to use the seasonal winds of the Indian Ocean the way Arab traders had long done. I felt as if these vessels were giving us a glimpse of the past, a glimpse that made our own travel seem comparatively simple and easy. But we weren't looking at the past. It wasn't a museum diorama. Indeed, four years later, on our next trip to India, we would see such dhows anchored in India's west coast port of Cochin during monsoon; they floated high in the water then, as they waited for the seasonal winds to change so they could be loaded with Indian goods for their return journey to the Persian Gulf or East Africa.

As much as we had loved Indian food, after being away from home as long as we had we were eager for a taste of Western delicacies. Our other ships had offered them. But the *Sydney* was a cheap, practical vessel, not a luxury liner; it had cooks, not chefs. What they served in the dining room was hearty fare rather than haute cuisine. One day, though, our hopes were raised: there were two soups on the menu, not just the usual pasta soup but consommé as well. We ordered it with glee. When the steward trundled the familiar tureen to our table and skillfully produced consommé for us by skimming broth off the top of the pasta soup with his ladle, we knew we would have to hold our impatience in check for another week and a half.

The vessel was at least full of life. We hadn't been at sea more than two or three days when Sikh men from north India and Italian women discovered they had virtually identical circle dances. It was wonderful. Night after night they whirled together on the deck to energetic hand-claps and songs. But our cabin, which was off an echoing stairwell landing, was no place to put sleepy babies to bed. Happy, intoxicated, and stumbling parties on the staircase were far beyond our control; indeed, they were beyond anyone's control. Our only option was to get the children so sleepy before bedtime that they didn't hear the ruckus. Although the scene was not one of total chaos, the shy, lanky assistant purser had to climb the mast one midnight, in strong wind and a rough sea, to coax down an incoherent and belligerent drunk.

April had been the start of India's hot season, so we were unprepared for the cool headwind that whipped our hair as we sailed up the Red Sea. We had to dress well to walk on deck. Nonetheless, I was tired of heat and found the air a pleasant reminder that we were beginning to approach our native temperate zone. The Ford Foundation staffer may have been right to talk of spring in Paris as something to which we must be looking forward.

Italy was special once more. The ship put in first at Naples, then at Genoa. There was time in Naples to take the children by taxi to Herculaneum, a prosperous town near Pompeii that suffered the same awful destruction in AD 79. Large, luxurious villas had been dug out of the ash and lava there and then restored, right down to their grassy atriums. Heather puttered about cheerily in sunny courtyards as we took in the surrounding sights. Then we went off in search of pizza.

We scheduled a couple of days in Christopher Columbus's ancient home port of Genoa before going on to Paris. With luck we located a sunny rooming house on the hillside, with a view across the ancient city and the sea. While Trudy unpacked, I rambled back down to the railway station to book our continuing travel. Afterward we could get some lunch. Luckily, the ticket man at the station knew some English, for his news would otherwise have been difficult to understand. He told me that a train was leaving for Turin in thirty minutes, and it would con-nect with an express that would get us into France before midnight. When I seemed uninterested, *he* asked *me* what I had heard about the pending rail strike. Whoops! All he knew was that Italian railways were going on a general strike, of indefinite length, in eleven hours. Hello Genoa, good-bye Genoa. I shall not attempt to characterize my run up the hill, our instant repacking, and our race by taxi back to the station. The whole family was starved, and Trudy's and my clothes were wet with perspiration, but we made it . . . barely.

It really was a delight to be back in a green land again, so we tried to soak it up as consolation for what we had been forced to forgo. Our train sped through the lush, low eastern end of the Apennine Mountains, then across Italy's manicured piedmont, its fields edged with mulberry trees, to Turin.

We did find food of sorts along the way; we managed to catch our next train in Turin with time to spare; and, by evening, we were ascend-ing the steep rocky river bottoms of Italy's alpine valleys toward snow-capped peaks on the French border. We would make it out of Italy at least an hour before the strike began.

That night, we sat shivering for three hours on the simple wooden benches of an obscure mountain railway station, waiting for our French train to pull in. Heather toddled away to make friends with two waiting nuns; one of them spoke only German, the other only French. She came back gleefully to show us she had a hard candy from the nuns in her mouth. She wasn't used to such treats. Not five minutes later, though, her face screwed up in something between a gag and absolute horror: her once delicious candy hid a shot of premium cognac.

We raced into Paris on a mainline train. After a bit of initial confu-sion, we settled into a well-run pension in Montparnasse that could provide us with breakfast and dinner. That simplified life for us. The pension was a few minutes' walk from three Metro lines and from places where Trudy could take the children to play, so we remained there for the full two months, with only one brief side trip to visit my brother-in-law in Berlin—going there by train and returning by air.

Before I continue with details of our time in France, I must wedge in a few words about our trip back to Paris from Germany. Living in India had taught us that, when traveling with children, we should always carry with us a gallon jug of good drinking water. Filling it each morning became a ritual. The day we went to Tempelhof Airport in Berlin was no different, except that we realized at the airport that we wouldn't need water on the flight, so checked the Coleman jug along with our suitcases.

Because of the time it took to get our two little ones' things together, we were the last to disembark from the plane at Orly Field in Paris. We walked into customs to find that the other passengers had already gone on their way and seven customs officers were clustered around our luggage. They pointed at the water jug and asked, "What is this?" When we replied that it was drinking water, they looked at us blankly and put the question to us a second time. They looked so troubled that I offered to drink some, just to show them. They gave me a blunt chorus of "No." Then I said it would be all right to pour it out, and I took the lid off. Again, they looked shocked and forbade that, too. But they did peer into it suspiciously, and they sniffed it carefully as if it might be toxic. The end of the story is that they finally all gave up trying to understand what we had done; they walked off still shaking their heads, releasing our troubling jug and us to the world.

Dumont's Gift

I found Louis Dumont at his desk at his Center for Indian Studies near boulevard St. Michelle. He ushered me in with a warm smile, and so began a hideous experience. Oh, yes, Dumont was welcoming, he gave me access to his resources and his time, and he was brilliant. But when he played devil's advocate, in order to push me to think critically about what I was doing, few of my preliminary generalizations proved interesting to him. My stated goal, to summarize all I'd learned about the Paliyan way of life, he found just plain dull. He pressed me to find and center on any elegant, underlying structures. But what might those be? Having no ready response was shattering. Here I was, already thousands of miles from my Indian sources of information, and everything was falling apart. To top it off, my 1960s ulcer diet dictated that I refuse French wines, European dark chocolate, fresh salads and salad dressings, plus a host of other delicacies that people around me were enjoying—most of them things for which I had yearned while in India. It may have been an ever-brightening springtime for Parisians, but it became a darkening season for me.

Despite the initial setback, I had far too many solid findings to resign myself to failure; I was able to remain focused as well. So, while Trudy went off with the children to the Jardin du Luxembourg, I spent long days rethinking everything: my body of data, the research problem, and all my previous lines of argument. One day, while a geographer was going on at length in Dumont's India seminar about the layout of a Maharashtran village, I had a sudden flash of insight about interconnections among diverse facets of Paliyan culture. Ignoring both the speaker and Dumont's apparent curiosity about my sudden burst of activity, I scribbled furiously for more than an hour. I saw, for the first time, the relationship among the Paliyans' valuing of individual autonomy, details of their loose social organization, and their practice of solving a problem by pulling back and calming down instead of acting in a way that aggravated the difficulty. Taken together, these constituted a coherent system. As we filed out of the seminar room I told Dumont I had made a breakthrough. He flashed me a knowing smile and proposed that I present a paper on it at the following week's session. I sketched out for the group, seven days later, a tidy portrait of a way of life that revolved around belief in the value of individual autonomy and respect of others. Questions afterward built on what I had said, rather than challenging it. That was a promising sign. When Dumont closed the day's session, he did it with a satisfied look and an unprecedented request that we all join him for a glass of wine on the street below. It was a ceremonial glass I *would* drink! The next week we could happily board the SS *France* for the final leg of our voyage home.

The Penn faculty let me run with the Parisian synthesis. There was a great deal of comparative work to be done, but I had momentum. On May 24, 1965, eleven months after arriving back in the United States, I received my Ph.D.

Lured Back to India

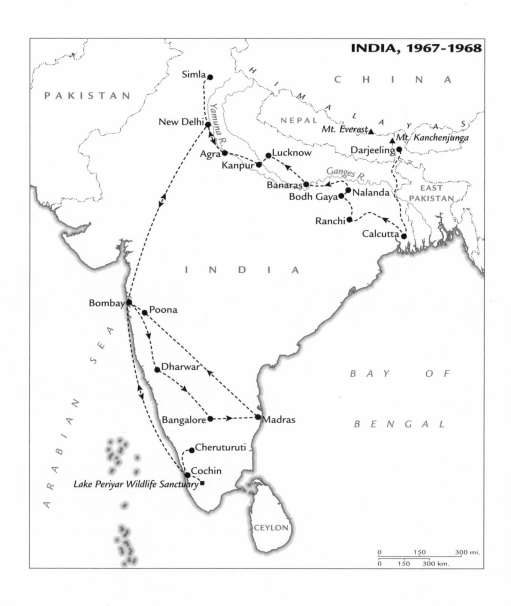

INDIA, 1967-1968

PAKISTAN

CHINA

Simla

New Delhi

Yamuna R.

NEPAL

HIMALAYAS

Mt. Everest

Mt. Kanchenjunga

Darjeeling

Agra

Lucknow

Kanpur

Ganges R.

Banaras

Bodh Gaya

Nalanda

EAST
PAKISTAN

Ranchi

Calcutta

INDIA

Bombay

Poona

Dharwar

BAY OF

BENGAL

Bangalore

Madras

ARABIAN SEA

Cheruturuti

Cochin

Lake Periyar Wildlife Sanctuary

CEYLON

0   150   300 mi.

0   150   300 km.

Through Alice's Looking Glass

A Hindu Challenge

With my doctorate finally in hand, I taught for the summer at Penn, then bustled off to a tenure-track teaching post at the University of Texas in Austin. It was another world, balmy and relaxed, really relaxed. During my first week on the campus, I heard a passing student tell a companion, "Do you realize, I have actually been enrolled for three consecutive semesters!"

Because I had one foot in South Asian Studies, one of my duties at Texas was joint coordination of a group-taught course on Asian civilization. My co-coordinator in this venture was Raja Rao, a Hindu novelist who was known, especially, for *Kanthapura, The Serpent and the Rope,* and *The Cat and Shakespeare.* Raja, thirty years older than I, held a position in Texas's powerful philosophy department. Ours was an amiable, productive partnership, despite Raja's being troubled by my faith in "mere empirical knowledge," and despite his more than once labeling my stance "materialist" and "that socialist, sociological nonsense." Because I did not think of myself as being what anthropologists called a materialist, I wondered just what those teasing epithets meant to him. My attempts to draw him out led to long tales about the nature of "reality." He and I evidently defined *that* term differently too. How were we to organize a course together when our terms and assumptions were so incompatible? We each yielded a good bit, but, at the beginning of our second year of working together, he urged me to return to India and spend time learning to view the Hindu way of life from what was termed its Vedanta perspective. He hoped this would allow me to appreciate the shortcomings of my alien social science perspective. Being curious enough to go along with his suggestion, I applied for a research fellowship from the American Institute of Indian Studies for 1967–1968 and was awarded the support I sought. My project, ironically, was entitled "Indic Culture: An Anthropological Synthesis." Although the end product of the year turned out to be far more Hindu than anthropological, wasn't that precisely what Raja had hoped would happen?

Arriving via the East

The project was enhanced with university funds so that I could spend a month en route discussing Hindu India with Japanese scholars who had undertaken extended research there. My reason for this was straightforward: if I truly wished to divest myself of inappropriate Western perspectives on Hindu civilization, perhaps other viewpoints on the civilization, such as those of Japanese scholars, would stimulate me to begin my rethinking. They might direct me along avenues I had not previously considered and, in so doing, start to free me from what Raja had been calling my misconceptions.

Up to this time, we had always crossed oceans by ship; now we were traveling by air. It felt weird to have breakfast at dawn in Texas, fly more than a third of the way round the globe in sunlight, and sit the children down for dinner in Tokyo before the sun finally set. Trudy and I knew that, because we had traveled with the sun through nine time zones, we were having dinner fully twenty-one hours after we had eaten breakfast. But imagine the effect of the stretched day on our five-year-old and our three-and-a-half-year-old! They had napped on and off in flight without getting a fraction of the rest they needed. Neither of them managed to eat much at dinner or even to keep their eyes open once they knew that beds were available. Needless to say they fell immediately into a deep sleep . . . and slumbered soundly until 3:00 a.m. They awoke at three with their energetic little bodies telling them it was noon, lunchtime! They were starving. "Mummy, Daddy, let's go and get breakfast!" they sang. The International Guest House where we were staying happened to be in an affluent and westernized residential neighborhood, with a few embassies scattered through it. We walked in the brisk predawn air for miles in search of an all-night restaurant. All we saw were tall, inhospitable walls and, through the gates, massive dormant buildings. The children grew so frustrated, cold, and weary we had to turn back.

Hours later, at our long overdue breakfast in the Guest House, we received unpleasant news. A senior staff member came to our table to inform us bluntly that our room booking must have been made in error. They ran a residence for senior scholars and had no way of catering to children. They asked that we move right away. Since I heard no apology, and was too tired to handle this mischance very well, I bristled and replied that I did not know Tokyo. I had never been there before. Since we had received from them a written confirmation of our booking for a "family of four," I would be happy to move out *if* they could locate something suitable for us in the vicinity of Tokyo University. By noon they had found us the perfect place.

We sped across the city in a taxi just as we had done the evening before. The cozy *ryokan* (inn) they had located for us was halfway down a street of modest, snugly packed houses—a street so narrow that taxis had to slow to five miles an hour to manage its corners. A young, graceful willow hung over the entrance. For the children, it was close to the back gate of Ueno Zoo; for me, it was a comfortable walk from the University of Tokyo. Streets of shops and restaurants were located nearby, and the neighborhood itself was lovely. It was precisely what we needed! Although we had not had a part in negotiating the arrangement, it was apparent that the proprietor had agreed to house us for as long as we required.

Naturally, I began with my own roster of India specialists whom I hoped to meet in Japan. Professor Chie Nakane, head of the anthropology department at the University of Tokyo, would not hear of me doing it all unassisted. I had written to her about my plans, and she greeted me on arrival with a list of diverse scholars to append to my own. She also introduced me personally to two India specialists from her own institution, one being a junior researcher of my own age who could take responsibility for me, and she made sure I had access to Tokyo University's stellar library.

All the anthropologists, sociologists, geographers, and Sanskrit specialists I conferred with in Tokyo, Nagoya, and Kyoto were generous with their time and ideas. They were open to the questions I posed, and their hospitality was gracious. Two geographers and I, after an intense and sober day of professional talk in Tokyo, went to a private room above a tempura restaurant and, between us, finished off an embarrassing number of sake bottles. The real question we faced at the end of the evening was who would be able to help whom to a taxi or train. But how we had talked! A senior Sanskrit scholar at the University of Kyoto walked me to what had been one of his favorite haunts in student days. We rested on tatami mats by a placid, tree-shaded temple pond and feasted on extraordinary preparations of tofu and sake as we talked on into the summer evening about India. While I had yet to come to grips with Vedanta, my Japanese colleagues did, collectively, offer me various new insights about India, especially about the Hindu joint family. They also nudged me into recognizing the limitations of my training. It was a rich and productive month.

The time was rich for my family as well. Even though the inn staff knew absolutely no English and we were equally untutored in Japanese, we were led through the day's routines without much confusion. If breakfast arrived in our room at a time of the staff's choice, it was at least a thoroughly Japanese meal to be eaten with chopsticks. We never saw eggs and bacon, or a knife and fork. Some mornings, to be sure, we were brought raw eggs, but they were to be whipped with soy sauce and cooked by stirring them into steaming rice. We could bathe either in a small, deep bath in our suite or in the huge, piping-hot public bath downstairs. Heather and Eric took special interest in our translucent paper windows, which they could easily slide open in order to watch and wave to the back-street vendors with their varied goods and cries. There was much novelty to savor and a great deal for each of us to appreciate.

The children took regular advantage of Ueno Zoo, the back gate of which was a mere two or three minutes' walk from our lodgings. It was the perfect place to run and play. There were attractive playgrounds near us, too, boasting slides and jungle gyms. On warm evenings we often strolled as a family around temple gardens and the peaceful lotus- and goose-filled pond that figures in Ogai Mori's early novel, *The Wild Geese.*

We were even more fortunate during the week we spent in Kyoto, for we located an inn there that was elegant as well as convenient. Our two rooms were hung with pieces of calligraphy and had sliding doors that could be opened onto a minuscule private garden. The food was special, too. Imagine morsels of smoked salmon with breakfast!

We certainly faced problems in our inns. We might be sent to the communal bath before others took their turns, which sounds fine until you realize that the water would be even hotter than usual—at times it felt not far off the boil. Dipping a toe in was beyond any of us on such days. All we could do was scrub down using the faucets and buckets along the side of the room.

More difficult yet, we found it impossible to prevent middle-aged serving women at our Tokyo inn from pouncing noisily on our three-and-a-half-year-old son and snatching at the front of his pants. We adults knew they probably meant well; poor Eric found their practice incoherent and frightening. It disturbed him in ways they probably could not comprehend, and we lacked the words to ask them politely to desist.

Our travel to Nagoya and Kyoto was by the famous "bullet train," or *shinkansen,* which we all loved. It was silky smooth, even at 141 miles an hour, a speed it attained before we so much as got out to Tokyo's suburbs. The bullet trains did not operate independently of one another; they were integral parts of a tightly organized system run by computer. Expresses with only a few stops leapfrogged the locals at certain points en route where the locals made additional stops. I had never before seen public transport operate on schedule right down to the second. My recall is that it functioned like this: Say one's train is due in at 9:03. At 9:01:45 it can be seen entering the station; by 9:02:30 the engine glides silently past; by 9:02:50 one's designated car is already beginning to come alongside; by 9:02:57 the door arrives at its premarked spot on the platform, where you stand waiting; and at 9:02:59 the door begins opening. Expresses, at that time, ran every twelve minutes from 6:00 a.m. to late evening. Along the three-hundred-mile line from Tokyo to Osaka there are numerous rain gauges and seismographs. If they register either too much rain during a limited time period or too large an earth tremor, the entire system comes off the computer. Lights flash and horns sound in the cabs of all the engines in the system, and the trains automatically drop to speeds that human drivers can manage conventionally, but it leaves the trains still interlocked, with expresses still leapfrogging the locals. For 1967, it was a marvel.

Because we kept busy, it was a short month. All too soon came the time for repacking our three suitcases and boarding our onward flight. We flew to Calcutta, in eastern India, by way of Taipei, Hong Kong, and Bangkok. Several experiences were particularly memorable.

For us, Taipei was little more than a day in the National Palace Museum, which houses the world's premier collection of ancient Chinese artworks. Because their holdings are displayed seasonally, we had to be satisfied with pieces on summer themes. What a feast it was, though.

The Cultural Revolution had left mainland China closed to most out-siders at that time. The sight of the forbidden land beside us was hyp-notic for me as we flew for two hours around its great, curved shoreline from Taipei to Hong Kong. The air was pure and clear; it was one of those days when the sky is an implausibly deep blue. And our Thai jet brought us close enough to the Chinese coast to get glimpses of fishing boats and villages, close enough to be teased by the immense size and age of this land that I hoped, someday, would be open to visitors.

We stayed for three nights in a tiny hotel in Hong Kong, on about the tenth floor of a high-rise building in busy Kowloon. Our first night, the proprietor banged impatiently on our door at midnight, crying, "Fill the bathtub! Fill the bathtub!" We obeyed her at once, but it was our first warning that water was going to be available in the city for only three hours at a time every few days. If all of us were going to share the same tubful of tepid water day after day, we were going to have to do our ut-most to keep our active little ones clean between baths. Our one and only luxuriant, truly cleansing bath in Hong Kong took place our sec-ond or third afternoon, at a glistening beach on the south shore of Vic-toria Island.

On arrival at Bangkok we were asked to disembark for two hours while the plane was refueled and serviced. The Thais made it worth our while. The spread of tropical fruit the airport laid out for passengers to enjoy during their break astonished me. While I knew India's fruits well, of the twenty-five or thirty sweet and succulent fruits the Thais offered us, I could not identify a single one.

Finding Another India

We landed in Calcutta near midnight and made our way slowly through the immigration formalities. I recall the rooms where they processed us as being small drab boxes and the staff as being officious, but I think having two tousled youngsters in tow sped up the routines for us. Even so, it must have been after 2:00 a.m. by the time we stumbled across the sleeping bodies on the sidewalk and entered the foyer of our Victorian-era hotel in the city's center.

Reputed to be "one of the East's finest hotels," it was a shock. The torn velvet drapes in our twenty-foot-high room had decades of dust in them; the air-conditioner produced little more than grating noises; I tripped over an enormous live rat on our first stroll outside the next morning; dozens of emaciated people with begging bowls lined the sidewalks along Chowringhee Road (something I had never seen before in India); and there was litter everywhere. What were we exposing our children to? It was mandatory that we look for something more welcoming before another night went by.

After four days of refuge in a suburban hostel run by the American Institute of Indian Studies for visiting scholars, we settled into a tidy Indian-style rooming house, with a spacious walled garden and lawns. It was located on Little Russell Street, a residential street on the very edge of the business and government hub of the city. We were not far from book and clothing stores, a great parade ground where the children could play on grass, a museum, and the headquarters of the Anthropological Survey of India—where I had colleagues to confer with. This was to be our home for nearly three months.

Three days after we arrived in India, a young scholar I'd just met asked me to accompany him to hear two Baul singers who were performing that evening at an architect's house. I went along knowing only that some Baul singers are Hindus and others are Muslims. They wander the steaming Bengal delta, singing to and about God in such abstract terms that their personal religious backgrounds are left ambiguous, yet in such ecstatic and intimate terms that one feels the mutual love between each singer-devotee and his Lord. They are welcomed into Hindu and Muslim villages alike, where, in return for dinner and a place to sleep, they will sing on into the evening and infect the villagers with their spirit of devotion.

It was a hot, humid monsoon evening. When we arrived at the house, there they were: two lean, turbaned figures, each with a small drum having a string for plucking attached to the middle of its head. About thirty well-dressed men and women filled the spacious living room floor. They extended me a warm welcome and opened a spot where I could sit cross-legged among them. By the time we began to hear the lilting, percussive sounds of the singers' instruments, my host had put a tall cool green drink in my hand. I relished the taste. But, soon, strange things began happening. First I noticed that I had exquisite awareness of the entire surface of my body—I could "feel my envelope"—a bizarre sensation. Then I thought I was beginning to understand the ecstatic words of the hymns. They were performed, of course, in Bengali, a language I had never even heard until three days earlier. What was happening to me? The air in the room was close, and I found the cool drink so refreshing that I soon asked for a refill. Why did my host chuckle as he handed it to me? And why did all my neighbors smile in friendly amusement? My companion told me the next day that I had innocently been sipping strong bhang, the mind-altering Indian hemp. India had thrown open for me a door that I hadn't anticipated.

Once I got in touch with my anthropological colleagues, the main question they asked me was the goal of my project. It was difficult to explain to them because most of them, it seems, were firmly committed to the very Western social scientific concepts I was attempting to escape. I should have realized that would be the case. So I talked with them of our need to come to grips with the structure of Hindu civilization *on its own terms.* My procedure was to spend time initially reading, observing, and thinking on my own. I literally wallowed in Hindu thought and practice, even Hindu psychology. Then I tried out my ideas on others.

Some of my more mature ideas led eventually to lectures or written papers on the traditional structure of Hindu society, politico-economic dominance, and formalization, in addition to distinctly Indian ways of maintaining tradition. I participated in a two-week conference at the Anthropological Survey of India in Calcutta and gave formal talks at Lucknow University, three colleges in Kanpur, the University of Delhi, the 1968 Indian Science Congress at Banaras Hindu University, the Deccan College in Poona, a conference in Madras, and a huge conference at the Indian Institute for Advanced Studies in Simla. I also talked with colleagues elsewhere. The meetings in Banaras and Simla exposed me to virtually all of India's leading anthropologists, from north, south, east, and west. I became friends, especially, with Surajit Sinha, K. N. Mathur, M. N. Srinivas, Indera Paul Singh, Irawati Karvé (whom I had met in 1963), Gopala Sarana, and A. Aiyappan. All did whatever they could for me professionally, and the last four of them welcomed me into their homes.

One of the papers I wrote was born at three o'clock in the morning, in a windswept hotel room in the ancient southern port of Cochin. The subject was power. I awoke having had a sudden synthesis, similar to the one in Dumont's seminar four years earlier. By breakfast, I had a rough first draft in hand. Later I came to realize that this paper was based wholly on the Hindu concept of *artha.* This can be translated as "power," particularly the power of one responsible for a household, for village land, or for a kingdom. What Raja Rao hoped for was beginning to happen. Should I have been surprised to come down from that same hotel room one morning to find Raja quietly eating breakfast in the dining room? He just stood up, beamed, and took my hands in his.

As Raja had anticipated, thirteen months in India provided me the time and opportunity to acquire a degree of understanding of Vedanta, the predominant and perennial philosophical perspective of Hindus. And, yes, Vedanta *did* turn Western social scientific thought on its head, as Raja claimed. The five senses, far from being a sure means for learning about reality—as many Westerners hold—can catch only misleading glimpses of it. Our ears hear only a small part of the spectrum of sound frequencies, our eyes are yet more limited in dealing with frequencies of light waves, we taste few of the chemicals about us, and we so easily mistake a stick for a snake. How can we place faith in our uninformative senses as we attempt to determine what is real?

At last, piece by piece, I was acquiring a foundation on which I could build a course on Indian civilization that would begin with Hindu concepts and remain relatively true to them all semester. I was to teach such a course annually for almost thirty years and found much satisfaction in exploring the ways in which it placed me in the role of an indigenous guide to the civilization. Following some years of experimentation, the course opened with elemental concepts, such as time and creation, matter and forces, truth, and ways of knowing. Next, the main body of the course was organized in terms of duties, power, pleasure and the senses, and spiritual liberation—each of these sections covering one of the four great Hindu aims of life. Finally, I closed with a look at Indian perspectives on the modern world. It was a challenge for all of us. The course necessitated that I lecture and answer questions (even when we were outside the classroom) from a consistent Vedanta perspective. This was not an easy task. Students were called upon to write a series of essays, each of which had to be from a clear and valid insider's perspective. These exercises always baffled a few at first, but they led to memorable experiences for most. Each year the class descended into an unfamiliar, inverted world, as if through Alice's looking glass, and then slowly made sense of it.

Savoring India Personally

Our Itinerant Year

The scattering of my anthropology colleagues is one reason our year in India involved a lot of travel. Another is that, even though people treat India as a "country" today, it has long been an entity on the order of Europe. It approaches Europe (minus Russia) in its size; its population is similar, too; it has even greater linguistic diversity than Europe; and, previous to modern times, just like Europe, it has had only two brief periods when empires gave it a degree of political unity. I knew only one Indian state well from direct experience, Tamil Nadu. One can no more visit a single Indian state, and then maintain that one knows the whole land, than one can visit just Bulgaria, or just Scotland, and say one now knows the continent of Europe. The landscapes differ in fundamental ways across India, as do foods, houses, tools, clothes, marriage arrangements, and patterns of worship. Aware of this diversity at the outset, I thought that savoring Hindu culture as broadly as possible would carry me a few steps toward comprehending it.

Family travel is not easy in India unless one has a great deal of planning time and a liberal budget. To reduce the expense and difficulty of our moves we bought a car in Calcutta. This also allowed us to schedule trips at our own convenience; we could take routes of our choice, even on short notice, and follow whatever meandering side roads promised to be fruitful. Because there were long waiting lists for new cars, the only one immediately available in Calcutta was a classy little sky-blue Triumph

Herald, assembled in India and marketed as a "Standard"—the closest thing to a sports car I would ever own. It would be easy to resell when we left for home. Admittedly, it was small, but with a luggage rack on the roof to hold our three suitcases, it was not too much of a squeeze.

We did have one problem with the vehicle. I returned it to the dealer the day before we were to leave on our first long drive, up into the Himalayan mountain range, because a persistent rattle beneath the right side concerned us. The sales manager asked a senior mechanic to go for a spin with me to see if he could pinpoint what was bothering the picky Americans. I had not gone a quarter mile when he turned pale, bellowed "Stop!" and crawled underneath, right there on the street. He emerged with oil in his whiskers to tell me that, when the car had been assembled, the body had been bolted to the chassis along one side, but not along the other. To put it in simple terms, we were flapping. I hate to think what *that* might have led to as we tooled around hairpin mountain bends!

With the car fixed, off we went to Darjeeling, within sight of both the border of Tibet and two of our planet's three highest mountains—Everest, of course, and Kanchenjunga. We would also visit Bodh Gaya (the site at which Buddhism was born) and the ruins of Nalanda (a vast monastic college to which Chinese monks came in AD 401–410 and 630–645 to learn the early Buddhist texts). Then there would be Banaras, Lucknow, Agra, New Delhi, and, by air, Bombay and Cochin. We were able to take in numberless palaces, temples, tombs, and monuments, enter a Tibetan lamasery in the Himalayas, drive through the deep forest of a tiger preserve, and picnic privately on the grassy ruins of an early fourteenth-century fort, doing all this as weather and circumstances suited us.

Shortly after we reached the midpoint of north India, in Lucknow and Agra, we began encountering language riots. It had been twenty years since India had won its independence from colonial rule; the prearranged time had come to knit the nation together with Hindi, India's new national language, in place of English. Yet license plates, clocks, signs in railroad cars, and much else still used the English letters and numbers of British days. "Indians must start honoring that which is Indian," the politicians and students cried. This impacted us when our car's name and license plates were smeared with tar while I was lecturing at Lucknow University. Although the university's vice chancellor apologized and sent over a staff member to scrub off the tar, I decided to break the law and avoid further trouble by fashioning my own Hindi license plates that I could fasten over the official ones. Passions were most intense in the north-central plain—the region of India where Hindi was the native tongue—for local pride was at stake, too. Because we would be staying in that very area for the next few months, I imagined even the local, Hindi-speaking police would be tolerant of my false license plates. They were.

For the most part, we stayed in centrally located hotels and rooming houses, with big gardens where possible. And the gardens saw heavy use by little feet. Our accommodations and their guests were often interesting. We shared a hotel in Ranchi with the amiable young family of a High Court judge from Bengal, a Bodh Gaya rest house with a conference of doctors, a Banaras hotel with the *choygal* (the reigning prince) of Sikkim and his bride, and a Lucknow hotel with a spirited troupe of Soviet circus performers. At lunchtime one day in Lucknow we asked Heather where her brother was. She said with a totally straight face, "On the elephant." We dashed out onto the Carlton Hotel's veranda, and there was our happy four-year-old, a hundred and fifty yards away, he and the gardener both astride the neck of the establishment's huge work elephant. In New Delhi we sublet first one spacious house from the American Institute of Indian Studies, then another. They were modern flat-roofed houses in the style that Le Corbusier introduced to north India. We were thankful that the second house had air-conditioning when the heat and dust storms of June hit us.

Deep Experiences

The drive up into the Himalayas, to Darjeeling, took me out on India's open roads for the first time since my youthful motorcycling in the south. The main roads, though narrow, were well paved. We did well until we reached the Ganges, which we had to cross by ferry. Monsoon rains were near their end, so the river was full and fast and its banks were muddy when we arrived. The ferry turned out to be nothing more than a World War II landing craft that could transport half a dozen or more vehicles. It was in the process of loading trucks and looked almost full to me, but the crew told us our light little car could easily ride across on this trip "if we put it on the ramp." Ah, but *I* would be the one to put it on. When our turn came, having seen their method of loading, I asked the family as calmly as I could to go ahead on foot. Then my task was to back the car down a steep, rain-slicked mud bank and get my wheels onto two large but wet and unsecured planks. More unsettling than the slippery approach was the obvious fact that our ferry was not moored to the bank. It was out in the raging river, held against the bank solely by the thrust of its engines. Let me not have to do that very often!

Later, we reached a stretch of road where heavy Mercedes Benz trucks were parked on the pavement, two abreast, bumper-to-bumper for more than two miles. The shoulder being firm and dry, I drove on it all the way to the front of the line to learn the cause of the holdup. There was a long bridge ahead of us that had been closed by the police due to monsoon damage. Uprooted lotuses, swept downstream by the powerful current, had collected so thickly on the supporting piles and struts of the bridge that they eventually constituted a dam. As the water level rose, it exerted enough pressure on the bridge that the entire structure was being pressed sideways. The once-vertical piles stood now at angles of fifteen to twenty degrees. Police were blocking the road until a civil engineer could be brought in to assess the bridge's structural integrity. How long would that take? Nobody knew. I saw that there were so many people on the bridge using poles to try to break up the matted jam of lotuses that they surely weighed more than our car. I asked the police if they would let our light vehicle cross slowly. They got together with spokesmen for the truck drivers and asked them this: if the barricade was lifted aside for us to cross, would the truck drivers attempt to follow? The truckers said "no" with one voice. None dared risk losing costly equipment or cargo. To our surprise, we were soon on our way.

Once in the mountains and halfway up the climb, at a spot where both road traffic and Darjeeling's miniature railroad make stops, we pulled over to fortify ourselves with tea. It was strong, sweet, deep-red tea, ladled by our hostess from a simmering thirty- or forty-gallon cauldron. I thought I knew good tea from south India; this brew was exquisite.

Darjeeling was worth all the trouble of getting there. We were at an altitude of about seven thousand feet, at the point where Indians encounter Tibetans. Tibetans were a lovely smiling people. We hadn't seen beaming faces like theirs for months. The sky smiled, too. As monsoon clouds cleared away we were treated to a clear view of Mount Kanchenjunga, an enormous white pyramid some forty-five miles away, across the valley of Sikkim. All about us were precipitous slopes, Tibetan

The shrine at Bodh Gaya, where the Buddha achieved
enlightenment. The tree on the right is a second-generation
descendent of the one under which the Buddha sat.

Buddhist shrines and monasteries, lamas, shops marketing Tibetan cu-
rios, tea plantations on the slopes below us, and clear mountain air.
There were also moviemakers and actors from Bombay, shooting a
song-and-dance scene on the plaza where a Tibetan was giving our children a ride on mountain ponies. We were glad to be out of the congested city, and we made it a peaceful week.

The stop in Bodh Gaya exceeded all expectations. A shrine has been
built beside the precise spot where the Buddha was seated when he

Worshippers at the Ganges in Banaras at sunrise.

achieved Enlightenment. Adjacent to this shrine stands a Bodhi tree grown from a seed from a tree from a seed from the very tree under which the Buddha sat. It is the "grandchild" of that venerable Bodhi tree. A shiver went down my spine just from resting my hand on its bark. As happened in Britain, we were touching the past, but were doing so this time in the company of earnest pilgrims from the farthest reaches of the Buddhist world—Ceylon, Thailand, Tibet, Japan, and beyond.

Banaras had a similar impact on me. Here was a city that was said to have been old when the Buddha walked the land. Indeed, it was at Sarnath, on the outskirts of Banaras, where the Buddha preached his first sermon, about the Eightfold Path by which we can end our sorrows. While much of Sarnath now lies ruined, Banaras itself forges on as the premier sacred center for Hindus. It is such a congested old city that we parked our car at once and asked a taxi to take us into the teeming maze of paths and alleys. To be sure, like any ancient holy city, it has its share of entrepreneurs and rascals; but what a place of purpose it is. Prayerful men and women stream down to the Ganges River at dawn to enter the water and make their ablutions. Their spirit is contagious.

I had to experience all I could of Hindu society, politics, art, and religion for the project to succeed. We happened to be in Calcutta in September, at the start of the music season, so Trudy and I procured tickets for all five nights of the All India Sadarang Music Conference, actually a music festival, to be held only minutes away from our rooming house. The fourth night was to be, literally, an all-night show. Dozens of India's greatest classical singers and instrumentalists were on the program. It was the final concert of his life for the aging and half-paralyzed Bade Ghulam Ali, with his still sonorous voice. And we heard ancient genres of music, such as *dhrupad,* which had as yet appeared on few Western recordings. This festival was the start of something important for us. Afterward, musicians we had enjoyed in Calcutta, plus others, gave recitals in Lucknow and Delhi as we traveled through. We took the children with us to an extraordinary *shenai* (oboe) concert in Delhi. Seeing members of the audience go onstage during the intermission, Heather and Eric asked if they could do so too. I escorted them up. Bishmilla Khan, the renowned master, was unused to this response from children. He asked his other fans to wait, sped over to the two little blondies, dropped to his knees, placed his palms together in a salutation, and, not knowing their tongue, thanked them with his eyes.

The most memorable music soirée was in the home of a member of India's Planning Commission in New Delhi. We were there to hear marvelously developed ragas by a husband and wife, the Kanans. Everyone present except an admiral, Trudy, and me was a serious and well-known musician, even our hostess. The singer Meera Bannerjee sat cross-legged on the floor beside me; the young man squatting with his back against the wall was the sarod genius Amjad Ali Khan; and so on around the room. Trudy and I were there almost by chance. At a conference reception in the British viceroy's old palace, at Simla in the Himalayas, the lady who was to be our hostess for that musical evening had walked across a crowded room, done a pirouette under my nose, looked up, and asked, "And who are you?" She had a profile so elegant, so distinctive, that I knew I had seen her before. I identified myself and, for lack of another ready topic of party conversation, I decided to answer play with play. I told her that, although she didn't know me, I could tell her that, nine months earlier and fully eight hundred and fifty miles to the east, she had been seated halfway back, on the left side of the audience, at the fourth night of Calcutta's Sadarang Music Conference. She just smiled. This playful interchange, bizarre as it may sound, made sense in context: in Hindu culture, arts and play are a single field. Our life during our year of soaking up India may have had moments of discomfort, but none of us would have called it dull.

In March we got a taste of something new, two nights of traditional *Kathakali* dance drama by an all-male troupe from Kerala in southwestern India. The performers presented abbreviated versions of India's two ancient epics, the *Ramayana* and the *Mahabharata*. It was a vigorous art form, with pounding steps and hypnotic drumming. Most of the main characters wore heavy costumes and makeup that symbolized their temperaments. Two months later, I paid a brief visit to the troupe's school at Cheruturuti and was given a tour of its tree-shaded retreat by one of the dancers, who happened also to be the art director. Although it was a state-supported school, training was a complex mix of gymnastics, aesthetics, and religion. Youths began their day with strenuous workouts in the gym at 5:00 a.m., during which, to toughen them up, their masters danced on their chests. Next they moved on to ancient hymns, then to dramatic theory. The young art director invited me to his home for dinner. His wife—also a dancer—he, and I dined alone on a veranda overlooking the forest, for their children were out at the movies. They portrayed themselves to me as a naughty couple, too amorous to live by the traditional social conventions of the region, which would have limited the time they could spend together. I will not try to describe the customs that link matrilineal landowning peoples of Kerala with the rest of the population; let it just be said that, as artists, they took much license. When distant thunder began to rumble, then came nearer and nearer, I excused myself as much for their sake as for mine. While I had to return on foot to my lodging before the rain hit, they possessed an aesthetic theory in which thunder is said to evoke feelings of amorous longing, and I saw that it was more than theory. As the storm advanced, so too did their bestowal on one another of soft, lingering glances.

Delhi also connected us with the burgeoning world of visual arts. We took in art shows, met artists who were taking bold new directions, and even bought one or two pieces. M. F. Hussain, a painter, poet, and art-film maker, had been much influenced by Picasso. G. R. Santosh and several others were looking back into Tantric Hindu religion and arriving at abstract representations of cosmic notions. Yet others were introducing vigorous folk elements into fine art.

There were weddings, too, those ritual moments that are crystallizations of Hindu concepts of duty. I was invited to three of them. Each turned out to be a different lesson for me in how Hindus manage to

The Taj Mahal. At right, Heather and Eric enjoy a mazelike path.

balance personal wishes against social constraints. One was a family-approved love marriage; another followed the unfashionably traditional whims of the bride, who happened to love those musical instruments used in weddings of the past; the third combined traditional practices with the current vogue.

India, and travel itself, stimulated Heather and Eric in diverse ways. While walking in the streets of Lucknow, I had memorable experiences with each. One morning, on the sidewalk, Eric (who was almost four) snuggled up to my leg and whispered, "Daddy, we just passed a monster." Looking back, I realized we had just passed a woman in full purdah, entirely veiled in black, even to the screen over her eyes. On the other occasion, Heather tightened her grip on my finger, pulled me to a stop, and stunned me with an innocent insight that repeated what I had read years before in Benjamin Whorf's description of the Hopi concept of time.[1] The concept Heather and the Hopi happened to share is astute astronomically, for they defined "day" as the experience of our being turned toward the sun. And "today" they defined as the present such experience. I later described this conversation in poetic form:

Hopi Star Date in a Hindu Bazaar

Noon heat:
We neared the bookstall.
   Five
          sudden
                    pudgy
                              fingers
                                        tug'd,
ground me to a halt
(not for tasseled toys,
not for elephants)
for thought.

"Daddy, tomorrow never comes."
"Oh?"
"Today is here. It goes round
        to Austin,
        then comes back."
When she begins first grade will Whorf be taught?

Thanks to one available pool in Bombay and a second in New Delhi, both children also mastered swimming and diving while in India.

Downers

Our one big problem on this trip was that health was once more difficult to maintain. Both children exhibited symptoms of stress from the constant travel, Heather was in the hospital briefly with gastroenteritis in Calcutta, and we all had nasty bouts of dengue fever.

To top everything off, Eric had a frightening time with cholera in Lucknow. He had received a cholera booster shot not long before, but these are not as reliable as we then believed. It took a lot out of him. We worried as much about the little fellow's apparent depression as we did about his dehydration. Eric's doctor was a marvel, though. He refused to send us a bill for his services, kept his cholera diagnosis to himself, and treated Eric in our hotel room. That way, the health authorities were not obliged to close the city's leading hotel. As for de facto quarantine, all that the doctor had to do was inform the manager that our child's meals were to be delivered and left outside the room. The manager knew him and cooperated. After all, the Lucknow Medical Society did not *have to* meet in the hotel's elegant dining room for its monthly luncheons.

That was not the end of Eric's health problems. A week or two before we were to fly down for our vacation in Cochin, Eric contracted chicken pox. He had some scabs left on departure day but, as a precaution, we carried a letter from his doctor certifying that he was no longer contagious. On our second day in Cochin's Malabar Hotel, Eric suffered a bout of gastroenteritis. The hotel called in a doctor and what happened next apparently had less to do with health than with retaliation over a recently lost local election. We were in a port, with its own strict health rules, and Eric was suddenly written up as having a suspected case of smallpox. Our family doctor's certificate was pushed aside, and we were ordered to take Eric at once to a government isolation hospital. Trudy and I visited it, to see what would be involved. We were aghast. The hospital reeked of urine, and a family member stayed with each patient, sleeping on a thin woven mat under the bed and cooking the patient's food on an open fire. No way! We balked. The next thing we knew, an officious sanitation inspector, in a khaki uniform flecked with lots of brass, strutted into our hotel room, without so much as a knock, and set about looking for the child. He was unsuccessful. I wanted to pick up the intruder and throw him in the harbor. All that held me back was the likelihood of my imprisonment for assault on a government officer. After he stormed back out, we found the worried child hiding behind a door, picking at his few remaining scabs. The hotel manager understood our plight; he offered to "check us out" and move us quietly to a staff bungalow behind the hotel. We chose instead to spend several days in the mountainous Lake Periyar Wildlife Sanctuary—just across the range from Shenbagatoppu—and not return until the scabs were totally gone. Nasty memories.

Because the whole year for me had become an exercise in appreciation of Hindu India, it was deeply disappointing to discover, during the eleventh month, the true facts about the source of my fellowship. All year, my Indian colleagues had been asking if I worked for my government, and I had told them I had no such ties. The American Institute of Indian Studies is a private organization, I said; it is nothing more than a consortium of universities that procures funds to support research. But, weeks before we were to head home, an AIIS officer I met in New Delhi revealed to me that various government agencies fund specific projects that interest them and that the U.S. State Department had funded mine.

Without my having been given the slightest bit of information about it, I *was* working for the government. So I had been telling my colleagues untruths all year. I was shattered.

India was abuzz then with research funding scandals. Some of my colleagues knew of Project Camelot, a social scientific study of potential South American leaders secretly funded by the U.S. military. Then, in Simla, I met Gerald Berreman, who had only just withdrawn angrily from a collaborative project to study the Himalayas. His reason was accidental discovery that his research was funded by the U.S. Air Force. His question was a simple one: "Why was I not told I was working for the military?"

Given the truth about the source of my own support, I came to understand why an American cultural attaché had befriended me and arranged to share my transport at the Indian Science Congress. It also explained why there had been a strange dinner in New Delhi, with the same cultural attaché and a senior employee of the U.S. State Department who claimed former acquaintanceship with one of my in-laws. Their probing questions about my research were less of a mystery than I had supposed.

Confirming what the AIIS officer had told me, soon after I arrived back in Austin I received a brief yellow questionnaire from the State Department, requesting debriefing on the research. I sat and looked at it for ages. How could I not feel deceived by the way I had been put to government use without my knowledge? If they had been open about what they wanted from me, I could have decided whether or not I wished to work for the government. Not knowing how to reconcile my hidden government ties with the untruths I had innocently been telling Indians all year, on impulse I put my name and address on the form and then wrote diagonally across it, in large capital letters, CLASSIFIED. After that, I went through my year's writing to screen it; anything that could conceivably be used to render the modern Indian state more easily manipulable by outside powers would never see print. I surely owed that much to my trusting hosts.

Braving Canada's North

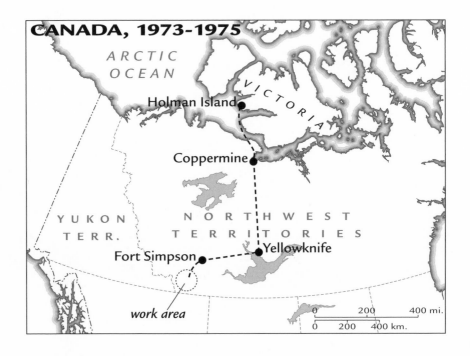

Toward Northern Forest

Another Point of the Compass

I would probably have been wasting my time if I had attempted to obtain permission for tribal research in south India in the early 1970s. The Indian government had become sensitive about its nation's humblest citizens, and the latest visa guidelines for scholars discouraged any such inquiry. Still, what I most wished to do was follow up on my earlier research with Paliyans. There were strong hints throughout my Paliyan notebooks that the individuals I knew best differed from one another in the ways in which they labeled and defined things. Was that *really* so? How marked were their differences? Were they greater in some subject areas than in others and, if they were, what accounted for that? Only formal study could reveal the nature, extent, and causes of such variation. It had not been among my goals in the 1960s to measure or explain these things. I was also curious in the long run as to whether there were differences across the world's societies in the extent to which people exhibited individualized concepts and beliefs.

Émile Durkheim told us almost a century ago, in *The Elementary Forms of the Religious Life*,[1] that sharing of concepts was necessary in a human society, and most of my fellows in anthropology had no apparent disagreement with him. They spoke comfortably about Navajo beliefs, or about Ainu concepts, as if these were standardized from one human head to another within each society. The general public did this too. Yet, only four years after Durkheim's theoretical pronouncement, young Bronislaw Malinowski, a fact-oriented fieldworker, painted a wholly different portrait in his paper "Baloma: The Spirits of the Dead in the Trobriand Islands." He reported that "personal opinion" varied from person to person within communities in the New Guinea area and it was only "public belief," as expressed in formalized myth and ritual, that was standardized. Some early twentieth-century pioneer scholars in sociology and folklore talked in the same vein.

If you stop to think about it, the nervous systems in which we take care of all our perceiving and thinking are inherently private. We also have entirely different histories and experiences from one another, even within a small community. A lot of our knowledge simply has to be idiosyncratic. To look at it from another viewpoint: how could one ever explain any of us having knowledge, concepts, or beliefs that are identical or even closely similar to those of our neighbors?

By 1970 I had moved to the University of Missouri, located in the attractive college town of Columbia. Mike Robbins in my new department and his student Richard Pollnac employed very different methods and language from those I envisioned using, yet I found them engaged in the actual study of interpersonal cognitive differences among the Baganda in East Africa. This line of research was far too fascinating for me not to pursue it myself.

June Helm had heard my description of the individualism and self-reliance of Paliyans at a 1965 conference on band societies in Ottawa. Her initial comment to me at the time was that I had just described her former Dene subjects, of the Lynx Point Band, in the Canadian Northwest Territories. For years, I remembered that response. Literature on the subarctic by yet earlier anthropologists bore her out. Later, I found a Dene leader, George Barnaby, saying something about his people that I would have expected to hear only in tribal south India: "No one can decide for another person. Everyone is involved in the discussion and . . . the decision [is] made by everyone. Our way is to try and give freedom to a person as he knows what he wants."[2] If my Paliyan friends were temporarily beyond reach, it could be rewarding to point myself north, rather than southeast, and undertake the follow-up research I so wanted to do with Helm's northern Dene.

Getting ready to work in a wholly new region, with a set of techniques I had never used outside a classroom, took me more than two years. I developed the plan jointly with a former graduate student of mine from Texas, Jane Christian, who was well trained in linguistics. Her approach to her work was something I had long admired. A linguist with prior northern Dene research experience, Marshall Durbin, helped prepare me for work in the language, and he agreed to join the project as a consultant during the summers.

With potential staff lined up, the next step was to do a pilot study, to see if the research setting was as promising as we had been led to believe, and to refine our choice of an actual work site and techniques. This would provide us with the details needed to write an effective research proposal. The University of Missouri gave me two small grants to do preparatory work on the language and to spend the summer of 1973 seeing to all of those matters.

Instead of going up alone, I bought a pop-top trailer and put the family in the car. It took us six days to drive the twenty-seven hundred miles to Fort Simpson, a small town in the Northwest Territories, right on the bank of Canada's enormous and fast-flowing Mackenzie River. The last third of our trip took us through almost unbroken forest, the tiny human communities we passed through being spaced hundreds of miles apart. Adventure time again! In those days Fort Simpson was at the very end of the gravel road that extended into the western side of the Northwest Territories. It was not far from Helm's Lynx Point Band, and a good portion of the town's population was Dene. We nested among the summer birds in a deeply wooded riverside campground at one end of the community. I worked on language, looked around for promising research sites, and conducted some initial interviews with adult men and women. The people seemed perfect for what we intended to do.

My loveliest exploratory trip took me miles down the Mackenzie River by outboard motorboat, traveling alone with a middle-aged Dene driver. We passed only two other boats in the first couple of hours, leaving us alone with the scores of bald eagles that teemed along the river. Whether they perched on the stately trees that overhung the riverbanks or swooped down in front of us to catch fish—sometimes three or four at a time—they paid us almost no heed. This was also the day I was to meet one of my most playful Dene consultants. Although taciturn at first, like all his fellows, what a raconteur weathered Old Jimmie could be when he finally relaxed enough to open up. What it took for this was a tin pot of coffee from his summer camp fireplace, dried bear meat from his cache frame, and a few hours of just sitting together on a log under the trees.

Northern Dene are more like Paliyans than I had dared hope, both in their thought worlds and in certain aspects of their behavior. I found immediately, for instance, that there was notable variation in their terms for birds and mammals, even between brothers or sisters. When I pursued a style of questioning that one of my regular consultants found baffling (he asked me *not* to use it lest I worry people), first he fell silent, then, the next morning, I found two padlocks on his cabin door. His neighbors told me he had gone off to visit his daughter, who lived in a community some nine hundred miles distant. What a Paliyan response! I was sorry to be saying good-bye to the helpful old fellow, but glad that June Helm had steered me to the north.

Fort Simpson lies at 62 degrees north latitude, and we were there for midsummer. This was a new experiences for us. During June and July the sun made a long, strange arc across much of the sky; then, "at night," it dropped just below the horizon for only about four hours, so that the sky never fully darkened. The glow of dusk graded straight into the glow of dawn. We found ourselves able to take color photographs without a flash at midnight. Daily change was dramatic, too. Except during those weeks nearest to the solstice, the length of time Fort Simpson enjoyed daylight changed a shocking five minutes or more each day. But not everything changed; there were days when the air was eerily still. Having grown up in windy places, I found it uncanny to look up at a cloud and see that its position and shape had scarcely changed over the course of two hours.

For children, summer means play. On long, golden evenings it was hard to convince Heather and Eric that bedtime had come. We adults joined them in one local game. Fort Simpson is on an island attached at one point to the riverbank. Mud banks, or "jelly bellies," extend from the downstream end of the island. Their smooth, firm surfaces have the elasticity of trampolines, and it was a summer sport to bounce and dance on them. Even breaking through means wonderful, cool black mud up to the knees.

Toward the project's end I identified an especially promising settlement in which to do our study. I flew in by bush plane and spent five days looking the place over. It was a community of some two hundred Dene in an undisturbed forested landscape, about an hour's flight from the nearest road. I had intended to spend a full week there but was so sure it suited our needs that I elected to return ahead of schedule to my interviewing in Fort Simpson. A bush pilot who had just flown in a party for the Forestry Department let me hitch a ride back out in his

Sunset becomes sunrise near midnight in July.

empty twin-engine Aztec. He sat me in the copilot's seat and, as the plane ascended, I looked back at the little community of log cabins and tents with the feeling that a dream was coming true. I was flying in two senses.

Once we reached cruising altitude, the pilot switched on the auto-pilot and laid his head back. Should I? Yes. I decided to tell him that, at age fourteen, I had read an uncle's book on flying and was certain I could manage a plane if I ever had to. He sat up and looked at me searchingly, broke into a grin, flicked off the autopilot, said "It's all yours," and laid his head back down. Because I experienced difficulty keeping our altitude steady, he roused himself long enough to provide a few tips. Then it really was mine! A swath of ominous rain clouds lay ahead; I scanned my instruments and decided to maintain my course using those. Some time later, after we came back out into open sky, the pilot sat up, peered out, and asked me if I knew the lake ahead. "Bischo Lake?" I tried. "No," he replied, "but that's close." And on I flew. Eventually the Mackenzie River became visible ahead. I was instructed to turn thirty degrees to the left and descend at three hundred feet per minute. I did. Then it was thirty degrees to the right and keep descending, then a couple more turns of thirty degrees to the right. It was a thrill to see the landing strip directly ahead and coming up at us fast. When we were five hundred feet above it, he asked casually if I knew how to put the wheels down. Not even knowing the stall speed of the Aztec, I had to be frank that I didn't. He waited as long as he could before taking over, then he did the actual touchdown. Stepping down onto the tarmac, I asked what I owed him. Laughing, he came back with "What did I do to earn it?" It had been an unbelievable ending to an extraordinary week. Packsack over my shoulder, I strode back to the campground with a very light step.

We drove out of Fort Simpson under difficult conditions on August 16. The wind was gusting, and balls of sticky wet snow were coming down so heavily that all road signs were obscured. As we neared the midpoint of a 240-mile stretch of gravel road that totally lacked villages and gas stations, all the red lights on the dashboard came on. What a place to have it happen! We had no idea whether it was it due to shorts in our electrical system or to failure of our generator or voltage regulator. We kept going with our fingers crossed. Not long afterward, we needed to top up the gas tank from a can we carried. I refueled without cutting the engine, for I feared that if we were running on the battery we might have insufficient juice to restart the engine. When we finally reached a small service station two hours later, we found to our relief that replacing all the fuses brought our systems back to life. The explanation also turned out to be simple: gravel tossed up by our wheels had damaged the electrical connections to our trailer. Some duct tape solved that problem in a moment. We could return to battling the snow and the long miles home.

The pilot project did, indeed, pave our way to obtaining major funding, from both the National Science Foundation and the National Museums of Canada. By the next spring, 1974, we knew our fourteen-and-a-half-month project was on course.

Showing Our Respect

Our chosen community was 105 miles from the nearest road. Like Fort Simpson, it had grown from an early nineteenth-century trading post on the bank of a large river, and the Catholic Church had been there almost from the start. Its population peaked seasonally at about 120 to 130 Dene adults. There were just over a dozen Euro-Canadians as well, including a government appointed settlement manager, two Royal Canadian Mounted Police officers, a nurse, two forestry staff, two teachers, a store manager, a Catholic priest, a Protestant minister, and a few of their family members. Depending on the time of year, a trickle of travelers came and went by boat, sled, bush plane, or on foot with pack dogs.

The community was quiet as well as isolated, and only a third of the adults who lived there at the seasonal population peak had developed much facility with English. We sought this, of course, yet it meant that most of our interviewing would have to be done in the people's own language, a Dene tongue distantly related to Navajo and Apache. It was a daunting prospect, for Athapaskan languages are notoriously difficult to learn—remember the "Wind Talkers" in World War II. More than the first half of our time would have to be spent acquiring the ability to undertake what we'd set out to do. If that was what it was going to take, however, we would simply have to do it.

Language was not the only problem. It was clear that we were going into a highly politicized environment. Many Dene people felt threatened by both researchers and certain ongoing developmental changes. One story that reached us concerned a Canadian ethnographer who had been thought by the Dene to have been deceitful when he explained his research objectives, this having occurred within the past few months in a band some distance downstream from where we wished to work. They felt the account he gave them in person was in conflict with what officials were saying about his plans. Even though the man had procured grant funds, a research leave, and government permissions, once the community he wished to study told him "No," he was forced to abandon his project. Several years earlier, a Canadian archaeologist had been discovered secretly removing human remains from a century-old native Canadian graveyard that was not far from our intended field site. There had been a furor, and he would not be coming back. This, at least, is what we heard. Whatever the truth was about these two incidents,

Dene reactions to our colleagues had thrown long shadows across the land.

Additional conflicts between the Dene and outsiders involved two related matters: developers' land and mineral claims versus the native treaty rights, and plans for a huge gas pipeline from the Arctic Ocean directly through well-established Dene hunting and trapping territories. A total land freeze had been put into effect throughout the region until native rights were clarified. One could not even build a cabin in the area without formal Dene consent. Any outsider seeking entry to the region was going to have to accept a variety of constraints and uncertainties.

Obtaining approval for our project at a time when Euro-Canadian outsiders were provoking suspicion and antagonism made it mandatory that we show clearly the respect we had for the indigenous people. The region had many gatekeepers. June Helm, who had seen our research proposal, advised us on all the people and institutions who would have to give approval to the study—more than we had realized. In pursuit of their permissions, we devised an approach that we knew was unconventional but we thought was fair and responsible. We worked our way *up* the ladder from the bottom, rather than starting by getting permissions from those at the top. After all, why should the potential participants in a study be the last ones asked to pass judgment on it? Being last, when everyone above them had given consent, would put them under undue pressure to go along with what the authorities had decided. If people approved a project under such pressure, while harboring reservations about it, or while feeling resentment over what felt like coercion, what sort of relationship would eventuate?

For us, inquiries and approvals necessarily began with the community itself, followed by the Indian Brotherhood of the Northwest Territories, officials of the territorial government, and, finally, federal officials in charge of Indian affairs. It turned out well, although the staff at Indian affairs did complain bitterly about being last on the list. Too bad! I chuckled to myself because there was no way they could raise major objections once the people themselves had already said "yes." Guess who had been coerced! We had turned the usual situation totally around.

For the sake of perspective, let me describe my initial diplomatic trip to take care of all this. A detailed statement about the "possible" project was sent on ahead. In early May 1974, I spent a week in the community. Although it was still cold, I tented among snowdrifts in the woods on neutral ground, rather than accepting the government accommodation

I had been offered. This was done to establish our lack of connection with government agencies. Word was put out that I would be available to answer any preliminary questions the people had and then would hold a public meeting to discuss the potential advantages and disadvantages for the people of participating in our study. Only a few came to my tent to talk during the week, yet many showed up for the public meeting. I told them that the project "might take place" but refrained from telling them that we already had the funds; doing so would surely be coercive. Then, I let them know who all of us were, demonstrated how the interviewing would be done (using actual examples from the pilot study), advised them how to abort our project should any major objections develop, told them their band council would be given two months to review all our scholarly publications before we submitted anything to a publisher, and guaranteed Canada's minimum wage for all interview time that people chose to give us. To my shock the Dene voted unanimously to try it. And their welcome was written all over their faces. For one thing, they had not been pushed. For another, they voiced interest in the possibility that some of the needy elders would get income from working with us.

The resident Catholic priest strode out of our meeting without a word to the assembly. A few minutes later, I got what I erroneously thought to be a request to come to his rectory, along with the band council, which he had *ordered* to meet with him. Councillors were already there when I arrived. The priest barred his door even before I reached the doorstep; his face was seething with anger, and he shouted for me to get away. It seemed best to keep silent and withdraw, so I turned away from his ranting. Next he contacted the Indian Brotherhood on his shortwave radio and demanded that it prevent our project's interference with his "children." Executives of the radical brotherhood, like the community, had received a detailed proposal from us, and they told the priest that they were meeting with me in two days, knew just what we were planning, and saw no problems with our project. The priest was rendered speechless. These specifics were relayed to me later. While the band council's deliberations with the priest took place, I was sitting atop the riverbank, playing with a puppy, where I knew they could see me through the priest's front window. It was experimental. Life with Paliyans had taught me not to respond to bullying behavior in a community where people place high value on self-reliance and independence. Half an hour later, the chief emerged and ambled over with a broad grin. He was a quiet, lanky fellow of about my age. His news was good. The band council was not paying attention to the blustering priest and had opted, instead, to give our team the green light. My Paliyan response to the priest's rage had accomplished just what I hoped.

Let me add that I never did learn the basis for the Parisian priest's opposition. He had been in the community for nineteen years and was its longest-term non-Dene resident. Besides serving as pastor, he filled out peoples' income tax forms and was expert at repairing their outboard motors. While he had to tolerate officials and the Hudson Bay manager having access to the community, our entry was optional. Perhaps he feared we would bring ripples to his little pond.

But we were in! Later we learned that this was not to be our last negotiation with the Dene. The government of the Northwest Territories issued licenses to researchers by the calendar year only, making a mid-term assessment necessary as well. It, too, went smoothly. I am glad to say that we kept to all our verbal agreements. This is jumping ahead a bit, yet let me mention that the people saw us off happily at the end of our study. In fact, it was an extraordinary farewell.

Colleagues have told me they were uneasy about our having given the Dene "veto power" over our publications. It would compromise scientific accuracy, they insisted. When it came down to it, though, we were not asked by the band council to consider *any* deletions or rewording; no vetoing took place. Certainly there were sensitive topics that we chose not to write about, but all anthropologists make decisions about scope, about what to include and what to focus on. And there was a great deal that we *were* able to study at a time when others could not even undertake their planned research. What we could accomplish, by engaging in respectful negotiation, put science that much further ahead. I am sure Jane fully agrees with me that the responsibilities of a scholar who works with human subjects are many, but highest among them has to be responsibility toward the people studied.

Getting Started

Days after we obtained all our permissions, I notified the band council that the project was now definite and provided its members with an arrival date. Jane and her fourteen-year-old son, Brian, picked up Eric and me in Columbia as soon as the boys' schools got out in late May. We drove up to northern Canada together, set up our living quarters, and got the research under way. Trudy and Heather would not fly in to join us until the end of the summer.

This time we proceeded north by a more direct route. Instead of looping around through Fort Simpson, we drove up the Alaska highway to a town from which we could fly due north by chartered bush plane.

It was a satisfying new experience for me to be expected by a community in which I was to do research, then greeted by a curious but cordial delegation on arrival. The band council had identified a nice spot for us during my diplomatic visit. It was in a loose cluster of tents and log cabins, near both the riverbank and one of the settlement's two wells. Half a dozen people helped us transport our gear to the site, where we could stash it in our tents until the trailer homes arrived by barge. The river was flowing well, so the barge came in right on schedule, about two weeks later. During that time we enjoyed a steady stream of uninvited visitors who called at our tents and volunteered to get us started on language. It was the smoothest beginning imaginable.

Subarctic Ways

A Peaceful Setting

We had found a serene place to do our work, so far from the bustle of twentieth-century Canada that, unless the radio was on or the mail had just arrived, we gave the outside world scant thought. After all, the Northwest Territories in those days had thirty-one square miles per person. This hideaway of ours was green with spruce, pine, tamarack, birch, aspen, and balsam poplar as far as we could see. Our settlement lay just below the confluence of two large rivers. The smaller of the two flowed in lazily, between high bluffs, from swampy lands to the east; the other was a wide, swift, cold, and turbulent river that rose at the continental divide and drained a sizable area in the northeastern Rockies. Low mountains were visible across the big river, to the west. Behind us, forested lowlands dotted with uncountable fishing lakes and scattered patches of muskeg stretched on and on for hundreds of miles.

Like many communities in the north, the settlement we worked in was small and had few resident outsiders. Because our project proved to be quite intense for everyone, and because the people were wonderful about it, I think they have earned a bit of privacy; it seems appropriate to leave the place nameless to help ensure that.

The community may have had a tiny population in any given season; that didn't prevent it from looking extensive and dispersed to a newcomer. It was a mile and a half long, made up of several loose clusters of log cabins and canvas tents, these being separated and spaced by groves of trees. A couple of the most distant cabins were located in forest on the far side of the river. I was unprepared to see tents in use right through the winter; this bore testimony to the toughness of the people—something about which I will say more later. There was also a small nucleus of public buildings that included a Hudson Bay store, a school, police and nursing stations, forestry buildings, a log-built community hall, the settlement manager's office, and several government houses. Inland from the river, beyond a dense stand of young trees, a grassy firebreak served both in dry summer weather and in snow as the landing strip for bush planes.

Most families spent two to nine months of the year away in the bush, so the segment of the population actually present in the settlement was usually well below its theoretical peak. Whole families went to fishing lakes for the summer; many more spent the winter months in trapline cabins and tents. Their comings and goings were timed in accordance with weather conditions: snow, ice, or dry ground was needed for easy movement on land, and open water for travel by river.

Perhaps because the Dene appreciated the rewards of living in both settings—town had its social and technological richness, and the bush offered personal freedom—people gave clear signs of anticipating each move eagerly. Anyone having a vacation retreat should be able to understand this; it feels good to get away from congestion and equally rewarding to return to the usual amenities and bustle. I accompanied the young chief to his trapline on his first trip of the winter, setting out on the very day that ice on our smaller river was deemed safe to cross. A scant five miles from the settlement, he stopped, built a fire to heat a frying pan of snow for making tea, grinned at me, and summed up his feelings in two words: "No boss!"

Nature's Plenty

Dr. Atkins could have developed his famous low-carb diet in the north woods. Lacking natural sources of carbohydrate, the northern Dene relied mainly on hunted food and let their bodies manufacture whatever carbohydrates they needed from the fat they ate. Even youths could tell you in which months of the year bull moose have the fattiest meat and in which months moose cows do; it is critical to know both. Fresh or dried moose meat could be found in 90 percent of the households on any given day, every month of the year, with caribou, bear, and beaver meat to supplement it, or perhaps rabbit meat in a pinch. Fishing for whitefish, lake trout, northern pike, burbot, and sucker was also an activity that went on all year, except in the late winter, both for human consumption and as food for sled dogs. There were also game birds plus berries in season. And people from the elderly down to the most modern youngsters still went through a meticulous ritual disposal of moose heads, fish innards, and other offal when butchering; they did so out of respect for the creatures they had been obliged to kill in order to sustain themselves. A youth might playfully have stood up in a moving boat and put a .22-long bullet through a moose's knee to bring it down, but the killing itself remained serious activity. Before they had guns, steel traps, and snare wire, the Dene used a variety of deadfalls and nooses to procure game, enormous ones being needed for moose. Knowledge of how to construct this traditional equipment persisted, even among the young adults, who eagerly built and demonstrated it for us.

The Hudson Bay store had expanded the local inventory of available foods. Dene showed little interest, however, in milk that was flown in frozen at $2.50 a quart, small cucumbers at $2.50 apiece, or hamburger at $5.00 per pound. Beef hearts they *did* buy, plus items they had learned about during the Yukon gold rush of the 1870s and 1880s: flour to make bannock pan bread; imported canned butter; and the beans, raisins, and yeast needed for making home brew. Given their taste for fat, how they used butter! Three of us went through three-quarters of a pound per day on one trapline trip.

But nature really was the big provider, offering far more than food. Most parts of the moose were turned into clothing and tools: long bones and rib tips were formed into scrapers for processing moose and beaver hides, shoulder blades became moose calls, sinew was used for sewing and hafting, rotten moose brain and bone marrow were utilized in hide tanning, bladders and stomachs were made into containers for rendered fat and blood, and much more. During our stay of fourteen and a half months, only two moose hides went to waste. Although a reason was offered for each lapse, these did nothing to forestall a public outcry. If it took a woman a hundred hours to process each hide, she deemed it worth every minute of her time and effort. People still made toboggan-like "sleds," snowshoes, drums, and baby rattles with birch wood, moose sinew, and skins. They created baskets and basins of birch bark and simple disposable canoes of spruce bark, stitched together with split spruce roots and sealed with spruce gum. The list is endless.

During the nineteenth century, the world market economy gave northern Dene new reasons to trap and snare furbearing animals. New equipment became available as well. Yet the fur trade offers a fickle market at best. Many families by the 1970s had learned not to rely on it and had begun to refocus their lives primarily on subsistence. Even so, they continued to use their modern tools. One large conservative family hired a plane to drop all of its members and their sled dogs into the Yukon Mountains for the six-month winter and arranged for the plane to return on a preset day in the spring to pick them all up again. They lived a simple life except for the plane. By and large though, more families used snowmobiles than dogs for pulling sleds.

Maintenance of the snowmobiles intrigued me. Most snowmobile owners knew little English and possessed no users' manuals, yet they kept their machines running themselves without the help of a mechanic. One fellow I traveled with in midwinter made emergency repairs on the trail using nothing more than simple pliers and a kitchen knife blade as a screwdriver. Looking into their labeling of engine parts, what I found were anatomical terms, such as *lungs* and *heart*. But their concepts of engine operation proved adequate.

Those people who still used dogs to pull their sleds had advantages, for their helpers could be used for ground transport in summer as well as winter, if fitted with packs, and mature lead dogs sometimes proved invaluable in emergencies.

Some years before, a priest's sled had arrived in midwinter at the isolated trapline cabin of a family I worked with during my pilot project. The priest's dogs were starved and scrappy, their harnesses were tangled, and the priest himself was delirious with pneumonia. The trapper faced a difficult situation. The fellow was already coping with difficulties, due to nasty weather, food shortages, his wife's medical absence, and his need to care alone for several young children. He could not ask his children to look after themselves while he made the 120-mile round trip to transport the priest to Fort Simpson Hospital. There were also too many in the family to consider taking them all along in a single sled. So he covered the ill man up with every blanket he could spare, hitched his own dogs to the priest's sled, and knelt down to talk with his lead dog. He told it to take a wooded route around the shoulder of the low mountain they lived on, and then follow the Mackenzie River to Fort Simpson and its hospital. We are not talking about following a clear, simple, much-used path. There were branching trails, the route around the mountain was a brushy one, and the river ice was perilously rough.

There were innumerable places for untended sled dogs to get into difficulties. How the lead dog kept to the right trail, how it managed to head off dog fights, how the team avoided getting its traces tangled in the underbrush, and how the dogs kept to their task for sixty miles without further human assistance will never be known. But Fort Simpson inhabitants can testify to the end of the tale: a sled with no driver, carrying a bundled-up and unconscious priest, ascended the steep riverbank and came to an orderly stop on the main street of the town. I learned about this feat some years after the fact from two of the daughters who witnessed the start of the trip and from residents of Fort Simpson who were able to tell me about the priest's arrival and his survival. The heart of the tale for me, though, is what turned out to be successful communication between the Dene trapper and his lead dog.

I have a companion tale about a much-admired man I interviewed and know personally. One winter night, he rolled into a fire in his open-air trapline camp. His face and one arm were severely burned. Despite extraordinary pain, he readied his sled, harnessed all his dogs to it, and instructed his lead dog to take him twenty miles upriver to the community's nursing station. Then he simply collapsed into the sled. As in the previous account, underbrush and rough river ice made it a treacherous and difficult route for the dogs, which had to make their way on their own. And, again, I heard the story that everyone in the community knew of the man's dogs arriving untended and coming to a halt directly in front of the nursing station with their unconscious load.

The lead dogs in both of these stories were asked by their masters to do a novel task—to travel to a distant but known place, without any further guidance—and both dogs are attested to have accomplished precisely what they were instructed to do. If I did not know the people and the places involved, and if the two stories were not so similar in their details, I would have to admit to quite a measure of skepticism.

The Forestry Department provided a few alternative jobs for those who qualified. A handful of men held regular, year-round positions with the service; others put their idle summers to productive use fighting forest fires. During the summer of 1975, more than one hundred forest fires were burning simultaneously within a hundred-mile radius of us. A perpetual pall of smoke hung above. Not all of the fires warranted attention, however; those in the swampy flatlands had little opportunity of spreading.

Being Together as Individuals

I described the settlement earlier as having loose clusters of log cabins and canvas tents. These tended to belong to sets of families that were not only closely related to one another but also associated with given hunting and trapping areas lying upstream, downstream, or toward the mountains. The loosest cluster of all, the cabins across the river, belonged to two amiable brothers who dwelled more than half a mile from one another. But, then, half a mile is only a few minutes' walk. People liked to live near relatives and spend time with them, but they exhibited what seemed to me to be an exaggerated need for space.

Within limits, the Dene held that households ought to be independent and self-sufficient. Nonetheless, because their main sources of food were enormous, it made sense to share any large animal kill with close relatives and with anyone else in the community who dropped by for a share. This was an absolutely routine occurrence with moose or caribou; I saw it done, too, when a trapper brought in the carcasses of ten beavers at one time, a substantial amount of meat. It was quite clear to us that one man who never hunted was given shares of meat hesitantly and reluctantly. We heard him scorned for living in a way that left him and his dependents perpetual recipients of food and never contributors.

Pairs or small groups of people worked as teams in tasks that were brief, such as hunting, butchering, hide scraping, and building cabins or sleds, as well as in season-long trapping arrangements. The lengthy partnerships had to be especially stressful for the individualistic Dene. If trapline partners were related—grandfather and grandson, or uncle and nephew—this might not happen, but it seemed inevitable that unrelated partners would experience difficulty in coping with disagreements and differences of opinion when coordinated work was required.

I learned about this from direct experience. The first person who took me out to his trapline for a few days found me puzzling at times. For reasons I did not understand, he would look at me now and then with a searching, troubled expression. I sought to participate as much as possible and be helpful, but my suggestions and actions weren't always received as I hoped. Perhaps I was not comporting myself in the way that a learner should. Perhaps I made too many suggestions, or made them too eagerly, or it could be that some of them struck him as being "off the wall." He also behaved as if he thought I was annoyed over his losing his rifle shells along the trail as a result of storing them too casually.

In truth, I was. By and large it was a good trip, however, and these were subtle little matters. Yet they passed without discussion and in that sense were not resolved.

In my mind, the biggest problem of all came when he asked me to stay at his house right after we returned, in order to have several rounds of drink. To his great dismay I declined. I did so on the grounds of my own culture-bound ideas: that our outing was now over, that it happened to be my customary mealtime, and that I owed it to my family to let them know I had returned from the bush in one piece. I had no idea why my companion appeared injured by my insistence on going home right away. Fortunately, he seems to have had a strong commitment to our association, and I believe he wrote off my walking out on him as a simple function of my ignorance and innocence.

What I eventually came to see was that it was usual for partners to hold their tongues over differences of opinion while at work, and then get intoxicated together when they came back to the settlement for a break. Alcohol relaxed them enough to overcome the restraint with which they had grown up, freeing them to express all that had been bothering them while working together. Loud arguments and fights were a routine aspect of these post-teamwork drinking bouts; injuries sometimes resulted. The sweet part of using intoxication in this way was that, the next day, one was permitted to claim amnesia for all that had been said and done. After they got disagreements and irritations off their chests, the partners could, and did, walk off together once more with a smile. Cooperating with other members of society, when one has been trained from childhood to be a quiet and undemanding person, an independent decision maker, and a self-reliant worker, calls for a high level of restraint on everybody's part. Suppressing one's discontent for days at a time has to be stressful. I came to see the practice of workmates drinking alcohol together as allowing them important and licensed moments of cathartic irresponsibility in a society that called otherwise for an almost unbearable level of responsibility.

I watched one courting couple use the same technique. They put aside everything else and staggered around in a totally drunken state together for two days while they opened up toward each other and began to negotiate the terms of their relationship. I kept an eye on them. They came to blows at one point; because he was considerably larger and stronger than she was, when she came to our door for refuge we let her sit down for a few minutes in our kitchen. Her fiancé followed close on her heels, searching for her. Lying through our teeth, we denied having seen her. After a few minutes the young woman thanked us and slipped back out with a smile to restart the process of their mutual opening. The next day her man, now sober, stopped by; he told us sheepishly, "Yesterday . . . you done right."

My understanding of all this came slowly. What a wonderful drinking bout three of us had after working for several days to make a new (toboggan-style) sled of birch we had cut ourselves! Although we did not accumulate much that needed to be resolved during this project, there were a couple of minor peeves, and I did have a sense that it would be good for us all to air them. It was when a grumble or two came out at the height of the party that I experienced my epiphany: I at last appreciated the fact that we were doing something far more serious than taking a celebratory drink.

I learned to play the game. Later in the project, an elderly man asked me to come over in the evening to share his home brew. I did, but I was welcomed with more than a constantly refilled mug. As we slowly fell into intoxication, he began to attack me bitterly for having included only one member of his family in my sample, his daughter-in-law. What a sharp tongue he had! For him it was serious; for me it was a technical matter. He knew nothing, of course, about our rigorous stratified sampling techniques or about the set of criteria by which we selected people to work with us. Realizing full well this time what was happening, instead of subjecting him to a defensive discourse on scientific method I let him get all his resentment off his chest. The next day, he sidled up to me hesitantly in the Hudson Bay store, wearing a tense, sheepish smile. "My wife tells me I didn't talk good to you last night." "I don't remember," I replied, in the requisite singsong voice. As it dawned on him that I was offering a culturally appropriate response, his smile changed character. It grew into a relaxed grin. The two of us walked off as buddies with other matters to talk about.

Leadership was low-key among the Dene. Everyone regarded it as an unpleasant characteristic of Euro-Canadians to act the boss. Dene chiefs were not only humble in manner, they were also often poor due to their mandatory generosity. I watched one young chief host poker games. Even when he held a near-certain winning hand, he folded in a skilled way that gave wins to the neediest players at the table. It was experiences such as this that made my return to our grabby, self-centered way of life in the United States hard to take.

One chief's election bears description. It was held the day that the government of Canada hands out its annual treaty payments to the tribe, so there was quite an assembly. Two twin-engine jet props flew in members of two nearby bands, and there were flags and Royal Canadian Mounted Police officers in dress uniform to grace the day. When the time came for voting, everyone sat on the grass and tallies were taken with a show of hands. Although more than one hundred had assembled for the purpose, only twenty-seven individuals participated in the voting, and nine of them voted in turn for *all three* candidates. The Dene put a great deal of social sensitivity into selecting who would be their leader and who their also-rans. I have never seen a more congenial election; the process ensured dignity for everyone.

Summer is a time for socializing with dances, stick games, and children playing on into the seemingly endless evenings. The season ushers in several great changes in the usual character of interpersonal relations. During the two and a half warm months the fewest people are tied up with work. It is also the time of year when the community reaches its peak size and its most relaxed and sociable character. After having emphasized the individualism of the Dene, I probably need to provide a glimpse of two summer activities to give a sense of the substance of the community as such.

Except for the New Year's Eve dance—a drunken, Western-style affair that was held in the community hall—dances generally took place on grassy riverbanks during the long golden evenings of summer. The only requirements were an open space, a fire, a couple of drummers, some dancers, and individuals who had "songs" to share. As the drummers gave a loud, hypnotic beat, a singer led a line of male and female dancers in a slow circle. They locked arms, swaying in a simple step together as they followed the singer. The spirit of sharing was what impressed me. Dancing, then, is an unusual activity in that it brings out the coherence of the community as an organic whole.

The "stick game" was a wholly different matter. It didn't unite, it divided; it didn't bring the two sexes together, it was just for the men. Yet there was, again, a wonderful spirit of excitement and involvement. The stick games were always played in a big tent near the riverbank, to several loudly beating drums. While, technically, the game involved gambling, the short willow sticks the men stood to lose had taken only a couple of minutes to make. Two teams of about four men each knelt facing each other across a central blanket. Each member of one team hid

Dancers share Dene dream songs on a long summer evening.

an object in one hand behind his back. It could be a penny or a pebble. Then, in unison, they put all of their clenched hands out in front of them, under the edge of the blanket. The captain of the opposing team taunted them and, using one of a large set of hand signals, he suddenly indicated the hand in which each opponent held his hidden object. All the opposing team members then had to open their hands immediately to show whether they had won or lost. The point was not accruing profit; it appeared to be a specially licensed way of competing in a society that otherwise discourages headlong competition.

Awesome Power

Power was a Dene preoccupation. Although I did not intend to study the subject, I kept encountering evidence that the Dene thought of power as abounding in nature. Some attempted to share what power they obtained, while others attempted to use it for personal advantage. I noted four aspects to their understanding of power in nature. First, there were creatures in the forest that seemed to be ordinary birds and mammals but were, in actuality, special beings able to protect particular individuals. Second, there were truly frightening creatures such as frogs and huge underground beings that, although alive, were incapable of consciousness. Third, people sought spiritual knowledge through dreams or altered states of consciousness. What they learned thus had practical value and might be shared with the community. Finally, there were people who manipulated power ritually for their own personal benefit. These several aspects of power are more closely linked than they may seem.

One day, while a sixty-six-year-old Dene man and I were leafing through a bird book, he launched into a tale about a weird happening in a quiet bush camp, years before. A lone American coot had waddled into the camp, right up to his tent and cooking fire. Everyone knows that coots are shy waterfowl, yet his new little companion showed not one trace of fear. His explanation for its boldness was that s^{h}ex^{h}atΘ^honne[1] ("my visitor") was in fact his personal protecting spirit.

A young man also talked about birds. He was a huge, heavy fellow, built like a defensive linesman for a professional football team. Some years ago, in midwinter, he had been running across the ice on a fishing lake some twelve miles from town. His leg suddenly dropped into a crevice in the ice that he had missed seeing on account of the glare. Because of the massive bulk of his upper body, he fell forward with enough force to snap both bones in his lower leg. Going back to his isolated cabin made no sense. Abandoning whatever he had been doing, he started crawling toward town on his hands and knees, on into the night, dragging his limp leg behind him. The pain and cold were awful. There were times when he simply had to halt for a rest and times when he probably collapsed unconscious. Although this was hardly the time of year to be seeing them, he soon realized that geese were flying along with him, giving him protection. As he relates the story, the details of his hours and hours of painful crawling are trivial; what is important is the tale of his geese. He takes for granted that their protection saved his life.

One elder I knew well, who was ridiculed behind his back for making birch-bark containers (he does "women's work" they said of him), once intimated that he never went out to hunt because he had no protecting spirit. He was savvy about power, though. Indeed, he asked if he could "give lessons" to my eleven-year-old, who had shown him a fossil he'd found; the old man thought Eric had a promising, pattern-finding mind.

But he was candid with me about his personal dread of going too deep into the forest.

People regarded it as confirmed that creatures resembling dinosaurs lived beneath the earth. For one thing, a man from our community had worked at the wellhead, on a gas drilling crew, at the time the well was due to blow in. He told his fellows afterward about the strange moaning he heard in the pipe when the well finally struck gas. He didn't mean "moaning" in a figurative sense; for him the wail came from something disturbed by the drilling. The great creatures were even nearby. Who didn't realize that beavers could not possibly survive in such a cold place? The mere presence of beavers in the ponds around us testified that something dwelt below each pond, warming the water sufficiently for beavers to live there. In midwinter, one occasionally sees yellow water overflowing the ice in forest streams. People became excited when they saw my aerial photo of one such overflow quite near us. The yellow liquid was, of course, monster urine.

There was understandable fear of small relatives of the huge beasts; even bold teenagers would not touch or approach frogs, which their classificatory verb stems told me they regarded as living, but unconscious, beings. They would look at a tiny frog, shiver, and retreat. For our neighbors there was ample empirical evidence of the creatures of a lower realm, and it was all around us.

Dreams are a means for getting knowledge, which, in turn, can be a source of power. It is understandable that dreams are valued and sought. Although dreams often come to us at night, we may also be visited by them when unconscious, a valued state. Unconsciousness was achieved in various ways in the past. Since the nineteenth century there has been the easy path of alcohol intoxication. I once watched a playful twelve-year-old lad with a Pepsi bottle in his hand staggering realistically down our street and telling a buddy in a slurred voice, "Maybe I pass out tonight." A game? Certainly so, but it reflected the goals of the adults around him. People who drank to achieve unconsciousness were labeled "alcoholics" by two welfare staff with whom I discussed this, a diagnosis that makes no sense medically if intoxication occurs only a few times a year. One has to bear in mind the value of trance states for many native North Americans. I acknowledge that inebriation can be a source of problems, but we are talking here about religion, not problematic recreation.

The settlement had two wells. Authorities wondered why the Dene used well water for washing clothes but went down to the river's edge for their drinking water, regardless of whether it ran clear or was thick with silt. But we noticed our neighbors going to the wells when they fetched water for making home brew. The explanation was simple. The subterranean world, including its water, is dangerous due to the power that is found down there. Remember the monsters. Yet, how attractive that power begins to look when one is pursuing the world of important dreams.

Earlier I described both the individualism that separated the Dene and the open-air summer dances that served to unite them. Let me return to the dances, for there is more that ought to be said. What I referred to as shared "songs" were performed in such a way that the term *chants* seems more appropriate. They were slow, simple, strictly in the Dene tongue, and each the personal property of a singer, for it was a text that had been received by that person in a dream. Everything I learned about the songs is consistent with what Robin Ridington has told us so eloquently, in his *Trail to Heaven* and *Little Bit Know Something*, about such songs among the adjacent Dunne-za peoples. In sharing them, the singer offered others spiritual knowledge that he or she had been given about the trail we all must follow after death. It was a precious offering that shortened the path. And what a gift for the anthropologist to have two smiling grannies step out of an ongoing dance, take him firmly by the elbows, and insert him into the dance line between them.

Allegations of sorcery are not to be dismissed, a subject I will return to in the final chapter of the book. Medical and other researchers have much to tell us about the actual effectiveness of certain rituals. There appears to be more than one physiological means by which a belief that one is under magical attack can have fatal consequences. Let me give an example. The endocrinologist Curt P. Richter has examined autopsy reports of people in the city of Baltimore who died *believing* they had consumed a lethal dose of some poison—when, in fact, it was proved later by the coroner that what they had ingested was either not a poisonous substance or had been taken in a far smaller dose than would have been fatal.[2] These Baltimore cases, medically studied deaths from magic attack in the Australian desert, and experiments with a comparable reaction in lab rats all show that being resigned to the inevitability of death can have a prompt and fatal effect. It leads to major production of an adrenal hormone that precipitates a rapid, well-understood syndrome called vagus death that usually takes a human life in about seventy-two hours.

Barbara E. Lex has hypothesized yet another physiological explanation of vagus death being brought on by what the medical world calls "tuning" in the autonomic nervous system. Reciprocal relationships between the sympathetic and parasympathetic systems can fail, so that "stimuli which usually elicit response in the non-sensitized system instead evoke a response in the sensitized system."[3] The body of the victim can precipitate its own demise in more than one way. We have a variety of scientific reasons to take magical death seriously.

Some evenings during the summer, elders could be heard drumming and chanting in the woods. People simply said they sought power. Although this subject was well outside the scope of what I chose to study, I kept tripping over it. A male neighbor of ours believed himself to be the target of someone's sorcery. His wife, however, was descended from a line of ancestors who had been famous for manipulating power. I have heard her say, in all earnestness, that her grandfather controlled the great and feared subterranean creatures. Apparently, she was using every means she had to counter the attack on her husband and save him. It was an ongoing aspect of their life.

One case I witnessed involved injury rather than death. Early during our study, a youth accidentally caused a companion to break his leg. The victim's mother came storming out of her house, wagging her finger at the one who caused the accident, shouting, "My son will not be the only one to break his leg!" In the next several months, young men in the community suffered six broken legs. The injuries went back and forth between the two families involved, on this side, then on that, then on the first side again. One break was actually self-inflicted: a youth had recently come out of the hospital where doctors had repaired his badly smashed leg and, in the course of demonstrating a karate chop to a friend, accidentally reinjured his own limb. Another in the series was still more bizarre. At our New Year's Eve dance, an intoxicated youth from one of the two families sped off on a snowmobile with his brother's fiancée astride the machine behind him. They hit a tree at high speed. Both were thrown clear, and the only serious injury was a broken leg for the driver.

Enough is enough, the two families thought. A powerful Cree medicine man was flown in at great expense from southern Alberta to try to bring the whole business to a halt. He was pale and huge, standing a head taller than most people in the community. Everyone looked at his ominous figure anxiously. After all, he not only had power, the Dene term for Cree even means "enemy." Once the awful visitor had completed his counter magical rites in private, our well-meaning chief attempted to get a dance going. We had the requisite drums and people—the Cree medicine man himself even started to play a drum—but the chief failed to entice anyone to follow him in the circle he trod. At least the long chain of broken legs came to an end.

Private Thought Worlds

Pursuing Knowledge

Amid all of these experiences, did we find answers to the questions about conceptual sharing and diversity with which we began our northern research? We certainly did. Although the way we approached the subject was scientific and rigorous, our findings turned out to be intriguing and fun; some are well worth passing along. First, though, just a few words about how we went about our work.

There is a delightful irony to the Dene project. Although we used formal sampling techniques and fairly standardized interview questions, those we worked with were seldom aware of this. We sat down with them, one on one, in pleasant settings, and ended up knowing them in terms of their diverse interests and their individuality, not as statistics. Many were playful in idiosyncratic ways even when they stuck to the business at hand. As I will show, this play even went as far as teasing. It was almost always the case that we concluded our interviews on such congenial terms that people welcomed us back to work with them on yet other subjects. In view of the enormous social gulf between northern Dene and most Euro-Canadians, I had not expected this.

An important aspect of our project is that we deliberately asked people about subjects we hoped they would find familiar, interesting, and relevant. This was a big help in making sure we didn't tire them; they rewarded us again and again with careful and serious responses.

Jane and I each worked with people of both sexes and a cross section

of ages, those oriented to the bush and to town, the full range of mono-
linguals and bilinguals, and families associated with different, named
parts of their habitat. Rather than dividing up the community between
us, we chose instead to complement each other by our choice of topics.
The way in which we each sampled the population as a whole gave us
rich, personally rewarding contact with people we might otherwise never
have encountered, people of disparate ages and experience, including
many who were unlikely ever to have initiated contact with us.

Private Worlds

There is no question that the Dene varied from one another considerably in their terms, their concepts, and even their broad frameworks
for thinking about familiar things. The ways they handled terminology
for birds, the moose skeleton, and trap parts should make that evident.

After having studied bird classification with five people in my pilot
project, I took it up with forty-five people in the main study. There was
a degree of consistency in the terms for many bird species; for other
species the variation was marked.[1] For instance, the distinctive pointed
crest of a waxwing was the basis for three quite different terms for the
bird: tʰitʰotsʰua, tϴʰilatsʰia, and cʰuabetϴʰicʰosa. Each refers in a different way to the same pointed head. Although more than half of the
people used variants of a particular term for the hairy woodpecker,
fourteen people gave me variants of a distinctly different term, four gave
quite another term, three gave yet another, and so on. The seven terms I
elicited were lʰoc'ee, lʰoc'ee texʰq'aa(li), etϴʰitetelli, tϴʰaxʰaa, tecʰiqʰaa,
tecʰitϴʰi, and tecʰi exʰqʰaxʰ. Although these could be looked at as manifestations of micro-dialects, they were all in current use within one tiny
community. Still more diverse were the ways in which people dealt with
bird categories from the approximate level of what biologists call families up to the yet more general level of orders, such as falcons or geese. I
found small modes of agreement at best. And people balked when I
fished for a term to cover *all* feathered flying creatures—that is, a term
comparable in scope to the English *bird*. At last, one wizened elder sank
into silence for a while to think about it, then burst out with the idea
that very general terms were used only in cases of ignorance or uncer-
tainty. A week later another senior told me almost exactly the same
thing. Neither man was comfortable utilizing such terms simply for the
purpose of generalizing. The two old fellows described their practice

like this: "When you see them from far you call them . . . ," "If from far you see him, you can't tell, so you call him . . . ," and "When you see something flying in the distance and don't know, then you see it's big one." So to tell a Dene "That's a bird" is to convey the message that you are untutored, or you are too far from the thing to identify it properly, or you have a serious vision problem.

This specialized use of generalization marked big chunks of the Denes' speech world. It also casts an interesting light on the modern school system. Euro-Canadian teachers draw the young into speaking in general terms. Might this not signal to elders that their children's ignorance is being fostered in school? Teachers also lead children into talkativeness. This too is problematic; to talk about a subject is believed by many Dene to lead to forgetfulness, especially if one does it as a young person.

The Dene delighted in birds. They leaped at my North American bird book. Yet because few of the 153 species that live in the area or migrate through it are sought for food or have other special significance, it could be argued that birds were not important enough to them to have become central to the language. So let me turn to something of unquestionable importance: Dene terms for moose anatomy. After all, the moose was every family's foremost source of meat; it was also the creature whose killing was marked by the most elaborate ritual of respect. Moose were hunted during every month and, weather permitting, by someone in the community every week. On any given day, fresh and dried moose meat was found in an overwhelming majority of homes. Just as everyone ate moose, every adult butchered it. Parties of male hunters did butchering as a group, as did husbands and wives if they felled one while traveling or while working on their trapline.

When I interviewed thirty-two people about moose anatomy, we always worked with a picture of a moose skeleton before us, and my subjects proved able to name even the minor bones. In one extended family, with which I did a trial run, three of the adults systematically divided a moose hind leg into two named parts and showed me the boundary; the other three divided it clearly and elegantly into three named parts. They came to learn about this variation in casual conversation with one another afterward, then brought me in on their discussion. Their two approaches could not be reconciled. It was not as if they had provided me with general and specific versions of the same thing, or with a classification of meat versus one of bone. They were surprised—and amused as well—to realize that their bush-oriented family was host to two contrasting ways of conceptualizing a valued part of their precious moose.

The spine of the moose and its main sections were labeled yet more variably, there being three principal terms for the spine as a whole and divergent approaches to naming its four recognized parts.[2] All characterized the spine and its lumbar segment in particular as "connectors," but there was more than one way to express this in their tongue. How divergent were they? Starting with the most prevalent terms for the spine as a whole and for each of the four main segments they recognize (these being cervical, thoracic, lumbar, and sacral plus coccygeal vertebrae), it would seem possible to come up with a "most representative" set of terms for the spine. Yet only one of my thirty-two consultants, an elderly woman, gave me all four of the terms that were most prevalent.

One last example: Everyone past the age of seven or eight could set what manufacturers call a "number one" steel trap quickly and proficiently. Although this tool was borrowed from European settlers, everyone in the community had grown up using it, and they employed only Dene terms for its parts. From person to person, the terms for the trap's parts were based on more than one master metaphor. For some of the forty-nine people I interviewed on traps, the capturing structure (composed of bottom frame, spring, and jaws) was given anatomical terms for spine, pelvis, and femurs. They could even show me the socket (acetabulum) in the trap's pelvis, where each femur articulates. Two different term sets were based on this general metaphor. For six other people, these same trap parts, plus the bait pan, were given a coherent set of terms for neck, jawbone, and tongue. Three named these head parts functionally, using the Dene term for "jawbone" for the jaws; two went by appearance, calling the spring "jawbone"; the sixth person was the only one to use "teeth" for the two curved jaws that were, indeed, like two opposed tooth rows. The remaining individuals had several additional patterns, including a mixture of the two main metaphors.

We also discovered that people, in their quiet later years, tend to develop slight divergences in their terms and concepts. This could be a result of the elderly living and working in relative isolation, with less feedback from others. A few of them gave evidence also of rounding out or organizing their lifelong accumulation of knowledge. They might, for example, start naming hitherto unlabeled things in terms of salient features. One elderly fellow in his bush camp delighted in giving me a phrase meaning "head-up-head-down-it's-all-the-same" for his previously unnamed nuthatch. It sums up the tiny bird's behavior perfectly!

This offers some glimpses of how they deal with objects; what about techniques? One example should suffice. When I interviewed a number of mature people about how they orient a trap in its three-sided "trap house," each of them placed the device differently. The animal, on entering the trap house, might find the spring located at the left front, the right front, the right rear, or the left rear of the trap. I then went around showing people drawings of the trap orientations others had given me. They responded to the portfolio with baffled disbelief, spelling out clear, firm, practical reasons for *not* placing a trap at this angle or that one—the preferred settings of their very neighbors and relatives.[3]

It should be clear by now that, for some of our world's peoples, especially for quiet individualists such as the Paliyans and the northern Dene, Malinowski was far closer to the mark than Durkheim regarding sharing and idiosyncrasy in human thought.

Understanding Others

In spite of the variations in their uses of language, the Dene do communicate adequately. One of their means is for speakers to pay rapt attention to their listeners. They are not so insensitive or oblivious to feedback as to blunder past all misunderstandings in their conversations. During a cigarette break, three house builders sat and listened in silence as a fellow worker described in Dene something he had seen on his trapline. Tracks and remains made it clear that a wolf had managed to free itself from the jaws of a trap by chewing its own foot off. In his account he referred to a particular trap part using what I already knew to be a rare term. I saw one listener frown; without so much as a pause, the storyteller used the stick he had been holding to illustrate which piece, by sketching it in the dust as he went on with his tale. I also heard occasional verbal equivalents of this barely solicited circumlocution for the sake of clarity.

Teaching on traplines was done almost without words. I watched boys given their first trapping lessons, and I was treated the same way when I myself was put in the position of learner. The "student" is given an opportunity to stand and watch an especially careful, but silent, version of the task. This is then repeated. Soon, one hears the teacher say, "Now you try." Although Dene have told us that paying attention is critical in learning, there is no initial insistence that the student pay attention. And, instead of verbal criticism, all the student usually gets in the way of feedback is a chance to watch the teacher silently touch up the project afterward.

Newly married couples have another way to ensure understanding. They know they come into their union with at least some differing labels; for a good year, they ask each other, "What do you call this?" "What do you call this?" It is the hallmark of newlyweds. Then, instead of converging, they persist in using their own, original terms. But they understand one another. I have heard new trapline partners doing precisely the same thing. Their apparent goal is to comprehend, not to emulate. The notion of there being a correct or standard form is alien to them. They have not had definitions drummed into them, as we have, by teachers who treat their dictionaries as authoritative.

Savoring Individuality

Many Dene used speech to establish their individuality. Marshall Durbin, our consultant, experimented with varying sentence word order so as to find out the limits of acceptability. When he tried one particular order of subject, object, and verb, several people smiled and said, "That is how [so-and-so] speaks." Durbin sought out the person they had named and, sure enough, he had his own delightful way of fitting a sentence together. No one else resembled him. A young man I knew well was famous for his repetition of syllables. He spoke at times like a poet, using his technique judiciously so as to achieve his own metered manner of speaking. Many enjoyed listening to Frank, yet no one copied him. Difference could be delicious. Despite scholars in the Western world persisting in talking about Europe as the birthplace of individuality, it is far from being a unique or recent Western phenomenon. What is more, we are hardly the ones who could be labeled extreme.

Tasting the North

Perched on a Riverbank

I located two clean used trailer homes on the Alaska highway at the start of the project—a twelve by forty-eight footer for Jane and her son and a twelve by sixty footer for my family of four. These, and a huge propane tank of cooking gas, were floated by barge 250 miles northward down a mountain river, and then hauled up onto the riverbank by an enormous tractor that traveled on the barge. During my diplomatic visit, the band council had identified a convenient spot for us to live if the project materialized. It looked perfect. They had placed us in a loose cluster of tents and cabins near one end of the settlement. We were only twenty-five feet from the bank of the river and quite close to one of the government wells. Thanks to a small community generator, we had electricity available too. And we were a scant five-minute walk from the store and even closer to the school.

We positioned both trailers so that the picture windows in the living rooms faced the river. For our family this window was to become a TV. It was a way to watch the changing seasons and the hurrying river: a brief and sudden autumn in late August and early September; ice forming on the river in November; winter storms and snowy landscapes; the ground-shaking breakup of the river ice in the early morning hours of May 2; the first green of aspens across the river as summer began; then motorboats, floatplanes, and the occasional barge in summer.

We fetched our water in buckets from the well. It had to be heated on

151

the kitchen stove for baths and for washing dishes or clothes. By digging a five-foot-deep hole down to a bed of gravel near our trailer, shoring up its sides with scraps of plywood, and covering it with boards and earth, I was able to construct a cesspool. Then, with some cast-off four-inch-diameter pipe and a juice can bent into an elbow, I built a drain line to it. This made it possible for us to use the trailer's modern bath and sinks. I spent only two days and five dollars on the project.

Setting up a toilet was also a snap, because we accepted an amiable neighbor's offer to dig a pit and construct an outhouse for a few dollars. But we were not ready for what it felt like to use the outhouse on the coldest nights. One consolation was the chance of seeing grand displays of aurora borealis, or northern lights, on our late evening ventures out back—searchlights and brilliant shifting curtains of green, pink, and ivory. There was one winter night when Heather hurried in from a bathroom trip and asked us to accompany her back out with a flashlight to see fresh wolf tracks right across her outgoing footprints. Since there were no pet dogs in the community and all the work dogs were kept chained, there was little chance we had misidentified the tracks.

The first summer Eric and I barged in a year's supply of storable food. We bought numerous cases of canned fruit, juice, vegetables, and cooked whole chickens, plus cartons of dried milk, cereal, rice, noodles, soup, pizza makings, and other nonperishable provisions. Boxes of groceries were stacked to the ceiling the entire length of our trailer corridor. We consulted Trudy and Heather only briefly about all this. They accepted it in an adventurous spirit when they arrived and were more than understanding about our purchases. A sweeter surprise we had in store for them was a shelf of jams we made in late summer from local berries, using recipes from our cookbook. Except in regard to the awful dried milk and canned chickens, I never recall hearing, "Daddy, not *that* again!"

One January night, when the temperature was about -50 Fahrenheit, snow was pelting down, and there was a howling north wind that gave us a wind chill of approximately -130 degrees, the heating oil for our furnace turned to jelly in the tank. The fuel would not flow, so the furnace died. Trudy spotted the problem at 2:00 a.m. There was no way for us to charter a plane and fly in a furnace repairman at that hour, especially in the midst of the winter's worst blizzard. And we could hardly have afforded to do so anyway. Because the temperature in the trailer was dropping about ten degrees an hour, something had to be done quickly. We hung blankets across doorways to curtain off the kitchen, moved both children's mattresses in there, and turned on the gas oven to keep that one room bearably warm. That offered a little relief while we worked on solving the problem. The most pressing need, of course, was to warm the fuel line between the oil tank and the trailer. Perhaps I could do that with shielded lightbulbs. I assembled a multisocket extension cord, stripped-down reading lamps, aluminum foil to shield the heating apparatus, and duct tape to hold it all together in the wind. Throwing a parka and snow boots on over my pajamas, I made a single trip out to rig up what I had improvised. Eventually, by sucking hard on the warmer pipe, I was able to get a reassuring mouthful of fuel oil. Oh, the pleasures of solving problems on one's own in the middle of nowhere!

Trial by Travel

For our families the isolation of this project was not easy. Being 105 miles from the nearest road made it necessary to come and go by bush planes when they were able to fly. Pilots did not always provide seat belts for children on their tiny overloaded planes. Once Eric and another time both children were asked to perch, unbelted, on luggage in the back of the plane, and we only found out afterward. I began to pay more attention. The next time the matter came up, I told the pilot in annoyance that providing passengers with seat belts was a straightforward matter of the law. He glared at me, gritted his teeth, clenched his fists, and said with barely restrained anger, "When I'm in the air, I AM the law!" Clearly it was time for us to turn to another carrier.

The first summer, before Trudy and Heather joined us, Eric and I had a 6:00 a.m. flight in a floatplane with a pilot who had just come in from his previous flight reeking of cheap bourbon. If we had been heading off on a straightforward trip this might not have proved quite so worrying. But we had to go through a thunderstorm as we approached our destination, and the pilot needed to put the plane down on turbulent rapids in a canyon. The machine skipped three times—the way a skimming rock does on the surface of a pond—before he got it to stick to the water. Eric's and my knuckles were white through all this.

In the course of an errand with us aboard, the pilot of one helicopter decided to show Eric, two other passengers, and me what he had learned during the Vietnam War about fast descents. As he took us across a mountaintop that had a sheer drop on the far side, he rolled the heli-copter on its side so that it was flying with its belly forward. This meant that the main rotor was stopping our forward motion. On our side, and feeling momentarily as if we were stationary, we fell like a stone for about a thousand feet. The pilot wasn't done with his tricks. On arrival home from that same outing, he tipped the helicopter slightly sideways, so that it slid edgewise and continuously off its supporting air pocket. We spun down in a rapid corkscrew to the firebreak that served as our landing strip. As one passenger dashed out the door to vomit, the pilot told us he had learned from experience that such descents are an effec-tive way of evading ground fire, but they are so disorienting for the pilot that pulling out of them is next to impossible. Maybe *that* is why he had consumed a couple of imported British beers before takeoff. Rest as-sured that we swore off bush helicopters for further family travel.

During the winter I went out on sleds to traplines with three men. Two were teaching their sons trapping techniques, and on one occasion I made arrangements for Eric to accompany us as well. The practice on traplines was to have an evening cooking fire in the cabin or tent. It might then be kept alight while one did things such as preparing the next day's beaver snares. After 10:00 p.m., however, it would be allowed to go out for the night. Even though we had covered the dirt floor of the cabin with fresh spruce boughs on arrival, to serve as insulation, Eric's and my down sleeping bags got quite a test. The temperature one night went down at least to -35, and we each told the other groggily the next morning that we had slept fitfully at best.

I discovered that people, even into their sixties and seventies, lived comfortably through the winter this way. The usual Dene routine was to sleep without heat; more about that in a minute. In mid-February, I set out for a trapline some time after midnight with a teenager, John. A Mountie had detained the lad for a few hours so that he could sleep off a bit too much alcohol, hence our late departure. John towed a sled be-hind his snowmobile; I stood on the back of the sled, with responsibil-ity for keeping it balanced and upright. I would not have agreed to travel at night had I known what the thousands of young willows along the trail would do to my hands and face in the dark at thirty miles an hour. We also both got mightily cold. John stopped about 2:00 a.m. at the trapline tent of his great-uncle and -aunt, so we could light their stove and try warming our hands for a few minutes. The temperature hovered around -30 to -35 degrees all that week; when we entered the

The chief's son and Eric help the chief
carry the take from a trapline trip.

old people's tent, it was more than obvious that their stove was stone-cold to the touch, while their moccasin-covered feet were projecting casually from under their single cover. The latter resembled a $29.95 American boy scout's sleeping bag, intended for the temperate zone, unzipped and opened up into a simple blanket. Beneath them was nothing but a cotton sheet spread over spruce boughs.

This was a memorable trip in other ways. After John and I resumed our journey and were midway across a small fishing lake, the engine started to cough and falter. John's only option was to halt for repairs.

Dene tent in the wilderness, February 1975. A moose hide is
being processed beyond the tent, and homemade snowshoes
stand near its door. A few days earlier, I stopped here with a
young trapper, John, to warm our hands at 2:00 a.m.

There being no way for me to help him, or even to see what he was doing in the dark, I went for a walk instead, to keep warm and to enjoy the
clear, quiet winter night. It didn't take long for my enjoyment to evapo-
rate. There we were, immobilized. Who knew how long we would be
stranded on the lake, and it was nowhere near as quiet as I had initially
thought. In addition to the wind hissing about on the snow-covered ice,
I began to hear the howling of a wolf pack not far behind us on the
shore. You can imagine my relief on hearing John, at last, mutter "good."

In the process of making and installing beaver snares my companions
often had bare hands at such temperatures for thirty minutes at a time.
In addition, their hands got wet when placing the snares. I may have
played in the cold for hours on end during my seven childhood years in
Canada, but now I found it hard to tolerate even ten minutes of such
barehanded work. It was not discomfort that got in the way, however;
after a short while my numb fingers simply refused to obey my brain as
I attempted to tie the intricate knots in our steel snare wire. It was obvious that Dene circulatory systems differed markedly from ours. Why not?

Their population has had thousands of years to cull out individuals with traits that are inadequately adapted to the conditions.

It is worth putting on record that winter travel by sled is only slightly less jarring to one's bones than the trip I described a few chapters back in a south Indian galloping-bull cart. I learned that with both one has to focus on the practicality of the conveyance and plan on coming home to a long soak in a hot bath.

Attempting Normal Lives

I did not do a spectacular job of parenting while Eric and I were on our own. My long and variable work hours were the biggest difficulty. But ten-and-a-half-year-old Eric was wonderful about it. He and two age-mates set up a snare line to catch squirrels, their original plan being to sell the skins. Much later I learned that the three little trappers were cooking and eating their catch. My liking the ease with which he established friendships was one thing, but the children's play schedule on the long summer evenings was quite another. One could hear groups of children playing far into the so-called night. On the longest evenings I often didn't manage to get him home until 11:30. Thank goodness he slept in. And he had projects. Toward the end of the summer Eric greeted me at dinner one evening with a touching gift, a basic Dene-English dictionary he had written himself.

When schooltime came, Jane's son, Brian, and our Heather were too old for the local institution, which went only through grade six. Thus, they had to be homeschooled. Eric took grade five locally, supplemented with advanced math materials from his school in Columbia. Heather was invited to attend the school just for sports and recess. It was an odd arrangement, to be sure, but it led to some nice friendships for her. She spent one weekend in a friend's log cabin. Returning home, she asked with a playful smile where the tub of lard was, to moisten up her dried meat. We were blessed with adaptable children.

Trudy, a professional librarian, was grateful to be given a nine-month leave from her job. She got on immediately with exploring the community, reading, teaching Heather, and making friends.

I, too, allowed myself downtime for friendships. We had the teachers over to play vicious but hilarious card games; our entire family accompanied the older schoolchildren on a mountain walk where we picked berries; I went swimming from a boat with the police; and we interacted with our Dene neighbors as neighbors. Sometimes, for me, this meant sharing their home brew just for the sake of sociability. One neighbor asked me to a big party. By the time I got over there, his cabin was crowded and he was out of cups. Unfazed, he dumped the contents out of an aluminum dog bowl and filled it for me with his special brew. Yes, I drank it; I didn't think Dene etiquette allowed me to say no. After a re-fill, though, I discovered that several-inch-long florescent pink streamers were getting wedged between my teeth. I held one up with a questioning look. My host flashed me a warm ear-to-ear grin and produced a hair spray can. Not wanting to alter my state of consciousness permanently with his exotic hydrocarbons, I faked tipsiness and called it a night.

The community threw me one duty that was impossible to refuse: service on the volunteer fire brigade. We had little more than helmets, waterproof coats, and a hand-pulled cart with a gasoline-powered pump on it that drew water from the river for the fire hoses. We saw action twice, and I can't say we accomplished much beyond getting rid of some of the smoke by inhaling it and providing the fires with an audience.

May came in dramatically. I mentioned the May 2 breakup of our river ice. The ice in the little river from the east had begun its breakup a week earlier. But its huge, helter-skelter, three-foot-thick blocks became jammed against the still intact ice of the big river. They constantly shifted due to growing pressure from upstream and formed an ever-denser dam. Scores of people lined the riverbank all day to watch and listen. The riverbank shuddered constantly. At the height of it all, another drama broke out. The nurse had to send a bottle of medicine to a seriously ill child whose family was camped on the far shore. There being no helicopter within easy call, a youth put the bottle in his jacket pocket and set out across nearly a thousand feet of shifting upended blocks of ice. We, who had been *wanting* to see movement of the ice, now stood silently, hoping things would remain still just long enough for the mission of mercy to succeed. It did.

Every day the wedged mass of ice at the juncture of the rivers grew higher. Finally, at about 1:30 a.m. on May 2, our trailer was shaken by a shudder and roar far greater than all the preceding ones. We dashed out, as did all our neighbors, and watched the big river finally start to go. The steep banks at our place were about twenty feet high initially, but the water level rose at least ten or twelve feet in the first ten minutes. It was frightening. By breakfast, though, there was an open channel down the middle of the river, and it would be only days before we saw boats weaving their way among the still colliding ice floes. Some simple arithmetic helped us understand the magnitude of it all. Given the thickness of the ice, a relatively modest ice floe, say 150 feet long and 35 feet wide, weighed on the order of five hundred tons.

Scattered snowbanks remained, but winter was over. It was warm enough to get out our cameras and photograph the many species of big, healthy mosquitoes—something I actually attempted. The Dene might roll up their shirtsleeves in summer, but we learned from them always to keep our long underwear in place, as protection against the clouds of flying nasties. From that viewpoint, the arctic winter had not been so bad after all.

Experiments, Puzzles, Exams

Experiments and Games

The lean young man who served as chief when we began our Dene study was fascinated by our precise Euro-Canadian handling of time. He began using me for experiments and inquiry. For most of his people, time was usually expressed in an approximate way; their predictions were meant to include the unspoken caveat that such and such would be good to do at a certain time *if* circumstances allowed. Flexibility was the word.

Not long after twenty telephones were installed in the community, the chief telephoned me to announce that he would come over to my place "in ten minutes." I thought nothing of it until, about nine and a half minutes later, I saw him inching toward our door while keeping an eye on his watch. I sensed what he was doing and let him be, going to the door only when he finally announced his arrival. He said nothing to me about performing an experiment and offered no reason for his visit. Because he seemed exuberant about something—almost certainly about his making a specific time prediction, as we customarily did, and then fulfilling it accurately—I put a coffeepot on the stove so we could both enjoy the moment.

On another occasion, he asked me, "Peter, what is mealtime?" I stopped to think before answering. He probably asked this as a result of working on firefighting crews; the Forestry Department fed the crews at specific times, at "mealtimes." What is more, each crew member was given the same precise portions of each food, as if anticipating that each person had the same appetite, manifest at the same moment. Put in those terms, our mealtime *did* look strange.

But I had an afterthought: perhaps his stimulus was *my* behavior. On more than one occasion, when we two had been out working together on his trapline, I rushed home right afterward because, as I put it, "It is almost my mealtime." If I had kept to the Dene custom, described earlier, no matter what time it was, the two of us would have taken time first to unwind together.

He saw appetite as a personal and variable thing, not as something time-bound. In one of the households that neighbored mine, I had seen a person get up at 6:17 and eat a handful or two of dry corn flakes straight from the box. At 8:51 another person came out of the tent, rubbed her eyes, and cut down a piece of stored dried moose meat from a cache frame. Then, at 10:07, a third person pushed aside the tent flap and strolled out opening a can of smoked oysters from the Hudson Bay store. I ended up telling the chief that our desires for food were no more standardized than those of the Dene; we behaved in a regimented way in our efforts to cope with our crowded society. I think this explanation was too much for him. It also was not wholly correct. I was forgetting that we are also conditioned to feel hungry at set times, like Pavlov's famous dogs, which the psychologist taught to salivate on signal. "It's noon. Let's eat," we say. As for our eating the same portions as one another, many of us accept servings of diverse foods on our plates because of the training given us, by our parents or by health teachers at school, about our bodies' nutritional needs. We let so many factors override our variable appetites and tastes.

As Viirappan had done to me twelve years earlier in the south Indian thorn forest, the Dene chief was turning the research situation on its head in a wonderful way. Why not? If we believe that knowledge and understanding of human variation justify research in cultural anthropology, surely it is so much the better if our fieldwork results in give as well as take—that is, if the work results in stimulation, inquiry, and learning on everyone's part.

One of my main elderly consultants said to me one day, "Peter, when you come over to my house, you don't bang on my door like the man from the store and demand that I open it for you. You noisily scrape the mud off your boots, open the door, walk in, put the coffeepot on the stove if you are thirsty, and then sit down. After a few minutes, you say something about your reason for coming." Frankly, I could not recognize myself in his words. I always behaved more like the demanding man from the store. I had to conclude that the old fellow was offering me a polite, indirect lesson.

There was a log cabin in the community that I had never approached. Its inhabitants were perpetually distant. They seemed to greet no one; it was not just me they shunned. I had long worried over the fact that my sampling requirements in the research would best be met if I was able to interview at least one adult male from what I regarded as "the ominous house." So I made a resolution: on the following day I would experiment with my helpful consultant's formula. With no slight anxiety, I walked up to the house in his prescribed slow, noisy way. My boots were dry and clean that sunny day, but I put on a good show of scraping them anyway. Using the rules I had been given, I simply turned the knob and pushed open the always closed door. Three men sat cross-legged on the floor, playing cards and drinking. They all looked up smiling as I entered. There was no awkwardness. I squatted on my haunches with my back against the wall, said nothing for what felt to me like a very long time, then asked what they were playing, and finally got around to my interest in interviewing one of them the following day. It worked.

It did start me thinking, however, about the ethics of research in other cultures. Would those committees that oversee American research on human subjects be able to accept the fact that, among northern Dene, knocking on a door (which is, for us, the polite *and legal* way of approaching someone's house) amounts to an unacceptable and alienating demand? Shouldn't researchers be obliged to forgo our customary practice so long as others view it as bullying, or intrusive?

Nicknames were a part of social life. People were not supposed to know what others called them, but we saw ample evidence that most did. Perhaps due to my longish hair, for it looked like a raggedy mess in the wind, some Dene started calling me Dl'óo T'oh (Squirrel's Nest) behind my back. We also heard that this name was used as well for my son, Eric. I was interviewing a forty-two-year-old woman at her cabin one day when her neighbor wandered in, the visitor being a female cousin about her age. As I was only asking about terms for mammals, which I deemed to be a totally innocuous subject, there seemed no reason to stop what we were doing. Although we continued, the tone of the conversation went through a subtle change. Eventually, one of the women broke into a naughty smile and asked if I knew what Old Seya's sixty-eight-year-old wife was called. I *should* know they both said. I could not help smiling. Everyone referred to the old woman as Dl'óomo (Squirrel Mother), a nickname that snuggled up nicely against mine. On a sudden impulse I blurted out, with intentional ambiguity, "We have been in contact." Remember that I was only thirty-six years old at the time. None of us could do much to control our laughter.

Mistakes and Mysteries

I made mistakes in the field, especially toward the end. Hearing a fight, I looked out my window to see a middle-aged woman on the doorstep of her cabin, two doors away, arguing with two men. This is the neighbor I described earlier as being heavily involved with supernatural power. Others had been attempting to kill her husband by sorcery, and she was using all she had learned from her famous father and grandfather to fight back in his defense. Although I usually avoid all surreptitious photography in the field on ethical grounds, I picked up my camera and shot the scene. There was a strange noise as I pressed the shutter release. For some reason, the camera stopped working. I borrowed a replacement camera and mailed my own to a repair shop in Chicago. In due course, the shop wrote back asking what I had done to the camera. Its entire shutter mechanism lay in a puddle at the bottom of the instrument, every single piece undone. When my film came back from processing, I got another shock. The picture of the fight was badly overexposed, but it had come out; over the powerful woman's head there was a slender black triangle that looked like a vortex. This I report as a skeptical scientist, for whatever it is worth. None of it was ever explained.

During some of my last evenings in the field, men played stick games in a big tent on the riverbank, to several loudly beating drums. After some hours, I was permitted to join the former chief's team. Later, when he announced his need for a bathroom break, I asked him whether I could serve in his place as an interim captain. This was a serious matter for him. He looked pained, hesitated for a long time, then awkwardly agreed to it. Knowing only a few of the signals, all I could do was make my best effort. I knelt, head down, wondering how to second-guess all my opponents. I even closed my eyes to concentrate. When I closed them, I had a strange sensation. It was as if there was a dark blob to the right or left of each opponent who faced me. For some reason, I chose my signals as best I could to match them. And my clumsy signals had a strange effect. I was right far more often than I was wrong and was devastating the other team. After several rounds of this, someone back in a corner of the tent suddenly called out, "You are cheating. You closed your eyes, so you can see." Embarrassed, unable to deny the charge, I had to terminate the game. Thirty years later, I still wonder about that one.

If we are lucky in our fieldwork, anthropologists obtain glimpses of other realities, and sometimes we manage to arrive at explanations of them that we can accept. That is one of the supreme pleasures of life in the field. Every once in a while, however, the glimpses we get are of such a nature that they only tease or baffle us. The dog tales described in an earlier chapter, the totally disassembled camera shutter, and the persistent "visions" I had in the course of captaining the stick game belong to the latter kind of experience. The last two, especially, leave me absolutely stumped. While the empirical facts of these cases are as clear to me as can be, and while my mind continues to ask for rational explanations of them, I am obliged to conclude for now that reality is more complex than the scientific side of me has been able to accept. But, then, I have never been one to ask that my experiences be simple or predictable. If I had asked that, I surely never would have ventured out into far corners of our rich planet. And life without such mysteries would be life bereft of much of its flavor.

Taking and Passing "Finals"

Some people were hard to track down. Toward the end of the project, I was at last promised, or so I thought, the interview I'd sought with a man who had worked for years with Euro-Canadians. "Come to my house this evening," he told me. There was no sign of life there when I arrived. Going in, I found him inside and drunk. He let me put coffee on his stove for both of us. So began an intriguing three hours. He immediately said, "No notebook!" I put it away. Then he began talking about his "secret." I knew nothing about this. He took off the cap, which was *always* atop his head, to reveal his balding pate. *That* is what his cap was all about! Baldness is rare among Dene; his gnawing secret had to do with his beliefs about his probable paternity. As if to get back at me for the awkwardness of this disclosure, he then challenged me. He told me I had been studying trivial matters and had learned nothing important about the Dene way of life. That put my back up. Maybe he was right, but I insisted that he give me a test. My request confused him, so I said, "If I am aboard a bush plane that comes down in this forest in winter, and the pilot dies, how would I survive?" He loved it. Now I had to think. He let me sketch out this difficult scene with only a few interruptions. Assuming I was not injured, the first thing to do would be to strip out all the wires from the plane, I said. There would be plenty of time later, I told him, to make a place where I could nestle in a snowdrift for the night. It was most urgent to put out snares right away for rabbits and squirrels. Picking up a piece of his snare wire, I showed him the knots and the size of the snares. He was insistent that I tell him also where they would be set and, for squirrels, how high off the branches. I made some educated guesses but kept on. It was a long test, covering many dimensions of survival. Eventually he smiled and brought it to an end: "You would not be comfortable, but you would survive."

Interpreting that as a grade of at least a B minus, I made my way happily home. Then I sat at the kitchen table for what must have been at least half the night scribbling out a record of my final exam.

At the beginning of my discussion of the Dene, I mentioned the gas pipeline controversy. The local handling of it illustrates well the relations we managed to establish with the people. Just before our departure, Mr. Justice Thomas R. Berger came to our settlement for a few days. Formerly of the Supreme Court of British Columbia, he had been appointed by the Canadian government to ascertain the environmental, social, and economic impact of what the petroleum industry wished to construct through the Mackenzie valley corridor. His hearings were held in all of the Inuit and Dene communities that might be affected; we received about two weeks' notice of our hearing, and a young lawyer was sent in ahead of time to generate testimony.

I thought I would be an onlooker, but two Dene elders came and asked me to tell the court what I had learned when going out to visit traplines. Because of the implications of the case, their expectation was a heavy one—namely, that I speak on their behalf to the outside world. It would have to be done carefully. A young woman from a nearby band would be providing the court with maps of peoples' official traplines. But straight lines on a map in no way summed up the interaction between humans and animals that I had seen. Animals that stray across traplines live in broadly defined areas—not just along the traplines themselves. There was much that needed to be said to flesh out the picture of actual Dene needs and interests. When hearing day came, I laid it all out as carefully as I could. Knowing that many in industry saw native culture as a trivial relic of the past, I spoke also about those Dene social values (such as respect for others) from which the rest of Canada had much to learn. That statement made Canada's national evening news! My colleague, Jane, responded to a similar invitation and provided important testimony on related matters.

The best Dene translator in the Northwest Territories was brought in to provide careful phrase-by-phrase translation of English into Dene and vice versa throughout the hearings. Jane and I were gratified to see attentiveness and nods of agreement from Dene elders as our words were relayed to them in their own tongue. Members of the community walked out from the hearing happy. Their case had been made. By 1977, it was apparent that testimony up and down the valley had, indeed, been persuasive. Mr. Justice Berger wrote, "No pipeline should be built now,"[1] and the Canadian Cabinet acted on his recommendation.

When I returned for a ten-day personal visit in 1977, two years after the research project concluded, I found myself faced once more by a smiling throng. I told them, "No notebooks this time!" People laughed at that and said all they wanted was for me to drop by and sample their home brew. As the week unfolded, it became clear that they had no axes to grind; they had been welcoming me from their hearts.

The Very Edge of the Inhabited World

Eyes Yet Farther North

Since my teen years, I had yearned to see the midnight sun of the arctic summer. The tundra would be carpeted briefly then with lichens, mosses, and uncountable millions of nesting birds. Although soft to the touch, all would look strangely crisp in the cool, slanting light of the never-setting sun. Early during my Dene research, I talked with my family about how the tundra beckoned me. For all of us to experience the real Arctic together would be impossible, they pointed out; the three of them would return to Missouri too soon. In their agile minds, though, my personal desire was quickly transformed into a more dramatic plan—but the precise opposite of what I had envisioned—for all of us. They suggested that we fly north for a break, but during the long night, say in December. What an idea! Rather than approaching the north edge of the inhabited world during its season of warmth and growth, we would venture there when harshness ruled. A place we might try to visit was Holman Island, an Inuit settlement (*Eskimo* is a rude, outsiders' label) on the coast of Victoria Island in the Arctic Ocean. It had a community cooperative providing rooms and meals for visitors. Of professional interest to me, the community was near the size of the Dene one I was studying, but I was to find that the resemblance ended there. From my work site in the Northwest Territories, the round trip would entail 1,840 miles of flying, all in light planes. We booked it.

The trip began with a fairly routine flight to Yellowknife, the busy capital of Canada's Northwest Territories. A night in a modern hotel there gave us our first taste of city life and our first opportunity for elegant dining in months. We intended to enjoy this break, especially the food. Because our supply of camera film was getting low, the stopover also provided an opportunity to restock before continuing. We held reservations for an early morning flight first to Coppermine, on the shore of the Arctic Ocean, then across Amundsen Gulf to our island destination.

All went well in Yellowknife until a ringing telephone woke us at 5:00 a.m. It was a man's voice. "Mr. Gardner?" "Mm." "I'm calling about your flight to Holman Island. We've got to leave early because of the weather. Can you be at the airport in an hour and a half?" It sounded serious enough that we leaped into action. Our morning outing to buy film was an obvious casualty of this rescheduling. We showered as quickly as possible and bolted down leftover travel snacks from the day before, all the while puzzling over how the airline had found us. Faces around the room disclosed that I was not the only family member worried by the matter of weather, but no one voiced our fears.

We raced to the airfield in an icy taxi, its crisp, crackling seats announcing that we were the first customers of the day. The good news was that we were to fly north aboard a STOL (short-take-off-and-landing) Twin Otter jet prop, a gem of a plane, fitted with plump balloon tires for putting down on snow. All but eight or ten seats had been removed so the rear half of the passenger compartment could be stacked with cargo. These goods were already in place when we arrived, and our fellow travelers were hurrying aboard.

Although the airline experienced delays in readying the plane, the morning sun was still well below the horizon when we lifted off. But the faint light that foreshadows Arctic dawn was sufficient to show us that we were approaching the northern limit of trees. Those growing in the deep dusk below us were tough, stunted little things; we knew that in minutes all we would see was the endlessly white, windswept tundra. Our plane made good time on its northward flight, good enough that eventually we realized we would not be able to witness dawn that day. We were leaving our friendly sun behind sooner than expected and would not see it again for a week. While it had certainly been our goal to experience the drama of the endless night, coping with troublesome weather at the same time was not something we looked forward to.

The plane descended toward Coppermine as we neared midday. The sky to the south of us glowed just enough for us to make out an enormous herd of milling caribou alongside our landing strip. A passenger said there were some seven thousand in the herd; they had been near the settlement for weeks. After school, Coppermine youngsters were shooting them for sport, he grumbled, and then they were simply abandoning the carcasses. For him it was a bad habit in the making. At the edge of the herd we saw wolves moving in with far more serious intentions.

Coppermine itself was not visible from the strip, and the airport was nothing but an expanse of flat snow with a short row of fifty-five-gallon fuel drums beside it. We were thankful it was not our destination. But it did have facilities. Going to the toilet was as simple as ducking discreetly behind the nearest fuel drum, a trip no other passenger sought to take, perhaps discouraged by the biting wind. When I mentioned to the pilot that our initial good weather had held so far, he was confused at first. It took him a minute to realize we had misunderstood the haste with which we had left Yellowknife that morning. He told me, laughing, that we had raced off the way we did in order to take full advantage of the *good* weather. It certainly was good, but cold. The stop probably lasted only ten to fifteen minutes, but unloading cargo necessitated opening the plane door too wide and far too long for the comfort of continuing passengers. When, at last, we began our ascent over the desolate ice of the Arctic Ocean, our eyes were sufficiently adjusted to the dark to make out for some time what lay beneath us. Enormous forces had been at work: cracks in the ice had opened for miles and miles, then refrozen. Then the blackness closed in, and on and on we droned.

Our Arctic Welcome

When a crescent of lights appeared in the distance, slightly to our right, all four of us leaped to the windows to see them. The settlement of Holman Island had been built along a small arc-shaped cove facing the mouth of Prince Albert Sound. In time we could see three rows of houses, each following the tight curve of the shoreline. The pilot buzzed the community, to alert the inhabitants of our arrival. It took only a minute for a swarm of snowmobiles to race into one of the streets between the houses and position themselves so that, as we made our final approach in the dark, two lines of red taillights edged the sharply curved street that would serve as our runway. But they were there for two purposes.

As we put down between them, the first two snowmobiles, then the next two, and the next on down the line accelerated just as we reached them and accompanied us along the street until we had a noisy swarm of the machines beneath each wing tip. Their combined headlights made it a remarkably bright and memorable landing.

Indian communities stood silently when planes came in. Holman Island, by contrast, was teeming with voluble helpers. Given all they had to do, unloading and reloading the plane, people got around to dealing with our needs about the time the loaded Otter was ready to take off again. The news they had for us was shocking. "You are staying in the Co-op? That can't be. It is full-up this month with carpenters who are here for a construction project." It was not at all clear what had happened to our request for accommodation for the week. No other plane would come in for five days. Someone piped up with a suggestion that we stay in the government fisheries shack. It would be possible, others said, *if* the key could be found and *if* the heater could be started. They were, and within half an hour we were able to move in. It was inelegant research space, though more than sufficient for our needs. We would have cozy bunks, and we could even borrow some of the fur outer clothing that was stored there. The Co-op did at least welcome us to the meals on which we had been counting.

Holman Island was well north of the Arctic Circle. With the winter solstice only days away, it would be a maximally dark vacation for this latitude, broken only by a brief glow in the southern sky during early afternoon. But the moon rolled round the horizon once each twenty-four and a half hours—a veritable clock hand for those able to read it. With little to budge it up or down, the temperature hovered at −37 degrees for the duration of our stay.

Our daily life was punctuated in several ways. We soon became used to groups of Inuit youngsters walking in without a knock when they chose, even before breakfast. It was awkward, but fun. One youth was the grandson of a famous Inuit printmaker. Another was the grandson of a woman who had traveled with the explorer Vilhjalmur Stefansson, serving both as a seamstress, to mend torn furs, and as a companion for him during his Arctic exploration. These were friendly visits that we grew to like.

Co-op meals were even more of a treat. We were served Peary's caribou cooked a different way each day for dinner: as steaks, in a rich stew, or as a roast. This white-coated, knee-high species, which dwelt solely on Victoria and Ellesmere Islands, was a local subsistence mainstay. In front of each house—in nature's deep freeze—was a great pile of the tiny caribou carcasses. The delicate meat was not at all gamey; it had its own character, but I would class its quality as being similar to that of the tenderest veal and lamb.

Inuit Images Transformed

We were invited for tea one afternoon by a friendly and chatty neighbor. She told us her husband had been in the hospital for some time, recovering from having tumbled his snowmobile into a ravine at high speed while pursuing a caribou herd. Arctic light is hazardous. The young family lived in a large, modern, prefabricated house with shag rugs, comfortable furnishings, and a fine stereo. Where we expected a living room ceiling to be, however, there were open rafters, draped from end to end with drying arctic fox furs. Although this was a strange mixture of images, we had already heard that individual hunters and trappers at Holman Island had made up to $75,000 apiece the previous year from arctic fox pelts alone. So long as the world fur market held, it was a good livelihood. The ancient environment supported a modern human adaptation.

After tea, our hostess asked if we would like to look through her photos of last summer's outing to their fish lake. These, like the rafters, were eye-openers for us. Warm weather brought a change of activities; although hunting and trapping were no longer feasible, fish were plentiful in the inland lakes, so many families moved there for a brief fishing season. The photos in her albums were, on one level, just vacation photos. The lake they went to was clear and clean, and it was surrounded by grass that most golf course managers would envy. She showed us shot after shot of family members splashing with their babies in the shallow warm water, wearing sopping wet shorts and T-shirts, looking like any vacationers. But the campsite was something else. Yes, they lived in a large, rectangular, canvas tent of the sort familiar to me in Dene camps. Beside it, though, stood an electric-powered washing machine and a small gasoline-powered generator with which to run it! The explanation was simple: diapers needed to be washed. The family rented a lumbering DC3 (which can land on the grass) to fly in all the gear they needed, then arranged with the pilot to pick them back up at a set time a few weeks later. What was revealed in her pictures was certainly not the enticing land I expected—of lichens, moss, and nesting birds—but no one could deny the beauty of their corner of the north during its momentary summer.

I had long been attracted by ivory and stone sculptures from the Arctic. The Holman Islander who arranged our air travel home let me pick up and examine an extraordinary piece that sat on his desk—a ball-shaped sculpture of forms within forms that combined geometric shapes with northern images. It would be given a place of honor in the world's premier museums. Just as exciting were the juxtaposed light and dark masses in so-called Eskimo prints. Prior to our vacation, I did not know that Holman Island artists were one of the sources of such prints. Once I learned this, I arranged to spend time looking through the studio where the prints were made. Although no work was going on at the time, it was possible to leaf through large portfolios of the studio's recent output. All the pieces were finely done and priced well beyond my reach. But I took my time and fully savored the viewing. The director of the studio also placed in my hands individual drawing portfolios of the community's leading artists. These were a shock initially. I saw interesting and informative line drawings, to be sure, yet I could find little in them of the forms characteristic of Eskimo art. There were, for instance, no elegant masses framing the subjects. Why? It took me a few minutes to come up with the rather obvious explanation. The much-erased pencil drawings provided no more than substantive content and rough compositional ideas for the eventual prints. It was the silk-screening that would allow a technician to bring out the elegance of the overall compositions. This printing, of course, was not an indigenous process. Yet I saw how perfectly the introduced medium had allowed the Inuit to realize the refinement in two-dimensional art that they had achieved over the centuries in their three-dimensional pieces. The prints lost none of their attraction in being a recent product of technical borrowing and change.

Hazardous Travel

Lured by the quiet cove, with its occasional dogsled, we went for a short walk on the sea. Our boldness grew. The following day we crossed the cove and climbed to the summit of the headland beyond, where an intriguing line of cairnlike structures seemed worth examining. The slope we climbed was steep and gravelly, covered in patches by small drifts of blown snow. With but four inches a year of precipitation, technically the area was desert. Yet the foot-high tufts of brittle brown grass through which the wind gusts hissed reminded us how lush it might look after the thaw.

Even this was not enough for us. Our last full day, we borrowed a hunter's snowmobile and sled and set off alone, in the dim early-afternoon glow, ten miles across sea ice to a small island in Prince Albert Sound. It was our most foolish venture in the north. Heather and Eric soon told us they were freezing on the sled; we ran them home and dropped off the sled. Setting out again, Trudy and I finally reached the cliff at the tip of our island destination. Once there, I shut off the snowmobile engine in hopes of photographing the passing sled of an Inuit. He stopped, let me photograph his dogs, and explained that he was training the team for a race. After he set out again, I found it had been a mistake to turn off our engine; it would not restart. I tried everything. It had a good spark and there was plenty of fuel, but I could not get it to fire. Eventually we began walking in the quickly diminishing light. Cold feet convinced us within a quarter mile to return and give the engine one more try. This time I got it to fire on one of its two cylinders, and we limped home slowly in the dark. How welcome the lights were when we rounded the last headland. That night, at dinner, an Inuit hunter brought a fresh polar bear hide into the Co-op. Folded up on the floor the hide had the approximate length, breadth, and height of a dining room table. He had shot it some distance away, then, ironically, on his way home he found himself crossing fresh polar bear tracks *ten miles away, near the cliff at the tip of the next island.* Although the pen may be mightier than the sword, the ballpoint in my pocket might not have measured up!

When we boarded the Twin Otter for the journey home we were quite unaware that another difficult day faced us. Until we reached Copper-mine everything went as it should. Soon after we left there and had gained cruising altitude, however, our plane abruptly lost use of all its navigation equipment. We were not far from the north magnetic pole, and it appears that extraordinary electrical disturbances had rendered our systems useless. And they remained that way. The pilot, who told me afterward that it was his first day as a chief flight officer, switched on an overhead light. He and the boylike navigator pored over a star chart, turned off the light, and took a manual sighting on a star with a sextant. We changed course at least thirty degrees. They repeated this process a quarter of an hour later. This time we swung back in the other

Inuit dogs on sea ice, ten miles from Holman Island.

direction about twenty degrees. So it went for hours, an endless and un-nerving zigzag across the dark, frozen waste. My knuckles were white on the end of the armrest. Finally, I went up to talk with the crew, for we were over an hour behind schedule. To my immense relief, as I ap-proached them, I saw the lights of Yellowknife on the horizon ahead. We had begun our descent into the cozy land of trees.

On the news, a day or two later, we heard that, on the afternoon of our return journey, a light plane had gone missing while flying from Coppermine to Yellowknife. It had not yet been found.

Quick Asian Postscripts

JAPAN, 1983

Wakkanai

Abashiri

HOKKAIDO

Sapporo

SEA OF

JAPAN

HONSHU

Tottori

Tokyo

Kyoto

Nagoya

Hiroshima

Osaka

PACIFIC

▲

Mt. Aso

SHIKOKU

OCEAN

KYUSHU

Yakushima

0   100   200 mi.

0   100   200 km.

Performers in Indian Bronze

South India Once Again

During the summer of 1978 I undertook a brief study of how south Indian artists who sculpt sacred images for Hindu temples go about their professional work. My two primary interests lay in their procedures for realizing the images and their ways of passing on and maintaining their professional knowledge.

Why art all of a sudden? There were two reasons, one personal and the other professional. I had grown up with art around me. My mother's maternal grandfather, Harry Roberts, had given up architecture at the age of forty-nine in order to pursue his real passion, painting. I had inherited many pieces of his. When his sight began failing, in his late eighties, he replaced working in parks or the countryside with daily trips to the Tate Gallery in London. Each day he undertook analytical study of a different painting or sketch, particularly those of J. M. W. Turner. Even those exercises were gems. Several others in Mother's family painted, including my mother herself. My father's sister was also an artist, and Dad had dabbled for years in both art photography and sculpture. It's little wonder that I painted in high school and college, counted artists among my friends, and had been a lifelong collector of artworks and books on art. I had been longing for years to find an excuse for doing an anthropological project expressly on art.

Professionally speaking, my project was motivated more by puzzlement than by anything else. I confess to being baffled by the existence of divergent perspectives on the images Hindu sculptors made. Art and cultural historians of several Western nations and India had been railing since at least 1858 at the "conventional," "repetitive," or "stereotyped" forms of those artworks made during the past millennium. Some who took this approach were V. A. Smith, A. L. Kroeber, S. Kramrisch, H. Goetz, A. De Riencourt, and M. Bussagli and C. Sivaramamurti. Their historical appraisals were, to say the least, cutting and dismissive.

My own experiences and those of south Indian friends and colleagues led me to believe that neither the teaching nor the practice of sculpture was moribund. It seemed possible that both were still being pursued vigorously in quiet, but long-existent, sacred places, such as Kumbakoonam. And one *could* find good recent pieces. Trudy had once given me for Christmas a subtle, elegant bronze of Bhikshatanar. It portrayed Lord Shiva as an ascetic who came out of the forest looking so handsome that the distracted wives of the sages inadvertently let their clothes slip off! This treasure was certified to be recent; even if the certifier had been in error, style alone indicated it could be no older than the eighteenth century. I had also bought for about thirty cents a lyrical image of Balakrishnan, Lord Krishna as a playful child, with stolen butter in his hand from his mother's churn. Sculptor friends of mine handled it with misty eyes. It, too, could not be very old. While neither was a "great" work, of the caliber that caught the eye of historians or museum curators, sensitive art lovers took them seriously.

Finally, there was a robust literature by specialists on Hindu aesthetics texts, such as Ananda K. Coomaraswamy and D. N. Shukla, who laid out the unique creative practices of the culture's artists.[1] Most art historians turned their backs on this literature; those who acknowledged it failed to discuss its relevance to recent times. If the texts on aesthetics were at all correct about creative processes in Hindu art, the region's sculptors were not merely emulating older pieces, as the sharp-tongued historians contended. I wondered, nonetheless, whether these texts adequately reflected the practices of artists during the past few centuries.

With reactions to the artworks ranging from disparaging to laudatory, how could I either reconcile what the scholars had been saying or ascertain the bases for their divergent opinions? Perhaps everyone was partially right, but they disagreed for reasons I could not yet grasp. The best way to clarify the situation was surely to do actual field study of the present practices of Tamil sculptors using the same techniques I had used in my earlier projects. Yes, it would be an abrupt new departure for me, but I did at least know the language, I had my professional tool kit ready, and I was able to get funding thanks to a Summer Research Fellowship from my university's Research Council and a travel grant from the American Institute of Indian Studies.

This time I flew off to the East alone, in part because it was to be such a brief study and in part due to the faltering of my seventeen-year marriage. Understandably, the project provided me with a stabilizing focus of attention during this time of shocking personal change.

Locating the artists was easier than I had anticipated, thanks to expert help from two seniors to whom I turned, Professor A. Aiyappan, the official sponsor of my research project, and Dr. V. Raghavan, another white-haired south Indian scholar. Aiyappan, decades earlier, had served as director of the Government Museum in Madras, home to one of the nation's finest collections of ancient sculpture. Raghavan, also long retired, was a Sanskrit scholar whose small living room was a veritable museum of Indian art. I had long held both them and their writings in high regard, and it was my good fortune that both had favorable memories of meeting me in 1968. When I sat down with each of them over cool drinks and detailed my summer plans, they expressed approval of the project and generously placed their time and knowledge at my disposal. They turned out to be fountains of information—on where to begin and with whom. Although our perspectives on the subject all differed, their practical tips and mature insights about the present-day art world got my research off to a quick start.

Happy Traveler, Amiable Knowledge Keepers

Soon I was out on the road with a small backpack and preliminary lists of names and places in my shirt pocket. Of the sculptors I hoped to interview and watch work, a number were well known in Tamil society; only a few of them turned out to be obscure. I was determined to find them all. Tracking down everyone was going to take me the length and breadth of the Tamil country by train and bus, through markets in thousand-year-old cities, and down the quietest lanes of venerable religious centers. What a delightful prospect! Being in the perfect frame of mind to lose myself in the experience, I set out with a light step.

The travel itself turned out to be a pleasant surprise. I was all too familiar with the congestion and bustle of India's main-line express trains. It had been a fight to so much as board them at times in the 1960s. The slow, lightly used local trains I rode in 1978 were peaceful by comparison.

I was not especially pressed for time, the ripening fields beside the railway were looking idyllic, and I was relaxed enough to take pleasure in everything along the way.

On my first trip out, as soon as the train had left the capital city behind, I gave up my seat and went to sit on the steps at the door where I had boarded the carriage. I could soak up the view directly from there, without having to peer through glass, and I could cool my sandaled feet in the wind. Farm families tended their crops a stone's throw in front of me; snowy white little egrets stood poised over irrigation channels in hopes of finding fish; and the breezes both brought to me the rich scents of this tropical land and played with my hair. Periodically interspersed among the farm villages lay small towns, with temple gates and coconut palms towering above their two-story business centers. In some of the larger such towns I knew I would soon find myself walking in search of my sculptors.

Never have I received such a welcome in the field. The sculptors were learned specialists. Perhaps because they realized that I, too, had gone through advanced studies and also knew something about their art, they swept me into their world with trusting smiles, treated me as an honored guest, never talked down to me, and delighted in showing me everything I wished to know of their life and work. I was able to locate all but one of those on my list, watch many of them do their bronze casting or stonecutting, and witness the teaching of novices and of advanced apprentices as well.

Such an artist is called a *stapati*. There were numerous subspecialties, and I was able to see them all. Besides the many *stapatis* who made bronze or stone images for temples, some did stone sculpture on temple walls and towers or built whole temples, a few did wood sculpture on the vehicles used to parade sacred images through the streets on holy days, and one was specialized in crafting the ornamental apexes for towers over the inner sanctums of temples. Given this breadth of work, we should clearly be translating the term *stapati* not as "sculptor" but as "sculptor-architect."

Texts

I had not previously encountered traditional specialists having such a degree of sophistication. In fact, the one impediment to my learning the

A Tamil sculptor with his palm leaf texts.

fine details of their art was that, even though they were Tamil speakers, most were also knowledgeable in both north India's Sanskrit and the ancient Tamil Grantha script, which had long been used in the region for writing Sanskrit texts on art. I had only Tamil.

But we did at least talk about the texts. The Tamil sculptors had a number of orally transmitted manuals that provided information on iconography, materials, and techniques—everything right down to the auspicious times for doing their work. And the iconographic works spelled out appropriate body proportions, postures, and other formal attributes for each of their many possible subjects. One basic text is called *Rupadhyanam,* literally "mental images." Students cannot get far in their studies unless they are able to commit these to memory. They were acquiring knowledge in precisely the same disciplined way that Brahmin youths learned holy texts; eventually, they even wore sacred threads across their chests as initiated Brahmins do. But some of the teachers had aids to their memory; they pulled out and showed me precious manuscripts, several centuries old and each meticulously inscribed by stylus on strips of palm leaf.

Sculpture as Performed Art

India's sacred art is text based, and sculptors taught me that making a new piece takes place just as Coomaraswamy and Shukla had specified. The *stapati* must begin in a ritually pure state and possessing thorough knowledge of verses that describe attributes of his planned subject. He must then concentrate on the verses in such a way that his mind is able to grasp a visual image. Finally, he employs his techniques and skills to fashion a substantive representation of what he holds in his mind's eye. However, so long as he is able to hold or recapture the mental image, he can go on to make additional pieces without repeating the early steps.

All but one of the *stapatis* I consulted could be called traditional in his use of these procedures. The exception was the well-trained son of a traditional *stapati* who had also begun experimenting with innovations that were inspired by what he called the "fresh forms" of folk art.

I routinely asked each of the *stapatis* to identify one or two outstanding artworks and tell me why each was special. Some of their choices I was already familiar with, others I went off to examine and photograph as soon as possible. The three different types of criteria by which they justified their selections told me a lot about the extent of their training. First, a few sculptors had studied to the point at which they were craftsmen who knew techniques. They tended to praise pieces that were technically exemplary—for instance, a renowned image of Dancing Shiva in the Government Museum. They told me it had "precise proportions." Second, some had studied further, going on into texts on theory of expression. *Stapatis* at this level tended to extol artworks that they found lyrical or expressive. Two of them actually got up and danced in order to illustrate a fleeting action that a certain artist had been able to express. Finally, the most advanced, most knowledgeable *stapatis* had reached a point in their studies at which a teacher had revealed to them that their own mind and eye were now ready to transcend the guidelines of the texts. The great pieces these *stapatis* lauded were truly rare: One included an element—a falling figure placed head-downward in the center of a battlefield scene—that was not mentioned in any texts but that enhanced the feelings of the work. Another, a faceted piece, achieved a kind of abstraction not otherwise seen. A *stapati* at this third level, whose family included long-established temple builders, then showed me a novel piece he himself had done in ivory.

Stop a minute! If Hindu sculpture is performed art, *that* must be why art historians panned it as repetitive or stereotyped. Think about how similar in form early seventeenth-century and early twenty-first-century performances of *Hamlet* would be. So would be performances of Bach's Third Brandenburg Concerto in 1721 and 2006. In performed art one works from a text. When Sir Laurence Olivier spent time studying and reflecting on Shakespeare's script of *Hamlet* in preparation for one of his great early performances of the title role, or when Wendy Carlos studied Bach's score for the Third Brandenburg Concerto and thought through how she might realize its sketchy second movement on the Moog synthesizer, how did that differ from some anonymous south Indian *stapati* studying and reflecting on a text that described the characteristics of Bhikshatanar as he prepared to perform the figure in wax, then bronze? And remember how rare the pieces are that *stapatis* tell us transcend the texts; ironically, only a few of the pieces historians praise fall in this category. How can we justify labeling a sixteenth-century bronze figure of Dancing Shiva "stereotyped" because it is similar to a twelfth-century piece that was made after reflection on the same text?

Dreamy Days

Families of sculptors had found peaceful spots in which to live and work, tranquil places for me to visit for a few days. Their studios and schools were mainly in small, attractive, centuries-old temple towns—places all south Indians will know, such as Mahaabalipuram, Swaami-malai, and KumbakooNam. Seldom did my thoughts carry me back to my own world.

One *stapati* asked me to accompany him to a nearby temple for the

The serene Tamil temple town where one sculptor worked.

quiet evening rites. The day's heat was behind us and, as pilgrims often do, we sat afterward under stately rustling palms beside the temple, eating sweet leftover food offerings that had been handed us by a priest after they had been sanctified in the service. Another sculptor, a man who leased space for his studio in one side of the main gate to an ancient temple, presented me with a thousand-year-old south Indian coin given him years before by a loyal patron. My research not only went well, it left me feeling like the Connecticut Yankee who had crossed a bridge into the distant past.

Time Edges in Japan

Toward Immersion in the East

For six years, I shared life with Carol, an artist. During the summer of 1982, we both took an accelerated two-year intensive Japanese course at the Monterey Institute for International Studies in California. My goal was to prepare for a seven-month sabbatical leave in Japan. We deepened the experience by living in a Japanese-language house. Japanese is a sweet tongue, with no difficult sounds to master, and I found several grammatical similarities to Tamil—as in the use of gerunds and the way of making conjunctions. These made learning the language easier for me than I had expected. Our class was pushed by four energetic teachers, all Japanese, who gave us seven hours of lessons each day. Then, each Friday, we had three and a half hours of exams. It was clearly the best and most productive language training I had ever had. Our final consisted, in part, of a five-minute talk in Japanese, without notes, before the faculty, students, and several distinguished Japanese guests. In order to make this presentation more meaningful for me, I spoke on "Sizuka na Hito," "Peaceful People," that is to say, my dear Paliyans.

I particularly enjoyed our written exercises. Having grown up drawing in ink as a self-imposed discipline, I approached writing Japanese characters with a somewhat experienced hand, as well as enthusiasm for the elegant forms. It was only a matter of time before our writing teacher took me aside to insist that I seek out a calligraphy teacher in Japan. I would certainly try to fit it in.

The only serious time we took off from our language studies was on Saturdays. Most of those we spent on the shore at the Point Lobos wildlife preserve, with cameras. I did not know it yet, but this, too, was preparation for Japan. The previous year, I had taught Carol how to use a camera. Now, during the summer's photography, she, the artist, taught me how to take photographs. When each film came back from processing she showered me with questions: "You took three shots of this. What were you attempting? What was it about this third shot that led you to make it your final one? How did it satisfy you?" With heightened awareness of what I was doing, I moved from taking several so-so photographs of each subject to taking a single shot that really pleased me. Surveying the work later, I found that half of my effective photographs from the summer were taken during our very last day at Point Lobos.

Only four and a half months after completing the language course, we disembarked at Narita airport. A few nights in Tokyo made it obvious that expenses in the metropolis were beyond our sabbatical budget, so we pushed along immediately to serene Kyoto, a city I remembered fondly. It would be possible to live there more modestly. We were fortunate to find a reasonably priced, nicely located, Japanese-style apartment within a day. Like the Japanese, we folded our mattresses and put them away in the closet each morning, then sat on the pungent tatami floor to work and eat. Food markets were located nearby; our neighborhood bathhouse was a minute's walk away, through the grounds of an eight-hundred-year-old Shinto shrine; I could reach Kyoto University in fifteen minutes on foot; and we were only three or four minutes from an entrance into the Imperial Palace gardens. All that remained was for me to locate my colleagues.

Unaware of Japanese protocol, I walked unannounced into the office of the senior Sanskrit professor I had visited at Kyoto University in 1967 and explained to him what brought me back. I know now that, had I been Japanese, this would have been an impolite, awkward, perhaps impossible thing to do, but I was an untutored stranger to the land. He rose to the occasion kindly and introduced me to two anthropological colleagues of my own age. They welcomed me warmly, ensured that I obtained access to their library, and insisted on staying in regular contact. One of them, Toshinao Yoneyama, served as head of the anthropology department. The other, Yutaka Tani, a mature specialist in cognitive anthropology, voiced great interest in the goals of my project. It was hard to believe that we had managed to accomplish all that was necessary to feel fully settled in only a few days.

Probing Mental Worlds

I had come to Japan to think about anthropological study of categories. Working twice among individualistic people, in India and in the subarctic, had prompted me to generate a wide variety of questions on the general subject of our mental worlds. As my earlier research demonstrates, I think anthropologists have overstated the case for what A. F. C. Wallace once called the "replication of uniformity" model of culture, in which it was taken for granted that there is standardization of concepts from head to head.[1] Wallace went on to point out that there are advantages to a *complementation* of peoples' concepts and beliefs within a social system. That, after all, is what specialization is all about; a system containing more diverse roles contains more knowledge. Wallace pointed out, besides, that our concepts do not have to be identical from person to person so long as others respond appropriately to our behavior. We still do not know how much testing of the adequacy of our concepts is needed as we grow up, or how much feedback from others we have to receive for us to participate effectively in a cultural system. Let me give one personal example of an error that went *un*corrected: I was in my midteens before learning that *reluctant* was a near antonym, not a synonym, for *relieved*. No one had ever challenged my misuse of *reluctant,* perhaps because precisely speaking parents and teachers imagined that my wording was meant to be playful or sarcastic. My occasional use of irony and sarcasm as a youngster may have thrown them off.

I had also seen two examples of cultural systems that are able to operate with relatively little explicit communication. This is why I took my inquiry to Japan. Admittedly, mathematics and language teachers soundly drill Japanese children, and the Japanese know how to behave with propriety. Nonetheless, in everyday conversation, Japanese are most comfortable leaving a great deal on a subtle, unstated, implicit level. I had long known that excessive explicitness is even judged as insensitive or rude in Japanese society. As a result, in pursuit of social responsibility, people may leave sentences vague as to their subject or object. This can be startling to foreign scholars when they first encounter it.

Given this vagueness, how can people ensure that their hearers achieve adequate understanding of what they say? I wondered if the logic and redundancy of their sentences take care of that. Not necessarily, I found. After I got tangled up deciphering who said what in a dictation test that contained embedded quotations (A was quoting what B had said about C's words), I was aghast to hear my Japanese grammar teacher tell the class that verbs did not have to remain in the same tense throughout a sentence. For any subsequent verb in the statement, the proper choice of tense was *not* a matter of the speaker keeping consistently to the tense of the initial verb. Usage depended not on logic; instead it was a function of the speaker's feeling as to what the most suitable form might be.

Fortunately, like Dene, Japanese are sensitive listeners. They pay close attention to the messages and frames of mind of those with whom they converse. They will often know what has *had* to be left out, as when a small-town resident says in English, "I saw you-know-who going into the loan office." Being tuned in may enable the Japanese to fill in missing subjects for one another and even to avoid difficulties with such things as inconsistent tenses. They use a variety of clues to triangulate on the meanings behind the words. Professor Chie Nakane told me during my 1967 visit to Japan that, when the Japanese interact with Indians, they have great difficulty with Indians who respond to them in logical and unfeeling ways, rather than sensitively. Conversely, she said, Indians are put off by what they consider the *over*sensitivity of Japanese. It is a two-sided coin. So, what are the limits of using sensitivity in place of explicitness and precision? In Japan, that may depend on the astuteness of one's listener.

I ended up doing more on the theoretical aspect of this project than on the methodological. Designing systematic and appropriate interviews was the main problem. I would not be likely to elicit natural speech of the sort I wished to study, in view of the fact that I was a foreign stranger asking people to perform a technical task. Responses under these circumstances were unlikely to have much vagueness. Putting heads together with my consultants yielded little in the way of effective techniques that could be used to escape this problem. My background work was teaching me a great deal about the world of Japanese speech, but, unless I switched to a very loose sort of study, say of natural conversation between others, I was going to miss the very phenomenon that interested me. I would have to accept either a drastic change of research design or a loss of rigor. Fortunately, this was a sabbatical leave to think, not a formal research project from which I was required to return home with a tidy set of findings.

There was other work to do as well. I was expected to give talks or seminars at Kyoto University and the National Museum of Ethnology in Osaka about the subject of my leave. These generated stimulating discussion. I also gave a major presentation at Kyoto University on the puzzle of pure Hindus showing respect toward hunting Paliyans, a talk I was able to introduce by using my Japanese speech from Monterey. This talk taught me a lot about politeness and sensitivity in Japanese academia; they do not at all prevent criticism. I received a number of courteous and enjoyable questions after I spoke and only realized the next morning, when reanalyzing them, that I had actually fielded some of the most serious scholarly challenges of my career. The university library, rich with Asian materials, made it possible for me to polish, refine, and expand an article that I was committed to completing right away for the journal *Human Ecology.* Here, at least, was one tidy finished product from the leave.

Where Past and Present Touch

Kyoto is an exciting place for anyone who appreciates Japanese traditions. In addition to being able to visit the old Imperial Palace and the ancient temples and princely retreats at the foot of the forested hills that ring it on three sides, one can enjoy frequent Noh plays and *koto* (lute) or *shakuhachi* (flute) concerts. In other words, the old is present and the arts of the past are cultivated. Shinto priests and Buddhist monks are common sights in the streets. At Daitoku-ji alone is a complex of twenty-four temples, monasteries, and offices of the Rinzai Sect of Zen Buddhism clustered together. The other Japanese Zen sects also have their headquarters in Kyoto. There are ancient and modern gardens of exquisite design in palaces, temples, tea shops, banks, and private homes. Traditional potters and silk weavers are active, as are famed makers of lacquerware and fans. There are calligraphy supply shops. Riding on a bus, one might see a gorgeously attired geisha or two, for their schools and places of entertainment still function in the Pontocho and Gion quarters. On top of all this, Kyoto is a modern city with exciting architecture, shining new cars, and all the conveniences, such as an immaculate new subway, efficient taxis, and up-to-date copy centers.

Kyoto, more than the rest of Japan, is a place where old and new intertwine. It is as if they feed on each other. Accountants in modern dress pack the Noh plays on Saturday afternoon. Executives of sake manufacturing firms take evening lessons in *shakuhachi* from great flute masters. Teachers in modern schools perform Zen tea ceremonies at their homes for guests. Police in immaculate modern gear hold back

Ryugen-in garden, Daitoku-ji, Kyoto, dating from the thirteenth century.

traffic for the processions of one-thousand-year-old festivals. Corporate employees in company sweatshirts do calisthenics in, of all places, the Imperial Palace gardens. Buddhist nuns and Shinto priests are driven about in long black cars. One can buy yesterday's cast-offs or World War II mementos at monthly flea markets in the grounds of Toji Temple or Kitano Shrine. Let me rephrase what I began with. Past and present are not just intertwined in Kyoto, they feel totally inseparable; perhaps this, being the ritual center of Japan, is one spot where the edges of past and present have to touch. Many who traffic in the ancient may feel obliged to make gestures to accommodate the new, but the agents of modernity seem to reciprocate by using the old to lend balance to their lives.

That will certainly not account for all juxtapositions of past and present. The concave faces of the tall stone walls around the Imperial Palace gardens have stood elegantly for ages, but, at 2:00 a.m., one occasionally hears strings of howling motorcycles racing along the street beside them. Perhaps the cyclists do it simply because of the way the concave walls amplify and project the high-pitched scream of their redlined engines across the sleeping city. Yet, considering where this is done, there could well be an element of defiance—a youthful rejection of the authority of the past. Or, were we listening to proud outbursts of ingenious samurai pretenders? It is your call.

For me, the texture of Japan was too rich to ignore. I tried to take in what I could during my breaks from work and allowed myself at least a couple of outings a week. Sometimes, the culture interrupted my labors on its own—as when a Hollyhock Festival procession, its huge horses and riders costumed in rich medieval garb, prevented my slipping across the street to my neighborhood copy center.

The religious sites of Kyoto defy any talk of a typical Japanese temple or a characteristic garden. Gardens may be composed of natural rocks, polished stone, raked gravel, heaped sand, mosses, live or dead trees, trimmed bushes, bamboo, ferns, ponds, bridges, and stone ritual washbasins, with a backdrop of forest, buildings, or walls. Dissimilarity does not end there. The walled rock-and-gravel gardens may impart tranquillity—as at twelfth-century Ryoan-ji—or unsettling turbulence—as at the Zuiho-in garden, dedicated in 1546 by a fanatic feudal lord. It was a stimulating feast for the senses.

An endless string of festivals demanded attention: a demonstration of classical archery in January, driving away demons in February, an April celebration of transient cherry blossoms, boisterous *ama sake* festivals during summer at Shinto shrines, and many more. They, too, defy summary description. For the cherry blossom festival, which we attended with a party of *shakuhachi* players, people set out mats, edge to edge, under the blossoming trees, picnicked on delicacies, and drank sake to great excess with their friends. People milled in happy confusion. Given all the drinking, the lack of bathroom facilities became for us just one more source of levity. For July's Gion festival, floats of up to twelve tons are draped with magnificent ancient tapestries from Belgium, Persia, and elsewhere, artworks that hang for the remainder of the year in the National Museum.

Traditional musical and dramatic performances are held regularly at recital halls throughout the city. We attended Noh plays at the Heian Shrine; watched *kyogen* farces at Sanpo-in; and, on an extraordinary night, heard one of the city's two *shakuhachi* masters jamming on a seldom-seen five-foot flute with a top Japanese pianist from the San Francisco jazz world.

The broad puns of the *kyogen* plays were just within our grasp linguistically. Almost by chance, we were among the fifteen people who knelt on Sanpo-in's ancient veranda one afternoon as a "living national

The view from a veranda at Sanpo-in.

treasure" performed a series of these brief and humorous plays. We had learned on a previous visit to the place that the screens that were now serving as his props were sixteenth-century Kano paintings.

I speculated above that agents of modernity use the old to lend balance to their lives in the new Japan. That is how it appears. A high-rise apartment may have a special room with a raised tatami-mat floor. Vast numbers of people learn arts, including martial arts, with a focus and dedication that suggest they actually feel necessity. But what really accounts for these seeming tokens of tradition? We know that Yukio Mishima, the novelist, argued fiercely that Japan should not leave the disciplines of the past behind. He felt Japan was losing its character, its strength and virility. He may not be representative, but he wrote *Runaway Horses* (part two of his grand tetralogy) on this theme, and later committed suicide in a martial setting to emphasize his point. Could being overwhelmed by the new, since the modernizing reforms of 1868, be responsible for this reaching back to tradition? Do practices of the past represent a source of revitalization, or an anchor of sorts, for those who need it? Surely they cannot merely be a matter of fashion; they are too old for that. Nyozekan Hasegawa, in 1938, contended that the traditional and modern in Japan are "invariably found to be flourishing side by side," and that interest in the traditional usually arises "as a reaction" to alien influences. He argued, for example, that, during the early period of Chinese influence, traditional Japanese forms revived. Then, much nearer to the present, the 1868 reforms stimulated a "compilation of national histories" in 1877 and a "tendency to revert . . . to the traditional literature" by the early 1890s.[2] Had he lived a few more decades, he would surely insist that I am seeing only the most recent manifestations of what he held to be a long-term tendency.

I spoke of old and new being especially intimately entwined in Kyoto, the old imperial capital, where a great many institutions serve to maintain traditions. Could it be that mere availability of the old makes the reaching back more conspicuous there? For now we will have to leave these questions open.

Brushes, Flutes, and Gardens

My writing teacher in Monterey did not have to push very hard for me to seek out a calligraphy teacher. It was an appealing idea. Within a week of my arrival in Kyoto, inquiries led me to Kosho-in, a fourteenth-century Buddhist retreat founded by an emperor's daughter and patronized by the royal household. One of the nuns there, Shin Ei, taught calligraphy. She accepted me as her student right away. All the others who came to her were women learning the cursive form of the syllabic hiragana script. For me, she planned to teach the complex kanji characters, and my lessons were to begin just as soon as I acquired my equipment.

For the remainder of my seven months, unless I was traveling, I spent Tuesday afternoons kneeling with my brush in front of the fifteenth-century garden. My sensei was a perfectionist herself and at times rejected ten or twenty of my efforts before sitting back, saying, "Aah," and putting great spirals and laudatory comments in red ink all over my successful piece. My very best works were left unmarked, but she tucked them all away for herself. When I moved up to writing phrases, they all reflected my sensei's faith-based Amida Buddhist beliefs. We realized later, though, that some pieces had sensual readings, one about love in spring.

I grew very fond of my teacher. When she realized that I had arrived

Kosho-in, where the author studied calligraphy.

in class distracted by a problem, she counseled me or responded with a Buddhist lesson. On a day when I had quarreled with my partner and could not focus on calligraphy for the first hour, she eventually prodded it all out of me, laughed heartily, and said, "Dogs bark." It took me some time before I could appreciate that particular Buddhist commentary on the natural. She was always eager to hear my accounts of personal exploration in Japan, unless they had to do with Zen. Then, she would shiver and say, "No, no, no." Knowing something of my past research, she asked innumerable questions about India, the birthplace of her beloved Buddha. She asked me, for instance, to draw maps for her, and

one place I located was Bodh Gaya, the scene of the Buddha's Enlightenment. She has these still. I was my teacher's senior in years, and she re-
spected that; it made our relationship ambiguous at times when we were
meeting casually, outside class, but I did have to accept her discipline
during lessons, even when she chose to toy with me.

As our friendship grew, I took her to a performance by a south Indian
Kathakali dance-drama troupe that came to Kyoto, and we began invit-
ing each other to dinner. Dining at Kosho-in meant sitting at a Western
hardwood dining room table, eating rice from a modern rice cooker,
and drinking fine scotch afterward with Shin Ei and the abbess. I was
amazed. We all laughed, though, when sensei came to dine with us. We
sat on the tatami floor and cooked our rice in a more traditional way.

Again and again, Shin Ei asked for an explanation of how and why I
came to study with her. Each time she did so, I attempted to tell her precisely how it happened, yet she never really accepted what I had to say;
she was searching for meanings. She also found it hard to comprehend
how I, wearing what the Japanese said were outrageously youthful shirts
for my age, sometimes produced acceptable pieces of calligraphy. My
producing them often triggered another round of her searching questions. But then she had never seen the tidy ink doodles in the margins of
my notebooks, which went back to my undergraduate days, or the ink
drawings that began seriously when I was about twelve. I received a de-
tention once, in New Zealand, for drawing my English teacher while she
was giving a lecture.

One Tuesday I arrived ten minutes early for class and entered without
thinking about a buzz in the background. There Shin Ei sat, shaving the
top of her head with an electric razor. Embarrassed by having invaded
her space at what I took to be an intimate moment, I backed out of the
room with an apology. She burst out laughing and sent two of her female students to fetch me. They grasped my arms, laughing themselves
at my confusion, and drew me back in, as ordered. Then Shin Ei smiled
slyly and put on a great show of checking the shave, touching it up, and
giving her pate a final polish with a cotton cloth.

There was another day, toward the end of my period of study, when I
arrived to find her head immaculately shaven. More striking than this,
she was wearing the magnificent ceremonial kimono of her religious
order. As soon as I knelt to begin work, she came over slowly and presented me with a carefully wrapped document, folded in three. I unwrapped and unfolded the sheet of rice paper to find three pieces of

calligraphy on it and three elaborate red seal impressions. Shin Ei had always been irritated by my way of signing good pieces; my name looked thus in Japanese hiragana syllables:

gaa
da
na
pii
ta

On this special day, she was endowing me with a Japanese name, Shin Gan. The first character was the initial character of her name. It means "truth." This was a touching gesture. The second character was tailored to me. She knew that *Peter* means "rock" in Greek; she was also aware of my passion for the rock gardens of Japan and for rocky seashores—a passion that goes back to my childhood in Falmouth, England. *Gan* is one of the most appropriate terms for such a significant rock. To establish the authority of the document, it bore the seal of Kosho-in. This made Shin Gan a fully legal alias. The certificate included Shin Ei's name, as well as her teacher's, establishing a lineage of calligraphers. I shall not attempt to describe how this felt. Professor Tani added an extraordinary touch. Using a piece of precious material he owned—ancient walrus ivory—he had a seal made for me with an archaic version of the characters in my name.

Almost as soon as I, Carol began her own lessons. She was accepted to study the *shakuhachi* flute with one of Kyoto's masters. This took her away once a week for a long group class, lasting from afternoon to late evening. But she mastered both the instrument and the traditional musical notation. Her progress stunned me. At a school recital, in one of the city's recital halls, she played a piece in a trio, with a fellow student and the composer of the piece himself.

One evening, the *shakuhachi* teacher invited some of his older students and me to a night of recreation in Gion, one of the two traditional entertainment quarters. We spent most of our time in two establishments, a geisha house and a cocktail bar, both run in the same fashion. It was interesting to watch how they cared for us. We did not order anything. No one asked crassly what we wanted, and no money changed hands that evening. The master was an established client of both houses, and all business behavior was banished discreetly to another time. Fine delicacies that suited the heavy drinks were brought to us at the first house as if we were guests at a private home. When we left, the two women who had served us as well as the proprietor of the house came out to the street to see us off, as if we were cousins visiting from out of town. It was beautifully soothing from start to finish. The other establishment was similar in character.

My stomach had not been able to tolerate much strong alcohol since my bleeding ulcer of twenty years earlier. Accordingly, I slowed down my drinking of scotch without mentioning it to anyone, not even to Carol. Out of nowhere, a geisha approached me with a cup of tea. How good it looked. No one else was given tea. It appears she had read subtleties in my behavior, in the same way that a mother becomes aware of a baby's needs before she has so much as a grunt to go by. I pondered this mothering, and, before we left, noted how the curious deep collar of a geisha exposes the back of her neck. And what does a Japanese child tied on its mother's back see in front of it? It sees the mother's neck. Could a geisha just be a super mother? That really challenges the common Western notion of an East Asian courtesan. Chalk it up as a theory.

Toward the end of our stay, I decided to do something systematic with my camera. I picked twelve of Kyoto's most exciting gardens and set out to photograph them all. Two turned out to be inaccessible, the private garden of an abbot and a garden open only to the religious. Two others required permission, but that was given, and I was lucky to obtain entry on perfect days for photography. The ten gardens I could shoot were more than enough. I walked to one, a seventeenth-century prince's retreat, on a drizzly day. For much of the day I was the only visitor, but the greens were extraordinary and I enjoyed the peace. I also spent a couple of hours alone on a veranda writing poems. Hakusasonsoo, the heavily wooded, little-known garden of an early twentieth-century artist, was another treat.

I was fortunate to be the first guest of the day when I went to photograph the gardens at Daisen-in. A young monk offered me a tea ceremony on arrival by way of welcome. While savoring the tea and enjoying the cup, I noticed an old monk peering at some twenty pieces of wild and angular Zen calligraphy on the other side of the room. Going over to see what he had, I learned that he was the abbot of the place. He welcomed me with a request that I stay to assist him. What he sought was satisfactory translations of each of the pieces into English. We worked on it long enough to reach some agreements. Then he turned to me and spat out, in Japanese, what can only be translated into English as "Do!" It was my first Zen lesson. When it came time for my photography, the abbot arranged that I shoot one part of the garden from his quarters. Yes, I *was* going to "do." The day became more precious by the moment.

Fast Trips from Ice Floes to Flying Fish

Three breaks allowed us glimpses of some of Japan's diversity. But the overall impression was almost chaotic. There was too much to see, and we foolishly tried to take it all in. Travel is expensive in Japan; we managed it, though, with the help of discount rail passes and membership in the youth hostel system. In February, we visited Abashiri and Wakkanai, on the north coast of Hokkaido, a land of Ainu hunters and gatherers, deep snow, and sea eagles. Even though they wore modern Japanese dress, the Ainu were well in evidence on the streets of Abashiri. We also saw near there whole flocks of white-tailed eagles wheeling about for fish over wave-tossed ice floes. The magnificent Steller's sea eagle was evident too. Its body is eight inches longer than a bald eagle's, its wingspan is sixteen inches greater, and the shape of its enormous beak can only be said to resemble that of an aggressive cartoon eagle. It is impossible to forget standing on a hillside in Wakkanai, being pelted by huge cotton balls of snow, and watching a Steller's fly by a scant forty feet in front of me. On the journey back home, our train through the northern forest ran six hours behind schedule, unusual for Japan, due to forty inches of new snow that day. A woman with whom we had not conversed bustled her belongings together and got off at one brief rail stop, then, less than a minute later, dashed back in to present the foreigners with two steaming bowls of noodle soup from a platform vendor. It was more than a touching gesture.

Three weeks later, we stood on the deck of a southbound ship, headed for the island of Yakushima. Once there, we spent a few days basking in the sun, swimming, watching tropical flying fish, and picking up coral along the beaches. This also became a volcanic venture. Yakushima itself is volcanic; our ship there passed by several other billowing cones; then, taking a break from our return trip across Kyushu, we walked up to the lip of one of the craters within the caldera of Mount Aso to peer down for hours into its active sulfurous bowels. We spent an eerie night at an inn on the trembling volcano's shoulder. The following morning our breakfast was served in a busy cafeteria, but we got our first taste of *jawan mushi,* an exquisite warm egg custard containing hard-boiled partridge eggs and shiitake mushrooms. Our journey took us next to the south coast of Shikoku, again warm and southern. This was a land of beaches, enormous fighting dogs, and *katsuo tataki*—a filet of albacore marinated in *mikan* orange juice, garlic, and soy sauce, tossed momentarily onto burning straw, and then sliced. At one youth hostel, as we all sat in a circle after dinner, to tell where our homes were and name our favorite food, I tired of hearing "Big Mac hamburger" and "ice cream." So, when it was my turn to speak, I just blurted out, in Japanese, "For me, *katsuo tataki* is most delicious." I fully meant it and was pleased to see several astonished but delighted faces nod in agreement. These youthful travelers may seldom think of abandoning their modern fast foods in favor of the rich offerings of Japan, but that is not an adequate guide to their sense of the possibilities.

A third train trip, much later, took us along the undisturbed west coast, to Tottori. There were sand hills at Tottori itself. Elsewhere, the forest came down to the rocky shore and beach. Tiny, craggy, wooded islets were scattered about on the water, each resembling a slightly overgrown bonsai landscape. It was so enjoyable that, on the way home, we jumped off our train at one quiet beach without checking whether we could catch a train out again, later in the day. Did that really matter? We were becoming almost at home in the countryside.

I have been emphasizing nature more than people. The trips exposed us as well to wildly diverse images of humans and their works. Let me give the kaleidoscope one more twist. Groups of boisterous Kyushu farmers come home from market towns by local trains, their goods all sold. Dropping now-empty homemade yokes beside them in the corridors, women and men mingle happily and noisily as they watch for their whistle-stops. The stern constraints of the samurai ethic seem not to have reached this corner of the countryside. Our companions on the train leap straight from the pages of a nineteenth-century pastoral novel, with its freedom for both sexes and its love matches. Fishing villages, nestled along the shoreline, with their old stone steps and their tiny cottages, also resemble visions from the past, until one comes close enough to witness synthetic fiber fishnets, Toyota pickups, and TV antennas. We sweep past extensive mountain orchards, where every fruit hangs tidily bagged on the branch, to ripen without pests. I had always wondered where the perfect goods of Japan's fruit stalls originated. There are miles of seemingly wild northern forest, until one notices that the trees all stand in rows. Whole cars on the bullet trains drop silent as we slide through Hiroshima, as when a film has suddenly lost its sound; all hold eerily still (frozen in prayer, sadness, hope, or raw disbelief) so long as the city remains in view. Geography and history, ancient and modern, pass by, all jumbled by the wayside, there to see and feel until our senses give out from sheer overload.

Treading Old Paths and New

Journeys That Converge

Pursuing Nature and Anthropology

From my earliest years, I have found calmness in nature. I have always thought of this as nothing more than a personal quirk. An isolated avenue of ancient beech trees behind my grandmother's three-century-old home in Norfolk, England, was a spot where my sister and I could play alone, happily, far out of sight of the house. Rustling leaves were soothing, not worrying; birds and squirrels abounded; memories of the sights, smells, and sounds are sharp enough to remain clear forever. We picked wild mushrooms in nearby meadows with Mum; when Dad was home on leave from the navy, we strolled along Norfolk's lanes with walking sticks, searching in hedgerows for ripe blackberries, hedgehogs, and red admiral butterflies. During the last year and a half of World War II my father was the port doctor in Falmouth, on the southwest coast of England; I had my sixth birthday there. One of my passions was lying on my tummy beside tidal pools on the rocky headlands, peering into their rich little worlds of crabs, snails, sea anemones, multicolored seaweed, and the occasional darting fish. Each pool was an enticing little world with its own character.

Later, in western Canada, I would wander into aspen groves in every season, or stroll on clear, breezy summer days around damp margins of the ruffled ponds, with their stands of cattails, nesting ducks, and redwing blackbirds—watching, always watching. The most idyllic place of all for me in Canada was Savary Island, a sand-rimmed, six-mile-long island some ninety miles northwest of Vancouver, tucked between the British Columbia mainland and Vancouver Island. Our Aunt Phyllis was one of very few people who owned a cottage there, nestling in tall conifers near the beach. We went to and from the island by small coastal vessels such as the *Gulf Wing* and the *Lady Cynthia,* enjoying three long, peaceful vacations at Savary in the late 1940s and early 1950s. Although the northern waters were too cold to stay in for long, they were where I taught myself to swim—from a homemade raft that a friend and I constructed, then moored to an abandoned pile near the dock. We would sun ourselves lazily on the raft until we were too hot, then roll off into the clear water, sinking down into the world of spider crabs, starfish, snappers, and shrimp. The shrimp we often swallowed alive—a bit of boys' bravado. Or we would fish from the dock, enjoying the pungency of the tarry piles, catching occasional snappers and dogfish. The forest, which blanketed virtually the whole island, had a clear lower story where we could wander, whittle sticks, or just lie on the dry needles and smell the trees. It was pure peace.

On our twenty-day voyage from Canada to New Zealand in 1951, it was creatures of the open sea that beckoned: flying fish by the thousands, phosphorescence in the ship's wake at night, a breaching whale that hung ever so long in midair near the Fiji islands, and milling sharks by our ship in Suva harbor later that day.

The very best part of my life in New Zealand was having a beach a hundred feet down the wooded slope in front of our house. We moored a homemade sailing dinghy directly below, enabling me to go out most days after school to learn sailing on my own, without lessons or handbooks. Our arm of the harbor was shallow enough and the weather moderate enough that I could discover both effective sailing techniques and the boat's limits by trial and error. I pushed enough that I frequently returned home wet. It was a happy and productive wet. On windless afternoons, if the tide was high, I often picked up a paddle and went into the saltwater mazes that wound endlessly through our pungent mangrove swamps. One school outing gave three of us the opportunity to disappear into New Zealand's strangely silent coastal sand hills. We found in the depth of the dunes a herd of lean, skittish wild horses that watched us, snorted, and then thundered off. And there were also the times I spent with a new reflex camera trying to capture the elegant forms in New Zealand's lush, exuberant forest.

At fifteen, I cycled more than once down a little used Canadian dirt

road to an active beaver pond I had discovered. It was possible to sit un-
noticed in the bushes and study the busy creatures as they made endless
repairs to their dam and put aside fodder for the winter.

During a time of academic stress and one too many existentialist
plays and films, when I was nearly twenty, I walked away from the intense pressures of my senior year in college and lay, buried and still, in
some luxurious, untrampled lakeside grass. I probably lay there without
moving for at least two hours. Eventually, I began to think of the green,
burgeoning life about me as a manifestation of optimism. Growth itself
was inherently optimistic. Brother Grass, as it were, bid me by example
to get on with my own growth. What a strange thought; but it gave me
the incentive I needed to rise and return to the world of my studies and
the world of difficult decisions about the future.

In Philadelphia, for a year and a half, I cycled to the university on
roads that took me near the zoo. It became my habit to stop in frequently
to see the primates. The city zoo had unusual success with breeding
orangutans, and it was them I looked in on in particular. One day our
human paleontology professor, Elwin Simons, came to class with a
heavy cold. Preferring not to lecture, he suggested that we visit the primate section of the zoo instead; he would have questions for us later on
primate anatomy. I used the opportunity to visit my orangutan friends.
One young male sat in a car tire swing, with eyes down, rocking gently
and periodically kicking some feces. At age twenty-two I had a bright
copper–colored beard—perhaps I should say a bright orangutan–colored
beard. The youngster looked up, stared for several seconds directly at
my face, arose from his swing, did what I can only describe as blowing a
kiss toward me, performed a backflip, then wandered off. While my
wording of this is outrageously anthropomorphic, what I am attempting to describe is not the feelings or intentions of the orangutan; I seek,
rather, to report on *my own* reaction to what happened. For me, it had
always felt most appropriate to refer to other primates as "our cousins."
After this experience, I found that I used the expression with yet more
personal conviction.

It would not be long before I was to make my way alone into Paliyan-
occupied valleys in the dry Indian forest, toting a backpack that contained nothing but snacks, writing gear, and a knife. The forest in the
Northwest Territories was to follow.

My relationship with the wild sounds unbelievably idyllic. This was
not consistently the case. I have to confess that, as a nine-to-ten-year-

old, I participated with Canadian friends in gleeful, bloody gopher hunts, using water buckets, BB guns, and slingshots. The farmers encouraged our hunts on their pastures, but their annoyance over cattle injuring legs in gopher holes may not have been the main thing that drove us. We lived in hunting country, on one of North America's major duck and goose flyways. As soon as the air turned crisp, people flooded in from hundreds of miles away to participate. Even my bookish father joined the autumn hunt. In most minds, our stealthy gopher massacres were probably nothing less than practice for the future. As such, they would certainly have held a special delight for the men-to-be.

I have mentioned having felt an early attraction to hunting and gathering cultures. But was it the cultures as such that drew me, or was it the natural settings and the peoples' interaction with seemingly unspoiled environments that caught my attention? I have never thought of asking myself that question before, but it is a reasonable one nonetheless, considering that I was drawn as well by Antarctica and the Central Asian Gobi. In *A Personal Record*, Joseph Conrad recalls the fascination the edge of the world held for him as a nine-year-old: "while looking at a map of Africa of the time and putting my finger on the blank space then representing the unsolved mystery of that continent, I said to myself with absolute assurance and an amazing audacity which are no longer in my character now: 'When I grow up I shall go *there*.'"[1]

That was in 1868. Two years later, in a letter to his sister, eleven-year-old Franz Boas reported that "after he has taken his doctorate of medicine he would like to go on an expedition to the North or South Pole and travel to Australia or Africa."[2] Look at what the future would bring for them—first their famous journeys of 1890 and 1883, into the lands that had intrigued them so in boyhood, then their famed publications: *Heart of Darkness* by Conrad and *The Central Eskimo* by the anthropological pioneer Boas. Although I failed to foresee my future path with the same accuracy, I felt a similar pull to the edge of the known world. Perhaps cultural anthropology and research with hunters and gatherers were likely pursuits for me.

Then Taoism

About 1980 or 1981, I discovered in the university's library the Derk Bodde translation of volume one of Feng Yu-lan's *A History of Chinese*

Philosophy, a precious book. It had been published by the Beijing art press of Henri Vetch in 1937 and was appropriately housed in the rare book collection. I recall carefully opening the volume, printed as it was on hand-crafted paper, only to find that a less appreciative reader had mutilated chapter one and part of chapter two with a brilliant yellow highlighter. Recovering from the shock of that discovery and turning to the content of the book, I ascertained quickly that Feng provided the insider's overview of China's philosophies needed for my research on what I was later to call "predictable theories." I was distracted, however, by Feng's two chapters on Taoism, especially the Taoism of Chuang Tzu. Feng gave me glimpses of powerful treatises on relativism that rejected the notion that our human species should be set above all others. Never had I read anything resembling this except within the field of anthropology. A Taoist way of life also accorded with my personal ideals, and it had much in common with the Paliyan prescription for a good life— residing in a natural setting, cultivating a mature and independent self, respecting all others, and fostering a peaceful society. I made extensive notes above and beyond those needed for my theory project. These I would return to at various other times.

Soon after reading Feng, in December 1982, I had a chance to talk with a Chinese visitor about the continuing existence of Taoist type societies. Ying Ruocheng, the noted Chinese actor and translator of Shakespeare and Arthur Miller into Chinese, was at the University of Missouri as the Edgar Snow visiting professor of theater. While assuring me that Taoism was dead in present-day China, Ying listened to my ideas regarding people such as Paliyans persisting in the hills today in a curiously Taoist manner. He remained reluctant to accept their "way" as a close equivalent to Taoism, but the idea was one I could not dismiss.

In 1987 I married a woman, nicknamed "Shaf," who had Southeast Asian and Chinese roots. Imagine my astonishment, one evening, when I found Shaf curled up in a chair after dinner reading Ming-dao Deng's (properly, in Chinese, Deng Ming-dao's) *365 Tao: Daily Meditations.* In response to my questions, she eventually revealed her belief that her mother had, in subtle ways, passed down to her the perspectives of Shaf's Chinese grandfather. Because she had not been aware of my interest in the subject, it was a fortuitous and totally unexpected convergence for us as a couple, and it triggered my own return to personal study of Taoism. Deng is a Chinese American who spent thirteen years studying Taoism with Kwan Saihung, an elderly master from China. In the midst of the destruction of China's ancient traditions, Kwan Saihung had been chased off to America by his own master, ostensibly to find his purpose, though ultimately, perhaps, in order to safeguard Taoist ideas from the purges of the Maoists. The move to America brought one problem after another for him during the early years. Once he acquired an able and devoted American student, their shared goal seemed to come into focus—to provide cultural and linguistic translation of Taoist thought for the Western world. That, at least, is my interpretation of what occurred.

I eventually purchased my own copies of *365 Tao: Daily Meditations* and *Everyday Tao,* Deng's two ventures into writing philosophical texts, then expanded my reading to his *Chronicles of Tao* and *Scholar Warrior.* The *Tao Te Ching* was already in my bookcase, but I went on to acquire translations of other Taoist texts of the fourth to second centuries BCE: the *Hua Hu Ching,* which, along with the *Tao Te Ching,* is traditionally attributed to Lao Tzu; the *Chuang Tzu,* named for the author of its first seven chapters; the *Lieh Tzu,* also named for its author; and the *Yüan Tao,* by Liu An. Shaf's interests and mine were restricted to what Taoists call the "right-hand" or "internal" path, which has to do with philosophical concerns, as contrasted with the "left-hand" or "external" path, which entails the use of ritual techniques. Studying Deng's philosophical texts alongside the traditional ones, I was struck repeatedly by Deng's skill at rendering Chinese Taoist ideas into terms that I, as a contemporary westerner, could comprehend fully. There was no question that Kwan Saihung's assigned task in America had more than borne fruit through the writings of his gifted student.

As happened when I first read Feng, my reactions to Taoist literature, Deng's included, were both personal and professional. *Chronicles of Tao* is a detailed account of Kwan Saihung's life, first in China, then in the United States. Taken in hand by his Taoist, martial artist grandparents as a child of nine, he had ascended Huashan, one of the proverbial mist-shrouded mountains of China, to begin his studies. One thinks of such things as occurring only in the distant past. For me, Deng's lucid, philosophical writings and his history of the master did much to impart immediacy to the Taoist way. I was even moved to contact Deng, in order to talk with him directly about my deepening interest and to clarify a few points. Taoism was in curious harmony with what I had come to believe about the nature of reality and human existence. The more I read, the more I felt that I had been a Taoist for years. Although I had most of my growing still to do and possessed no formal teacher or guide to aid in that growth, I was comfortable considering myself as at some point along the Taoist path.

Looking at them professionally, I found the older texts to be rich with ideas that anticipated later anthropological theory. *Chuang Tzu* and *Yüan Tao* developed the notion that perspectives and values are relative to one's species. For instance, a fish, bird, or deer would not view Lady Li as the attractive beauty Chinese men saw. They would flee her rather than draw close.[3] Summarizing this line of thought, Feng says, "Each individual thing . . . thinks of itself as exceptional and other things as ordinary."[4] While that admits only to the existence of species-specific perspectives, Chuang Tzu went on to liken those to the "self-pride" one sees among humans.[5] Early Taoist writers also acknowledged the cultural specificity of patterns of behavior and criteria of judgment. Thus, the *Hua Hu Ching* urges us to "abandon any mental bias born of cultural or religious belief,"[6] and section nine of the *Yüan Tao* takes up the local character of customs, providing specific examples of culturally variable tools, practices, and values. Any anthropologist should be able to tell you that the admonition that we abandon bias "born of cultural or religious belief" is equivalent to the anthropological concern with avoiding those biases that are due to our cultural training. That is a matter of productive field method: if we wish to comprehend what people in other systems are doing, or wish to discern their motives for behaving as they do, we must avoid evaluating their actions solely in terms of the cultural frameworks with which we have grown up.

The *Yüan Tao* goes beyond this. Specific "local needs" are taken up; people are said to take "advantage" of the resources of their regions, to "avail themselves" of the means of subsistence and clothing that are "suitable" for local conditions, and so on. Even values were integral to the overall task of coping with survival, such as northern barbarians placing a premium on virility, they being people who had always to keep their weapons and themselves ready for war.[7] These very ideas, on need fulfillment and on the interrelatedness of diverse aspects of life, are fundamental to the functional thinking of two of anthropology's key twentieth-century figures, Bronislaw Malinowski and A. R. Radcliffe-Brown.

There is more. Roger T. Ames, one of the two translators of the *Yüan Tao*, justly characterizes that work as an ecological treatise.[8] He says, for instance, that "human beings do not act upon a world that is independent of them. Rather, they are interdependent with the world in which they reside, simultaneously shaping it and being shaped by it."[9] I would go further than he did and insist that the *Yüan Tao* approaches being ecosystemic, due to the author's clear beliefs that we are but one of many interlocked species and that even the grasses and trees have their needs.[10]

Taoist texts accord in a surprising number of ways with my own views about the world and with diverse and significant, instrumental perspectives of anthropology. Thus the name I have given this chapter.

Adapting to the Path of Cancer

My Misbehaving Cells

I began seeing a doctor in early May 1996 because of recurring pain in my bones. It would appear in one spot (a rib, a shoulder blade, or the rim of my pelvis), linger for some five days, and then vanish for two or three weeks. All the rheumatologists who looked at me confessed that they were baffled by my migrating symptoms, but we found that the pain did at least respond to medication.

Because I was also anemic, my doctor sent me for an endoscopic examination of my colon in May 1998. We drove off immediately afterward for a relaxing vacation in Florida, a time spent swimming, building sand sculptures, and teaching Andrew (Shaf's and my ten-year-old) how to sail a catamaran. I came home to word that my colon was clear, but they would have to go in again and biopsy "abnormal-looking" tissue in the last part of my small intestine. I sensed what that wording probably meant. The procedures were scheduled for June 24, the following week. On June 23, and not wholly by accident, I bought my second volume of Deng's work. It would be a suitable book to read during my anxious wait.

On July 1, my doctor called me to say that an appointment had been booked for me the following day with an oncologist at Ellis Fischel, our state cancer hospital, a mere six minutes' drive from our home. So it all began. Dr. Michael C. Perry, head of the Division of Hematology and Medical Oncology, took on my case. He was a gem. To be sure, he was brisk and painfully precise, but how reassuring it was to be in the hands of a perfectionist.

Diagnosis and assessment of the stage of the cancer were based on the biopsy, blood tests, a CT scan, study of my bone marrow, and a general physical exam. It was serious. There were many lymphomas in my abdomen and one under my arm, two cancers in my spleen, a cancerous wall in my small intestine, plus cancerous bone marrow throughout my body. This spread, both above and below my diaphragm, told us the disease was well advanced. While it was a "slow-growing" cancer, which sounds reassuring, it was a kind that could not be eradicated. At best, it could be pushed back from time to time. I was fifty-nine, with a young wife and a child, making the situation consequential for us. We were all staggered for the first few weeks, including Andrew, who had recently lost a warm kindergarten teacher to cancer. Not surprisingly, Andrew asked me earnestly for straightforward information; I honored his request.

The details of the treatment are of less interest, I suspect, than the results. I will, at least, outline the former. There have been four rounds of treatment so far, each with its own character. First, I had six doses of chemotherapy with CVP (Cytoxan, Vincristine, and Prednisone) that reduced the cancer mass by 50 percent. Cropping my hair short the day before it began, I escaped most of the usual hair loss. Short hair is not as easily pulled out. And the bone pain I'd had for more than two years vanished! It must have been due to my bone marrow cancer.

Just over a year later, in October 1999, pressure on my bladder and kidneys told me that the cancer was building up again. A CT scan confirmed it. "Dr. Gardner, you don't cry wolf," Dr. Perry said, leaving me feeling like a useful participant. This time, I received two doses of Fludarabine chemotherapy. It had little apparent effect, so we went immediately to a third kind of treatment—eight doses of Rituxan, cloned antibodies of cancer cells. These took hours to administer, and I had to be watched throughout, due to the possibility of a shock reaction to the foreign protein in my blood. It was, however, easier on my body than chemotherapy had been. For a few days after each treatment I had mild flulike symptoms, but my immune system was undamaged. As with CVP, there was marked reduction of the cancer, and a second relatively comfortable year passed.

By January 2001, I sensed pressure building up once more and with greater speed than previously. I was right. This time the cancer had crushed my kidneys and the vessels that drain them, shutting down my urinary system. Urgent action was called for. Indeed, Dr. Perry informed my wife that I had only a couple of weeks to live. All he told me was that, if my bone marrow was suitable, I met the other criteria to be eligible for treatment with Bexxar, then an experimental drug with unknown potential side effects. I would be the hospital's first recipient of it. Because my bone marrow turned out to be sufficiently free of cancer and because it was obvious to me that my situation was critical, the choice was easy. Proceed. Bexxar consists of cloned antibodies of cancer cells carrying tiny "backpacks" of iodine 131, a radioactive isotope with a half-life of 8.3 days. The antibodies would search out the cancer cells and deliver their "bombs."

There was a complication. When the Bexxar arrived by air, my medical insurer refused to give prompt approval to my being treated in the costly isolation room that would protect others from my radioactivity. Neither the rapidly decaying isotope nor I could wait for the insensitive bureaucratic wheels to turn. So my physicians devised a way of providing immediate treatment without the isolation room. A crowd of specialists greeted me on the day of the procedure, and the curious scientist in me found it all more intriguing than worrying. Present were a professor of nuclear medicine, a nuclear medicine technician, a physician participating in the national clinical trials of the new drug, a clinical trials nurse, a scientific consultant to the drug company (who had flown in to make sure the efficiency-minded actions of my insurer did not derail my treatment), and a safety officer with a Geiger counter who checked that treatment without an isolation room did not leave me too radioactive to return to the world. The naughty me dreamt of being left dangerously radioactive by the procedure, walking into the insurance office, perching on the manager's desk, and asking how it felt to chat with a monster of his own making.

With the Geiger counter held a meter away—it actually looked to me more like 1.1 meters—my post-treatment radiation level was barely within the permitted ceiling for public safety. For many, many weeks I had to sleep in my own room and avoid coming within ten feet of children and pregnant women. A scan after twelve weeks confirmed what I felt; the Bexxar had given me a major reduction in the cancer.

I had to go through four precarious and weakening dips in my red blood cell count, plus four equally precarious dips in my white blood cell count that left me with little protection from infection. I took refuge at home, and Cheryl, my caring clinical trials nurse, telephoned me daily to see how I was faring. I went to the hospital only when problematic symptoms or blood tests required it. It was a time to curl up in a cozy chair and read. Initially I read a dozen novels by Nobel laureates from Japan, Egypt, Finland, Yugoslavia, Germany, France, England, Portugal, Trinidad, and the United States; then I moved on to masterful works by the likes of Chinua Achebe, Isabel Allende, Hanif Kureishi, Michael Ondaatje, and Leslie Marmon Silko. Time flew.

Pursuing Life My Way

After three months, I was back to life as I knew it. The only long-term side effect, so far, has been that efforts to protect my thyroid gland from the damaging radioactive iodine proved ineffective; after seventeen months it stopped functioning. That was easily remedied.

There were ups and downs—times of worry and times during which life returned almost to normal. My students were wonderful about keeping their distance when I was most susceptible to infection. They also accepted my occasionally being slow at grading. I could not have asked for more. But, when the university made me a generous early retirement offer in May 2000, my thirty-five and a half years of teaching came to an end.

I developed an approach that I would recommend for facing seriously threatening cancers. It is simple: banish both optimism and pessimism; have nothing to do with either. To be pessimistic is to admit defeat, and this can become self-fulfilling prophesy. There are a variety of means by which a belief that one's illness is fatal may cause death. Think back to Richter's and Lex's research on vagus death and voodoo. Magic cannot kill people; the patient's own belief that death is inevitable can. Why inflict this on oneself?

And optimism invites a profound shock when there is a setback. Most cancer patients face disappointments along the way. If our reaction is "I am not tough enough after all to manage the fight," "God is not listening," or "It was stupid of me to have dared to hope," this only compounds the problem. Then we have two simultaneous difficulties—the worsening of the medical situation and the burst of the bubble of confidence or hope.

What is left if we give up pessimism and optimism? Since it is a waste of time and energy to predict, hope, or worry about a future we cannot know, why not simply live the richness of each present moment? Allow that stream of experiences to dominate. Focus on the enjoyment of what each day brings, whether that is an incredible sky, the fresh smell of the garden after a rain shower, a nurse's smile, the delicate touch of a grandchild's hand, or a Nobel Prize winner's carefully crafted tale.

A central aspect of Taoist thought, which I previously found agreeable, but had not considered fully, is recognition of natural cycles. Cycles of the day and year, for instance, have been sources of delight since my childhood. Dawn and dusk are magical; so is the calm just before dawn. I know why Japanese appreciate a short-lived spring snow and the transient cherry blossom. Almost every fall, you will find rich autumn leaves of many hues and textures on my desk. Change is to be savored. But what of the cycle of our birth, maturation, reproduction, and death? Since my cancer diagnosis, I have come to appreciate Taoist acceptance of life stages—all of them. Why do we always wish to be older or younger than we are? Enjoy a snuggle from a parent when small, a first buddy's friendship at school, those lingering fascinations at adolescence, the unexpected opening of doors for us by our teachers. Later, take satisfaction in coming home from a hard day's work well done, in watching your children develop their capabilities, in trimming fingernails for a tired and aging parent who finds the clippers awkward, or in spending quiet time after retirement with things one previously always felt too busy for. Enjoy them when they happen and savor their richness one at a time. We cannot have a baby's smooth skin and an elder's depth of perspective simultaneously. Each stage is unique, and each can be celebrated in turn.

The last seven years include some of the best moments of my life. After I learned of my cancer, on July 1, 1998, I devoted the rest of that summer to writing the final four chapters of a book on the Paliyans that I owed to science and was compelled to finish. My focus was incredible. It felt satisfying to see the book come out in 2000, and when I moved on to other projects I remained better focused than at any time in my career. Things went just as well personally as they did professionally. While family members were stunned initially, we all managed to work through our shock. We increased our activity as a family and learned to talk about the cancer in a matter-of-fact way. Once the book marathon was behind me, I gave up most of my evening and weekend work routines to maximize family time.

One of the biggest family treats was a four-week trip Andrew and I took to south India, from December 2000 to January 2001, just before the Bexxar treatment. Andrew had read my Paliyan book, but, unlike my other children, he had never had the chance to accompany me on my field research. We looked in on my main study group of Paliyans precisely on the thirty-eighth anniversary of my initial work with them. My impetus for the trip was information I had received from colleagues that my forest friends faced increasingly hard times with resource-hungry India. Twelve bands were being denied their traditional rights to find food in forest that had just been designated a wildlife preserve, yet no alternative life had been provided for them. And profit-minded Hindu intruders had stripped Temple Paliyans on Saduragiri of their inherited priestly duties. What is more, Paliyan youngsters in one area had been denied the educational benefits that rightfully belong to all India's tribal children "until such time as they showed land deeds" to prove their tribal status. Yet there is no way semi-nomads could acquire such deeds. Despite this harassment, they had not lost their smiles and continued to live in terms of their values. As hoped, an interview by a reporter from a major south Indian daily newspaper was enough to bring public attention to the abuses.

When we arrived, a few hours went by before a Paliyan man finally realized who I was—the person who had lived there in the green tent. Suddenly the visit blossomed into an extraordinary reunion. They swept my son into it too. Smiling youngsters took him by the hand to see the nearby stream and groves and then roped him into their games. The next day we presented the community with a copy of their ethnography, and they poured over the photographs. Then, on New Year's Day, a fifty-two-year-old man, who had spent a lot of time with me at age fourteen, and four younger men walked with Andrew and me for five and a half hours into the jungle. We passed giant squirrels in the treetops, fresh tracks of an enormous south Indian gaur, monkey troops, and a snake. And the Paliyans gleefully showered Andrew with wild fruits. We returned sunburned, exhausted, enriched.

People ask if I have tried using my mind to overcome cancer. While the subject interests me, my answer at this juncture has to be "no." Yet my maternal grandmother may have done just that. At seventy-five, she found radiation therapy for uterine cancer intolerable and walked out on it; she was given a scant six months to live. Ignoring her pessimistic doctors, she returned to her normal routines and enjoyed fifteen more years of contentment. When arteriosclerosis ended her days, the autopsy showed her to be cancer-free. What a model!

I find that we can do a great deal with our bodies, just by talking to ourselves. Science teaches us that. Years ago, I read a paper by John M. Roberts on autonomic ordeals.[1] He noted the frequent use of ordeals involving heat and responses of the skin to assess innocence and guilt in law courts of traditional Africa and Eurasia. The accused might, for instance, be asked to reach into a pot of boiling water to extract an object. The severity of any burns was deemed to give a measure of the person's guilt or innocence. In this culture we, too, look at the skin in weighing guilt. Lie detectors measure an increase in perspiration that science holds to indicate a guilt reaction. Our police have confidence in this autonomic nervous system response to their questions, for the effects on the skin are measurable. There is a parallel literature on engineers from Drexel University in Philadelphia experimenting with "fire walking" on hot steel under controlled laboratory conditions. At a high enough temperature, moisture on the feet develops into a cushion of steam that protects the skin from severe damage. I have witnessed a day of "fire walking" at a Hindu temple festival in India, on a long, walled bed of coals so hot it scorched my face from twenty feet away. Some participants crossed the coals not once but several times and walked off normally afterward. A nearby ambulance sat idle. Whether or not rough coals had an effect resembling that of smooth steel at Drexel, the piety and expectations of the subjects may also have figured in their protection.

Looking at all this, I asked myself why I could not tell my body "pain and blisters are not needed" when I burned myself on the kitchen stove. I tried it the first time I had a good, sizzling burn on the stove top. It worked. While I could see some damage to the skin, and while the burned area hurt briefly whenever I got it wet during the first two days, there was no blister and no other pain. Further use of the technique always worked, even if the skin looked seared. When Andrew was five, I told him about the technique. The next time he got a burn he used it with the same success. This applied science has not let either of us down.

I tried controlling hiccups the same way. Our digestive system might derive some practical benefit from, say, three hiccups, but why should one go any further? Why not decide that three is enough? For years now, only rarely have I had to put up with a fourth or fifth hiccup; they generally stop obediently after the third—all this without any held breath or special concentration. More recently, I have been able to rid myself immediately of calf cramps at night. Stress pain in a neck or back muscle vanishes permanently in a matter of a minute or two. Possible applications of this technique are many. But for cancer? I am unsure I can do anything comparable to my other body talk in order to harness my runaway cell growth. Flinching is *not* a promising start.

Can these intersections of my recent paths, including the medical one, be summed up? I see them as running smoothly together. Appreciating nature has been a preoccupation of mine since childhood, yet it may underlie what I chose to do in my anthropology, working as I do with people who live *in* nature rather than trying to control it. There is also a harmony between the chosen paths of my initial research subjects and me. In addition, the Paliyan pursuit of noninterference with others and individual self-sufficiency has a curiously Taoist ring. We might even say that my respect for Paliyans was instrumental in drawing me down the Taoist path. Taoism's so-called right-hand path entails nature appreciation, too, centering as it does on natural cycles and respect toward other living beings. Again, the paths run in similar directions.

Let me suggest a new way of expressing this. Although I say that I have been engaged with several "paths," they are hardly separate from one another. My image of separate paths has allowed me to speak about each in turn, but in fact there is really one single trail, with several ways of viewing it that I had to learn about with time.

We must not leave cancer out here. I was stunned, at first, to learn I had been experiencing cancer for two years without knowing it. Yet the shock was replaced surprisingly quickly by a savoring of each day. It was as if the cancer had awakened me. Taoist concepts of natural rhythms gained deeper meaning for me as I went through my treatment. Every new dawn became an opportunity for awareness, appreciation, and growth.

A combination of my various perspectives is, I believe, what allowed me to find deep satisfactions in the last few complicated years. If I felt for the first time that my life course was finite in length, this was also my best reason for spending my time well. According to the Law of Supply and Demand, rarity made each step precious. Indeed, I had nothing more valuable than time to offer my family, friends, students, and passersby. And a Taoist view of life has brought calmness to that walk we share together.

A Note of Thanks

There are many to whom I am indebted. I am deeply grateful for the patience, accommodation, and kindness of innumerable Paliyans, northern Dene, Tamil sculptors, and Japanese who offered me their time and companionship when I lived among them. Special thanks are also due to my collaborator and consultant in the Dene project; hospitable colleagues in India, Canada, and Japan; and officials and private individuals who aided me when I was far from home. Then, too, there were teachers who encouraged me; friends who taught me informally along the way; a former teacher, Ruben Reina, who pressed me to pen this account of my personal journeys; Jane Lago of the University of Missouri Press, who patiently helped me bring the manuscript into readable form; and Andrew Dolan, who made my maps. My greatest debt, however, has to be to family members who traveled with me. Their forbearance, suggestions, and endless encouragement made all these shared experiences possible.

The fieldwork and travel described in this book were supported by generous grants, fellowships, and contracts from several agencies: a Ford Foundation Foreign Area Fellowship administered by the Joint Committee of SSRC and ACLS; a renewal of the Ford Foundation Fellowship; a University of Texas Research Institute grant; a Faculty Research Fellowship from the American Institute of Indian Studies; two University of Missouri Research Council grants (URC NSF 1201, URC NSF 1209); a National Museums of Canada Urgent Ethnology Programme contract (jointly with Jane Christian); a National Science Foundation grant (GS-43057; jointly with Jane Christian); an extension of the National Science Foundation grant; a Faculty Summer Fellowship from the University of Missouri Research Council; an American Institute of Indian Studies Travel Award; and a University of Missouri Research Council sabbatical grant.

While expressing deep appreciation for these various kinds of assistance, I must, nonetheless, take sole responsibility for all statements of fact and interpretation to be found in this book.

Notes

Seeking the Quiet People

1. Tamil is shown with double vowels for long sounds, c for the sound ch, and uppercase letters for retroflex consonants (said with the tongue curled back, these heard only medially or finally in words). The spelling of the tribe's name is properly "PaLiyan."

2. Gardner, *Bicultural Versatility as a Frontier Adaptation among Paliyan Foragers of South India,* 26.

Utopia in a Thorn Forest

1. Lao Tzu, *Tao Te Ching;* William Godwin, *An Enquiry Concerning Political Justice;* and Herbert Spencer, *Social Statics.*

2. Gardner, "The Paliyans," 432.

3. Ernestine Friedl, *Women and Men: An Anthropologist's View,* 7; Morton H. Fried, *The Evolution of Political Society,* 32, 33.

4. Colin M. Turnbull, *The Mountain People.*

With Princes into Wilderness

1. Gardner, *Bicultural Versatility,* 211.

Savoring India Personally

1. John B. Carroll, ed., *Language, Thought and Reality: Selected Writings of Benjamin Lee Whorf.*

Toward Northern Forest

1. Émile Durkheim, *Les Formes élémentaires de la vie religieuse.*
2. Thomas R. Berger, *Northern Frontier, Northern Homeland,* 95.

Subarctic Ways

1. I have written Dene words using several conventions: c stands for ch; q stands for a k-like consonant far back in the mouth; x is close to English h; and Θ represents a "voiceless" th (as in English "thin"). Several consonants can be accompanied by either a glottal stop ' or a very audible and explosive gust of air [h].
2. Curt P. Richter, "On the Phenomenon of Sudden Death in Animals and Man."
3. Barbara W. Lex, "Voodoo Death: New Thoughts on an Old Explanation," 820.

Private Thought Worlds

1. Gardner, "Birds, Words, and a Requiem for the Omniscient Informant."
2. Jane Christian and Peter M. Gardner, *The Individual in Northern Dene Thought and Communication: A Study in Sharing and Diversity,* 268–81.
3. Ibid., 147.

Experiments, Puzzles, Exams

1. Berger, *Northern Frontier,* 200.

Performers in Indian Bronze

1. Ananda K. Coomaraswamy, *The Transformation of Nature in Art;* D. N. Shukla, *Vastu-Shastra, Volume II: Hindu Canons of Iconography and Painting.*

Time Edges in Japan

1. Anthony F. C. Wallace, *Culture and Personality.*
2. Nyozekan Hasegawa, *The Japanese Character,* 59–61.

Journeys That Converge

1. Joseph Conrad, *A Personal Record,* 13.
2. Clyde Kluckhohn and Olaf Prufer, "Influences during the Formative Years," 6.
3. Chuang Tzu, *Chuang Tzu,* 41.
4. Feng Yu-lan, *A History of Chinese Philosophy,* 234.
5. Chuang Tzu, *Chuang Tzu,* 25.
6. Lao Tzu, *Hua Hu Ching,* 9.
7. Liu An, *Yüan Dao,* 83–85.
8. Roger T. Ames, introduction to *Yüan Dao,* 7, 20–21, 41–42.
9. Ibid., 20.
10. Ibid., 65.

Adapting to the Path of Cancer

1. John M. Roberts, "Oaths, Autonomic Ordeals, and Power."

Bibliography

Ames, Roger T. Introduction to *Yüan Dao* by Liu An, trans. D. C. Lau and R. T. Ames, 1–58. New York: Ballantine Books, 1998.

Berger, Thomas R. *Northern Frontier, Northern Homeland,* vol. 1. Ottawa: Ministry of Supply and Services Canada, 1977.

Boas, Franz. *The Central Eskimo.* 6th Annual Report, Bureau of Ethnology. Washington, D.C., 1888.

Carroll, John B., ed. *Language, Thought, and Reality: Selected Writings of Benjamin Lee Whorf.* Cambridge: MIT Press, 1956.

Christian, Jane, and Peter M. Gardner. *The Individual in Northern Dene Thought and Communication: A Study in Sharing and Diversity.* Ottawa: National Museums of Canada, 1977.

Chuang Tzu. *Chuang Tzu.* Trans. Burton Watson. New York: Columbia University Press, 1964.

Conrad, Joseph. "Heart of Darkness." In *Youth: A Narrative; and Two Other Stories.* London: William Blackwood and Sons, 1902.

———. *A Personal Record.* London: J. M. Dent, 1923.

Coomaraswamy, Ananda K. *The Transformation of Nature in Art.* Cambridge: Harvard University Press, 1934.

Dahmen, F., S.J. "The Paliyans, a Hill-Tribe of the Palni Hills (South India)." *Anthropos* 3 (1908): 19–31.

Deng Ming-dao. *365 Tao: Daily Meditations.* San Francisco: Harper Collins, 1992.

Dumont, Louis. *Une Sous-Caste de l'Inde du Sud.* Paris: Mouton, 1957.

Durkheim, Émile. *Les Formes élémentaires de la vie religieuse.* Paris: Alcan, 1912.

Feng Yu-lan. *A History of Chinese Philosophy.* Vol. 1. Trans. Derk Bodde. Peiping: Henri Vetch, 1937.

Fried, Morton H. *The Evolution of Political Society.* New York: Random House, 1967.

Friedl, Ernestine. *Women and Men: An Anthropologist's View.* New York: Holt, Rinehart and Winston, 1975.

Gardner, Peter M. *Bicultural Versatility as a Frontier Adaptation among Paliyan Foragers of South India.* Lewiston, N.Y.: Edwin Mellen Press, 2000.

———. "Birds, Words, and a Requiem for the Omniscient Informant." *American Ethnologist* 3 (1976): 446–68.

———. "Creative Performance in South Indian Sculpture: An Ethnographic Approach." *Art History* 5:4 (1982): 472–79.

———. "The Paliyans." In *Hunters and Gatherers Today,* ed. M. Bicchieri, 404–47. New York: Holt, Rinehart and Winston, 1972.

Godwin, William. *An Enquiry Concerning Political Justice.* London: G. G. and J. Robinson, 1793.

Hasegawa, Nyozekan. *The Japanese Character.* Trans. John Bester. Tokyo: Kodansha International, 1966. Originally published as *Nihonteki Seikaku,* 1938.

Kluckhohn, Clyde, and Olaf Prufer. "Influences during the Formative Years." In *The Anthropology of Franz Boas,* ed. W. Goldschmidt, 4–28. Memoir No. 89. Menasha, Wisc.: American Anthropological Association, 1959.

Lao Tzu. *Hua Hu Ching.* Trans. B. Walker. San Francisco: Harper Collins, 1992.

———. *Tao Te Ching.* Trans. G-F. Feng and J. English. New York: Vintage Books, 1972.

Lex, Barbara W. "Voodoo Death: New Thoughts on an Old Explanation." *American Anthropologist* 76 (1974): 818–23.

Liu An. *Yüan Dao.* Trans. D. C. Lau and R. T. Ames. New York: Ballantine Books, 1998.

Malinowski, Bronislaw. "Baloma: The Spirits of the Dead in the Trobriand Islands." *Journal of the Royal Anthropological Institute of Great Britain and Ireland* 46 (1916): 353–430.

Richter, Curt P. "On the Phenomenon of Sudden Death in Animals and Man." *Psychosomatic Medicine* 19 (1957): 191–98.

Ridington, Robin. *Little Bit Know Something: Stories in a Language of Anthropology.* Iowa City: University of Iowa Press, 1990.

————. *Trail to Heaven: Knowledge and Narrative in a Northern Native Community.* Iowa City: University of Iowa Press, 1988.

Roberts, John M. "Oaths, Autonomic Ordeals, and Power." *American Anthropologist* 67:6, pt. 2 (1965): 186–212.

Shukla, D. N. *Vastu-Shastra, Volume II: Hindu Canons of Iconography and Painting.* Gorakhpur: Gorakhpur University Press, 1958.

Spencer, Herbert. *Social Statics.* London: J. Chapman, 1851.

Turnbull, Colin M. *The Mountain People.* New York: Simon and Schuster, 1972.

Wallace, Anthony F. C. *Culture and Personality.* New York: Random House, 1961.

Index of Places

About the Author

Carole Patterson

Peter M. Gardner is author of *Bicultural Versatility as a Frontier Adaptation among Paliyan Foragers of South India* and coauthor of *The Individual in Northern Dene Thought and Communication: A Study in Sharing and Diversity.* He is Emeritus Professor of Anthropology at the University of Missouri–Columbia.